UNFINISHED LINES

UNFINISHED LINES

Rediscovering the Remains of Railways
that were Never Completed

Mark Yonge

PEN & SWORD
TRANSPORT

AN IMPRINT OF PEN & SWORD BOOKS LTD.
YORKSHIRE · PHILADELPHIA

First published in Great Britain in 2021 by
PEN & SWORD TRANSPORT
An imprint of
Pen & Sword Books Ltd
Yorkshire – Philadelphia

ISBN 978 1 39901 853 1

A CIP catalogue record for this book is available from the British Library.

Typeset in 10.5/13.5 pt Palatino
Typeset by SJmagic DESIGN SERVICES, India.
Printed and bound in India by Replika Press Pvt. Ltd.

Pen & Sword Books Ltd incorporates the Imprints of Pen & Sword Books Archaeology, Atlas, Aviation, Battleground, Discovery, Family History, History, Maritime, Military, Naval, Politics, Railways, Select, Transport, True Crime, Fiction, Frontline Books, Leo Cooper, Praetorian Press, Seaforth Publishing, Wharncliffe and White Owl.

For a complete list of Pen & Sword titles please contact

PEN & SWORD BOOKS LIMITED
47 Church Street, Barnsley, South Yorkshire, S70 2AS, England
E-mail: enquiries@pen-and-sword.co.uk
Website: www.pen-and-sword.co.uk

Or
PEN AND SWORD BOOKS
1950 Lawrence Rd, Havertown, PA 19083, USA
E-mail: Uspen-and-sword@casematepublishers.com
Website: www.penandswordbooks.com

Contents

Foreword
Professor Lord K.O. Morgan

Britain's railways are a vital key to aspects of its history, present development and future expansion. Historians of other countries, notably of the United States, have focussed on large-scale transcontinental tracks spanning an entire continent as the industrial domain of 'robber barons'. However, one of the many attractive features of Mark Yonge's survey of Britain's regional railways is that it focusses on local services and surrounding neighbourhoods – many of which did not succeed at all, for reasons he discusses in detail but which have nevertheless left their legacy on the countryside, urban and suburban landscape of England.

He considers many of the factors that stimulated their growth: the emergence of local, small scale industry and the need to replace canals for freight purposes, the growth of suburbs around major cities, the claims of possible national and international defence considerations (which led to intense and often bitter debates between rival schools of international thought), the needs of a growing aircraft industry and the pressures exerted by local transport, most notably the London Underground on either side of the First World War.

Mark Yonge also deals, with humour and relish, with some of the great personalities of England's railway system, bent on the massive profits to be gleaned from it, most notably the buccaneering pioneer, Sir Edward Watkin, Gladstone's ally and Liberal MP over many decades and prophet of the channel tunnel, Charles Yerkes, Isambard Kingdom Brunel and the aircraft pioneer, Handley Page. They include crooks such as George Hudson, professional engineers like Cubitt and the idealistic prophet, Dame Henrietta Barnett, devoted perhaps to simple capitalist exploitation, perhaps to social rehabilitation.

The influence of the nonconformist, free trade Liberal tradition comes clearly across. All are dealt with in picturesque, colourful detail. Not the least enjoyable aspect of this work is that it is a kind of gazetteer as well as work of local history whereby the curious or intrepid traveller may examine at close quarters the partially constructed lines, earthworks, tunnels and bridges that remain as legacies of this local, and often forgotten survival of the industrial greatness of the United Kingdom in its first industrial revolution.

Mark Yonge, a passionate railway enthusiast to his Kentish finger-tips, local historian and industrial archaeologist, has written a fascinating account of this vital aspect of our local history, and has performed a valuable and valiant service in reminding us all of the local glories of our industrial and commercial past. Very many readers will be much indebted to him in doing so, and in so lively and graphic a manner. This attractive work deserves a wide readership amongst general readers as well as railway specialists, and they will surely find it here.

Professor Lord Morgan, D.Litt. (Oxon), Fellow of the British Academy, Vice-Chancellor, University of Wales

Acknowledgements

This book has been written during one of the world's great natural crises. History will record that in the years of 2020 and 2021, thousands of deaths from a pandemic which spread rapidly to all countries led to a large amount of casualties as yet unknown. This tragic event meant that people at large were confined to their homes, forbidden to socialise or to take holidays. In addition, the national closure of museums placed a major restriction on the ability to carry out documental research.

Writing a book under these conditions has proved to be challenging, and without the help of family and friends would have been impossible.

My stepson, Alex, has excelled in his talent for the creation of map illustrations, the sourcing of images and for helping with the layout of this book. To my children and their spouses, a debt of gratitude is owed for their trudging through rough country areas to source photographs of abandoned earthworks or structures, particularly as these subjects were not naturally of their first interest. And to friends who took pictures on my behalf in parts of the country where travelling was allowed. The generosity of photographers who granted permission for their railway images to be used has greatly contributed to the completion of this publication.

Finally, love to my wife Alison who resolutely 'kept me at it!'

Preface

I have for most of my life been fascinated by railways and am fortunate in clearly remembering the age of steam. But unusually for someone of my generation, I never became a train spotter, preferring to study the history of railways and their place in the industrial development of Great Britain.

It was clear when railways became an established method of travel and the scars of their construction healed, they frequently became places of great beauty within the landscape. This was enhanced by the provision of opulent Victorian stations, ornate tunnel mouths, bridges and magnificent viaducts, many of which are still with us today. It is hard to believe that most communities within the United Kingdom were provided with regular passenger and goods services, making the local station an important place of social contact.

My interest was enhanced by the early railway pioneers who forged the first primitive iron ways, this feeding my fascination for the politics and rivalry between personalities. I was sufficiently intrigued to study them and their works in more detail, particularly in regard to the politics at the time of the early industrial revolution.

Throughout the golden age some railways gained a romantic status, such as Brunel's Great Western Railway, often referred to as 'God's Wonderful Railway', or the London & North Eastern Railway upon which the iconic '*Flying Scotsman*' raced to the capital of Scotland. So inspirational were steam trains and their place in the landscape, that for many years after their inception, modern railway companies still capitalise on their former glories.

Some years ago I began to develop an interest in railways that were planned, partly constructed but never completed. I collected papers and references to these projects, keeping them stored in a box with the idea that I would one day write a book about them. They were dated and tabulated, eventually to be disinterred when the time was right. These covered a thirty year period during which time I was travelling the world during my burgeoning business career. However, faced with retirement, a serious illness and much encouragement from those around me, the book has finally been written.

I hope you enjoy reading it and find the visits to the archaeological remains fruitful. Please stay on footpaths or seek permission to visit items of interest on private land, as an angry farmer can ruin a pleasant day out!

CHAPTER 1

The Cranbrook &
Paddock Wood Railway

The Weald of Kent in early times was a somewhat forbidding place and little penetrated before the settlement of the Jutes during the fifth century. Initially this great forest known as Andredswald was settled in small clearings, and a casual glance at a map shows the many hamlets and other settlements in the Weald, the name corrupted from the word 'Wald', meaning Wood. Some grew into large communities such as Tenterden, Horsmonden and Biddenden, the 'den' at the end of each name denoting 'a clearing in the wood'. Nowadays the tortuous road network in the Weald is in reality a series of widened footpaths throughout this ancient forest. Originally populated by mature oak trees, this source of timber is evident today in many of the hall houses and cottages throughout the county. The beams in these dwellings themselves are from the Weald and in many instances are on their second life, having first been used in the construction of Tudor warships in and around the port of Rye.

Kent today is seen as a wealthy county and Wealden village houses are keenly sought by commuting city traders who value their idyllic retreats. But this was not always so, as a glance at property prices 150 years ago reveals that Bradford in Yorkshire sported land costs twice those of Kent, directly as a result of nineteenth century industrial mill development in the north.

The first railway in Kent was a local scheme to connect Canterbury to Whitstable, and its claim to fame was that it became the first line in the United Kingdom to open for passengers as well as goods traffic. It was engineered by the Father of the Railways, George Stephenson. In reality, he contributed very little by paying only one visit to Canterbury prior to its construction, but it did enable him to attach his name to this and several other national schemes, thereby enhancing his reputation. Kent's other railway, London's first main line, was opened between London Bridge and Greenwich in 1836.

The first company established to provide railway access across Kent to the coast was the South Eastern Railway (SER) formed at the same time as the London–Greenwich (L&GR) line in 1836. In those early days it was envisaged that the county would be adequately served by one railway between London and the port of Dover, with ancillary branch lines to other large communities. Commencing from London Bridge station it initially headed eastwards before branching south from the L&GR close to the capital where it ran parallel with the London, Brighton & South Coast Railway, turning eastwards across Kent from a junction south of Redhill station.

Engineered by William Cubitt, later Sir William (1785–1861), this railway, in later years known as 'the boat train route', was unusual in that it ran almost without curves between Redhill and Ashford before continuing to Folkestone and spectacularly running along the base of the famous white cliffs to Dover. At the time when the contract was due to be awarded, Cubitt, ever the master of the understatement, was woken late at night by a bang on his front door, to be told excitedly that he had been chosen to construct the line. The curt response from his bedroom was, 'I've gone to bed. Come and see me in the morning.' He then slammed the window shut before disappearing into the darkness.

On completion of this line, the South Eastern Railway made good on its plans and added other lines to Tunbridge Wells, Maidstone, Canterbury, Deal and Hastings. This monopoly was to be greatly challenged in the following decades as will be seen later in this chapter.

A glance at the map of the time identifies where substantial gaps existed, one of which was the Weald of Kent. The Dover and Hastings lines skirted around this area to the north and west and for years there was little interest in constructing new routes. The low population of the Weald, along with a lack of heavy industry, and where most of the towns were situated on rising ground, notably discouraged investment. The only proposal which nearly became a reality was the Weald of Kent Railway, which in 1864 was granted Royal Assent for a line to be constructed from Paddock Wood to Cranbrook, Tenterden and Appledore. The national financial crash of 1866 put the lid on that scheme when several major banks collapsed, putting the final nail in the Weald of Kent Railway's coffin. This proposal was eventually abandoned in 1870.

Meanwhile, the Weald of Kent remained devoid of a railway connection until a new scheme, The Cranbrook & Paddock Wood Railway (C&PW), was promoted in 1876.

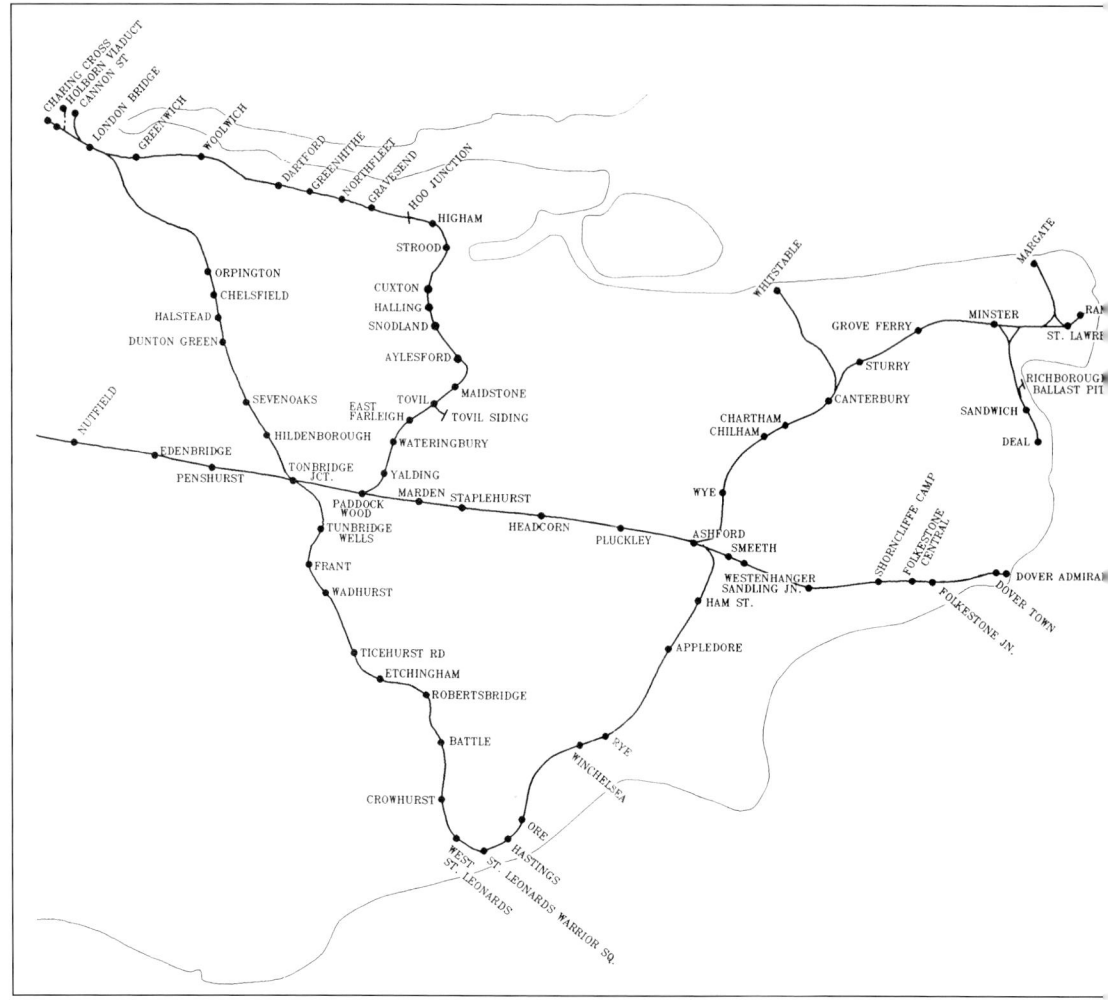

The South Eastern Railway as it was in 1851.

Pressure to provide a line to Cranbrook, in spite of earlier failures, continued to be applied. The town's population depended on horse drawn coaches and carts for passengers and goods which ran mainly to Staplehurst, the nearest main line station. As well as the town's 4,000 inhabitants, farmers in the surrounding area were still obliged to send hops, fruit and other crops to market and receive supplies in return by these beasts of burden. Pause to take pity on these poor animals having to tackle two steep hills, the first between Knoxbridge and Sissinghurst on the present A229 road, and the second ascending the long gradient from the centre of Cranbrook.

In 1876 a local group of eminent citizens joined forces to persuade the South Eastern Railway to support the construction of a railway from Paddock Wood to Cranbrook. This line would run through fertile land such as that found around Brenchley, Lamberhurst and Goudhurst, the promoters being convinced that it would prove to be profitable and an asset to the local community.

These luminaries were headed by Sir Gathorne Hardy, Colonel Edward Loyd of Lillesden, Hawkhurst, appointed High Sheriff of Kent in 1876, Major Joseph Hartnell of Hawkhurst, William Tanner Neve of Cranbrook, William Courtenay Morland and William Sharpe.

Hardy (1814–1906), who took the surname Gathorne-Hardy in 1878, was a prominent Conservative politician for most of his life, and whose family origins lay in their ownership of the Low Moor Ironworks near Bradford. His wealth, gained from industrial origins, enabled him to possess a country estate as his career in politics progressed. With a public school education followed by Oxford University, he was called to the Bar, Inner Temple in 1840 before concentrating on a political career after the death of his father in 1855. His most notable successes were as Home Secretary in 1867 to 1868 and Secretary of State for War from 1874–1878. He became the 1st Earl of Cranbrook in 1892.

With his experience and legal background, he was a highly articulate speaker and ambitious cabinet minister who made no secret of his aim to lead the Conservative party. In fact when Disraeli the Prime Minister was elevated as the Earl of Beaconsfield to the House of Lords, it was expected that Gathorne-Hardy would become party leader but he was overlooked in favour of Sir Stafford Northcote. Disraeli disliked the fact that Hardy neglected the House to go home in the evening to dine with his wife. His obituary in *The Times* read that he 'was not quite in the front rank of Victorian Statesmen and not the stuff of which Prime Ministers are made, but was a very eminent public man of his day'.

His family owned Hemsted House, a large country estate which today is better known as Benenden School, where Princess Anne was educated. As a large landowner and a prominent member of the establishment, he was a leading proponent for a railway to be laid to

Gathorne Gathorne-Hardy, 1st Earl of Cranbrook.

Cranbrook, particularly as his seat was close to the town. As such he was a natural leader of the group formed to promote such a venture.

John Gathorne-Hardy (1839–1911) was the eldest son of the 1st Earl of Cranbrook and followed in his father's footsteps by opting for a political career in the Conservative party. He was the Member of Parliament for Rye, a seat that he held from 1868 until 1880, then for mid-Kent in 1884 to 1885 then Medway from 1885–1892. Following his father's death in 1906, he took his seat in the House of Lords as the 2nd Earl of Cranbrook. As his father's political career was very active, John occasionally deputised in C&PW railway matters in his absence.

As someone who witnessed the birth and maturity of the railways of Great Britain, William Tanner Neve (1814–1899) clearly formed a bond with his colleagues when it came to promoting the C&PW Railway. His father was a farmer in the Tenterden area but William chose a legal path and became a solicitor in Cranbrook, where he lived at Osborne Lodge. This house was purchased in 1931 by Cranbrook School, later renamed Cornwallis House, and in Cranbrook Church a stained-glass window is featured as a memorial to his life. Clearly a wealthy man and a leading establishment figure, he was the ideal legal representative to handle the Act of Parliament necessary to build a new railway to the town.

As a local landowner of considerable wealth, William Courtenay Morland (1818–1909) lived at Court Lodge, Lamberhurst, where he managed a large estate in the area, embracing several farms. He was an active member of the community and a devout Christian, frequently attending church twice on the Sabbath.

He was an entrepreneurial farmer who embraced modern technology and indeed was an early advocate of steam traction engines, which he introduced to plough his land. As a leading local figure he sat on several local organisations such as the Maidstone Gaol and Turnpike

William Courtenay Morland a working farmer (minus a thumb.).

Committees and was a great supporter of the local school. He was undoubtedly very fit as his surviving diaries indicate his walking or riding great distances around his estate. For example, one entry on 7 April 1875 indicates that, after a day working in London, he took the train to Wadhurst and then walked without complaint, from there to his home at Court Lodge, Lamberhurst. His other great interest was the horticultural improvement of his gardens, where he spent much of his leisure time.

The Morlands, originally from Westmorland (now Cumbria), had judiciously improved their riches by marrying into wealthy families. Courtenay astutely realised that a railway across his land would offer great opportunities for financial gain, so naturally he was an ideal candidate to join the C&PW Railway promoters. He was instrumental in both the planning of the route and encouraging purchase of the necessary land by maintaining close contact with the farming community.

Joseph Hartnell lived in Hawkhurst and few background details can be gleaned except that he owned a considerable amount of land which would explain why he was on the promotion committee of the C&PW Railway. It is interesting that he would show such keenness for a railway that was destined to terminate at Cranbrook, several miles short of Hawkhurst, and we shall later see why this landowner was crucial in the fortunes of this railway.

In due time a letter was posted to the South Eastern Railway at their Tooley Street headquarters at London Bridge during September 1876, outlining the plans for the proposed construction of the C&PW Railway.

It was proposed that a low-cost light railway be constructed with an 8-ton axle loading and a maximum speed of 25mph. This is interesting because it mirrored the later Act of Parliament, the Light Railways Act of 1896, which set out very similar standards. Clearly, earlier schemes such as these persuaded Parliament to introduce legislation to enable railway development in rural areas to proceed more cheaply by allowing lower standards of construction. A further proposal was that the company would operate the line itself and provide its own locomotives and rolling stock. Once sufficient trade was achieved it was understood that the railway would be taken over by the South Eastern Railway and the promoters clearly believed that the line would be of value to the SER. They suggested that one third of the cost, around £25,000, should be provided by them.

Proposed route of the railway between Paddock Wood and Cranbrook. (Google. Imagery ©2021 Getmapping plc, Infoterra Ltd & Bluesky, Landsat / Copernicus, Maxar Technologies, Map data ©2021. By Alex Griffin)

The planned railway was to run from Paddock Wood on a rising gradient to a point east of Brenchley and then bear south between there and Horsmonden at Shirrenden Wood and thence towards Flightshot Farm. The railway would then head towards Goudhurst, crossing the Lamberhurst to Horsmonden road at Pullens Farm (known as Pullings Farm in Victorian times). The line was then to cross the Goudhurst to Bedgbury Road before following an easy gradient to Hartley on the Hawkhurst Road before swinging north into Cranbrook, arriving at a place adjacent to the present-day Dorothy Avenue. The provision and location of stations apart from Cranbrook were not outlined, but one can assume that these would be placed as shown on the map.

There then followed an ominous lack of response from the SER, clearly implying that this proposed railway was of little interest. At this stage, it is worth noting the staff from the SER with whom the C&PWR would have to deal with.

Sir Edward Watkin (1819–1901), Chairman of the SER, was a giant of a man in the Victorian age. As a young boy he witnessed the opening of England's first main line between Liverpool and Manchester, and in his twilight years, by then in a wheelchair, the opening of the last main line, The Great Central Railway, at Marylebone station in London.

Known as the Second Railway King, who at the Welsh Eisteddfod in 1888 described himself as a 'Welsh emigrant', Watkin busied himself with leading railway schemes and politics. He became a Liberal Parliamentary candidate at the age of twenty-six at which time he was involved with the Anti-Corn Law Movement. He was

Sir Edward W. Watkin.

born in Manchester on 26 September 1819, one of two sons and a daughter of Absalom Watkin. His father was by all accounts somewhat feckless financially, being more interested in reading, politics and philosophy than running his business in the textile trade. Edward therefore grew up in a house which provided much intellectual and educational stimulus in spite of his not receiving a formal education. Indeed this part of his life is hazy except that we can be certain that he left school and worked from the age of nine or ten years old.

It was soon clear that Edward was destined for greater things. His interest in liberal politics remained undiminished all his life and in early days he became involved in enhancing the City of Manchester by fundraising for parks and the restoration of the Athenaeum. He later fell out with his father by showing little interest in the family textile business, preferring a career elsewhere.

As a young child, his first experience with railways was when his father took him to view the Liverpool & Manchester Railway, England's first main line then under construction at Eccles near Manchester, some ten miles from his home. Later Edward was taken to see the opening of the railway on 5 September 1830, which proved to be a calamitous event when William Huskisson, MP for Liverpool, was run over by a train hauled by the iconic Stephenson's *Rocket*. Young Edward saw the severely injured man being rushed past in a horse drawn carriage to hospital, where he died. To this day a memorial stands beside the track at Parkside near Liverpool where the accident happened.

His career in railways began in an inauspicious way. As his marriage to Mary Briggs was fast approaching in 1845, Edward's finances were clearly not able to sustain a suitable living. He thus decided to speculate what little capital he had on the purchase of railway shares, and his first flutter yielded a profit of £110. 'God knows, I need it' he was apparently heard to say. Encouraged with this success he bought more shares, which yielded further substantial profits. This was the time of 'railway mania' when all manner of Parliamentary schemes were being proposed by, in some cases, scurrilous promoters. Money could usually be made in the short term by the buying and selling of shares. The railway stock market crash, when it came in 1850, hit a lot of investors hard and led to the bankruptcy of some major banks. But for the fortunate Mary, Edward's new found wealth enabled them to set up a comfortable home.

In these times of speculation, new lines needed staff and his first post was as Secretary of the Trent Valley Railway. He later took senior positions in several burgeoning railway schemes, including the London & North Western Railway, the Manchester, Sheffield & Lincolnshire Railway, the Grand Trunk Railway in Canada and the Great Central Railway. He was renowned for his dedication to work, and in fact in his early career he suffered from a nervous breakdown because of sheer exhaustion. However, he was seen as a solid pair of hands and rapidly progressed to take senior positions in the companies in which he was involved.

By 1864 Watkin became involved with the South Eastern Railway, initially as a shareholder, but later a director and Chairman in 1866.

He could clearly see that the company was weakly managed and had allowed much of its territory to be invaded by The London, Chatham & Dover Railway (LC&DR).

For several decades the SER had the territory in the South East on their terms, and unlike other regions, was protected from competitor incursion as it was surrounded by the sea on three sides. When the London, Chatham & Dover Railway, initially known as the East Kent Railway, started to build competitor lines in the London area, the SER's response was flaccid. Thus emboldened, the LC&DR pushed eastwards into north Kent via the Medway towns to Rainham, Sittingbourne, Canterbury, Margate, Ramsgate and Dover. Although the Dover route was a tricky railway to operate with severe gradients and curves, the company was able to claim that their distance to the capital was shorter than the SER by twelve miles.

Watkin, the newly appointed Chairman, aggressively set about shortening the SER route by building a new line with a substantial tunnel between Sevenoaks and Tonbridge in 1868, thereby challenging its new competitor and reducing the mileage to London to well under that of the LC&DR's.

The antagonism between the two companies was so intense that co-operation was only achieved by amalgamation at the end of the nineteenth century. Because of this animosity, Kent is unique in the United Kingdom where nearly every significant town has or had two separate stations. For example, Maidstone, Canterbury, Bromley, Dover, Ashford, Margate, Greenwich, Tunbridge Wells and Ramsgate and for a mere twelve years, Chatham, were blessed with this dubious honour. Each company's lines passed over and under with little intention of linking up.

Watkin is on record as saying that he always wished for an amicable working relationship, but by the time he joined the SER in 1862, most of the damage had already occurred. This may be so but his later actions were to prove how combative he was capable of being.

Watkin's most ambitious unfulfilled venture was of course the Channel Tunnel. Plans for a tunnel under the sea were actually mooted in the Napoleonic era as early as 1802, but these were originally envisaged for horse drawn traffic only. Later on, when land tunnels had proved effective and comparatively easy to construct, attention turned to the ambitious scheme to connect England to France and this venture is covered in a separate chapter. In any event before the advent of the Channel Tunnel, Watkin was much keener to develop ports on both sides of the Channel to handle ferry and train facilities.

This was a turbulent period in Edward Watkin's life with not only strife on other proposed railway developments, but also trouble caused nearer to home when he placed his somewhat feckless son Alfred in a managerial role at the SER Ashford Locomotive works. This action caused much anger with James Cudworth, head of the works and an early renowned engineer trained by Robert Stephenson, who resigned in protest, much to the irritation of the SER board. Later, young Alfred did not acquit himself well by interfering with train movements at Ashford station whilst clearly intoxicated late one Saturday evening. An even more bizarre account of Edward's machinations was his attempt to bounce Alfred into politics by arranging for him to stand as Liberal candidate for the Parliamentary seat of Grimsby in 1877. They both arrived by train at the launch of the hustings and witnessed placards reading 'Vote for Watkin'. Alfred naturally assumed that his father was standing for this seat, only to be told that the Watkin on the posters referred to himself. With no speeches or arrangements prepared, it was no surprise that this led to his failure to be elected. With that in mind it was clear that Edward's thoughts were not entirely involved with tasks in hand.

James Byng (1818–1897) was Chairman of the South Eastern Railway until Edward Watkin took over in 1864. Regarded as a genial man but lacking business lustre, his main failure was to allow the LC&DR to invade their monopoly between London and Dover. However, he remained on the board and was wheeled out as a safe pair of hands whenever Watkin needed someone to pour oil on troubled waters. This was never more true than on the Cranbrook and Paddock Wood Railway.

About Robert Perks, little can be gleaned but his position on the SER, although shadowy, clearly indicates that he was used by Edward Watkin to negotiate difficult situations. As a solicitor by training, he was able to undo damage that the impetuous Watkin was capable of causing. Watkin seemed to have accepted that his brusque dealings were antagonistic and thus used Perks to front important meetings, several of which were held with William Courtenay Morland in regard to the C&PWR.

So, what one may ask is all this to do with the Cranbrook & Paddock Wood Railway? Well, as can already be seen, Edward Watkin was deep in many problems throughout this time, so to be confronted by a scheme to build a line in the Weald did not go down well. His initial reaction was to reject the idea of a light railway because a more substantial one would be 'infinitely preferable'. Because of his other commitments, he asked James Byng to convey his thoughts. The promoters, when faced with this, agreed to the change, thereby receiving provisional backing from the SER.

In spite of Watkin's interjection, the conditions laid out by James Byng of the SER were that the line would be single track of standard gauge, the sale of land to be at reasonable prices and level crossings constructed instead of bridges. If this was secured the SER directors would recommend to their shareholders the subscription of one third of the cost of construction. This would not exceed 50,000 pounds and it would be worked at fifty per cent of receipts. Accommodation at Paddock Wood, the junction station, would be provided.

The C&PWR succeeded in gaining authority to proceed in August 1877. Immediately Ian Brady, the SER's chief civil engineer, was appointed as a consultant to the proposed line. He travelled to the area on 12 March 1878 and met Messrs Harcourt and Butler, engineers to the C&PWR, for a tour of the district. He was initially optimistic that a 'good line to connect Paddock Wood with Cranbrook, with all necessary intermediate stations and sidings', might be achieved for the sum of 140,000 pounds.

The remains of the bay platform on the up side at Paddock Wood, which served trains to Cranbrook and Hawkhurst.

Paddock Wood
looking towards
Ashford.

However, on closer inspection Brady was alarmed to realise that the C&PWR had made changes that would undoubtedly increase costs. In a letter to John Shaw, the SER manager and Secretary, he reported that:

> 'I can give no opinion as to the probable cost of the works until I obtain the amended plan and section and a copy of the quantities of earthworks. These have been promised to me by Mr Butler shortly. The Parliamentary deposit is no guide in this matter, as the line has strayed outside the Parliamentary limits of deviation in several places. Roads which were originally intended to be crossed on the level have now, under the act, to be carried under or over the railway by means of bridges and approaches of a somewhat heavy character. I think it would be well to reserve in the agreement power to the SER to deviate the line between Paddock Wood and Goudhurst as they may see fit. This would enable us to shorten the line and improve it.'

Clearly it was apparent that in spite of Watkin originally insisting on a conventionally engineered line, Byng had taken a different view when surveying the works.

Two months later after intense discussion the joint agreement between the SER and C&PWR was finalised with the appropriate seals affixed. At that time both Watkin and Byng were elected to the Cranbrook board which clearly boded well for the success of the railway. In spite of this, problems were experienced in finding people to invest so that land could be purchased. Thus powers for an extension of time were granted to the C&PWR.

In 1879 the board of the SER reported that 'some progress may now be made in the commencement of works of this railway' and in September Watkin reported that the promoters had purchased nearly all the land at agricultural value whilst 'alterations were being made as to the location of Cranbrook Station in order to save costs'.

Clearly, there would appear to have been some economy of truth in what had been reported to the SER board, because when Watkin, accompanied by Robert Perks the SER company solicitor, toured the works it was obvious that insufficient land had been purchased. It was at this stage that the actual site of Cranbrook and other stations were agreed 'where convenient approach roads could be made to the passenger and goods stations without disturbing any important trades'. Undoubtedly it was at this time that placing the station in the centre of the town was being abandoned in favour of a site at Hartley which would reduce costs. During the same year Morland was in frequent involvement with progress on the railway. His diary notes indicate several letters to his colleagues on the board and those at the South Eastern Railway. He was right to be anxious. He notes on 6 October that he 'went with Charles Bell to meet Watkin with Gaythorne Hardy (at Benenden) but Watkin did not come!' His instincts relating to Watkins's untrustworthy nature were thus clearly exposed.

In spite of Watkin's doubts about the railway, work finally commenced during the spring of 1880. George Furness, a trusted contractor, began by building an embankment and cutting near the B2162 road between Lamberhurst and Horsmonden close to Pullens Farm. This land was provided by Morland and it is recorded that he saw development potential on his land with not only the provision of a station and goods yard but other related buildings. It was further reported that tenant farmers in the district had received compensation for their loss of crops. In June, chairman John Gaythorne-Hardy reported that Furness received a payment of £200 9s and 6d and that 'everything is progressing favourably'. He confidently continued to reveal that 'the South Eastern Railway had spent £12,000 on the project so far and were unlikely to let the line remain uncompleted, especially as they were planning an extension of the Cranbrook line from Hartley to Dungeness'. According to company minutes, crops were being purchased between Goudhurst and Hartley and the SER was allegedly negotiating to buy land between Hartley and Cranbrook in order to enable the railway to gain access to the centre of town. This was in contravention of Watkin's earlier plan to site Cranbrook station at Hartley.

The residents of Hawkhurst on hearing this news became very alarmed at this unexpected development. What remains a mystery is why this should be the case as the plans and activities associated with building the line had been well publicised. The inhabitants, upon suspecting that the railway would not proceed beyond Cranbrook, petitioned the SER to alter their plans, demanding that they construct the line south from Hartley and place Hawkhurst on the railway map. It is likely that the local population had taken the SER at their word when the company vaguely referred to extending the line to Appledore via Hawkhurst in early discussions, and this plan was clearly not going to materialise.

This dispute now provided Watkin with just the ammunition he needed to withdraw support for a railway which he clearly never wanted in the first place. As described earlier, Watkin was experiencing a sea of troubles with other railway schemes, the Channel Tunnel and matters of a personal nature with his son Alfred. The last thing he needed was a wrangle in the heart of the Weald of Kent and so soon after, work spluttered to a halt.

As referred to earlier, Major Hartnell was one of the early promoters of the railway and he owned much land in Hawkhurst. Aware that Watkin and Perks had shown interest in developing the line from Hartley to Appledore and Dungeness at which point a new port would be established, he was confident of making profits from developing his land at Hawkhurst when the railway was built. There is no doubt that matters in the village were seriously 'stirred up' by Hartnell when this extension was dropped.

At the same time, Watkin had additionally suffered a further humiliation by failing to secure his railway extension from Sandgate to Folkestone Harbour, thus thwarting another of his obsessions with continental rail traffic. But as fortune would have it, another promoted scheme came to light which would not only be of benefit to the SER but antagonise its major competitor, the LC&DR in north Kent. This was the Hundred of Hoo railway which would run from a place near Gravesend across the Isle of Grain and finish at what was later named Port Victoria. Designed to develop Dutch traffic this would upset the LC&DR by placing the development smack in the middle of their territory. Just two months after the C&PWR works had commenced this new line received Parliamentary approval and Watkin wasted no time in transferring the contractor Furness north to complete the new line, thereby abandoning the Cranbrook promoters to their fate.

In spite of this setback which rendered the work sites idle on the C&PWR, the residents of Hawkhurst were determined to reinvigorate their campaign to bring the line south to their town. On 12 July 1882 the Royal Assent was granted to the Hawkhurst Extension bill, but in spite of this, Watkin would not be deterred and persisted in the completion of the Port Victoria branch the following September.

Once again Watkin was overwhelmed with problems, including the latest threat of incursion by the LC&DR, which was seeking to build a new line at Alkham near Folkestone, thus threatening more of the SER continental traffic. This continued rivalry meant that the Cranbrook Railway works lay moribund while the besieged Watkin could only wonder at his misfortune.

But the promoters were not to give up without a fight, and after a hastily called meeting in Cranbrook in February 1883, Gaythorne-Hardy, by now Lord Cranbrook, wrote personally to Watkin to demand that works continue. In his surprising reply, Watkin apologised for 'the failure of the hops and fruit, and embarrassed by the loss of income' and that he 'would give the matter my immediate attention upon return from holiday'. Nothing further was heard until July of that year. However, in the meantime Watkin was clearly drawing up battle lines against his old adversary, the LC&DR, who were menacing traffic in the Ashford and Folkestone areas with their proposed line to Alkham. Watkin proceeded to promote a series of railways which included Appledore to Lydd in 1881, Appledore to Headcorn in 1882 and Headcorn to Loose (Maidstone) in 1883. The Lydd branch was the only one built but the final SER folly was the construction and heavily engineered main line, The Elham Valley Railway, between Canterbury (SER) and Shorncliffe (later Folkestone West), which opened in 1890.

With all this activity, Robert Perks, solicitor to the SER, wrote to the company Secretary on 24 October 1883 in regard to the Cranbrook Railway. He reported that, 'the time to complete the purchase of land expires on the 27th May 1884 and a request for an extension must be made through Parliament'. And further, 'it seems pretty evident that the £100,000 or more required to complete the line will be wasted which would be most unsatisfactory.'

In spite of this, Lord Cranbrook announced to Sir Edward a further purchase of land, at a sizable amount of £2,762.

Watkin, in his usual filibustering way, explained all his troubles to Cranbrook, concluding his letter by stating, 'What I recommend is that important work be done elsewhere before works continue.'

The 'work being done elsewhere', undoubtedly referred to The Elham Valley Railway (EVR). This venture was promoted and constructed to prevent any incursion by the LC&DR into SER territory around the Channel ports, including a railway to Alkham. The EVR was a double track main line which was constructed primarily through farmland with a few villages and little else. The cost was high to take account of two tunnels, one of which was constructed simply to ensure that the view of a wealthy landowner would not be compromised. At each end trains were unable to proceed towards London without running round but at least it could be said that Canterbury could now boast of having no less than three stations and Folkestone now offered a direct route to the Cathedral city. Needless to say, the line was never prosperous and reverted to single track within two decades, closing in 1947 after a life of fewer than sixty years. But it had at least kept the enemy at bay. It's ironic to contemplate that part of the Channel Tunnel complex has nowadays been built over the EVR track at its southern end, something Watkin would never have dreamed possible.

Whatever Watkin may have claimed as reasonable excuses for not proceeding with the C&PWR, the truth was unmasked at a shareholder's meeting on 25 January 1894. An elderly Watkin at the age of seventy-four was Chairman, near retirement and eager at last to draw a veil over the endless delays over the provision of a line to Cranbrook. One of his directors, Sir George Russell, defended the company's actions in a speech saying, 'It is stated that in the last ten or eleven years we, of this Board, have constructed competitive and useless lines to the benefit of no one but the landowner. That is an absolute misstatement'. He then proceeded to discuss the EVR and the C&PWR in particular and went on to say that the board were forced to take action against threatened incursions by the LC&DR because 'it was essential that the ground should be occupied'. No one at the meeting challenged Sir George as to why a main railway line was ever believed necessary or indeed why some sort of mediation could have been initiated. All became clear when it was revealed that Sir George had cut the first sod of this new railway, so defend it he would with all his energy.

Ultimately the SER, having run out of excuses, had no alternative but to build the railway, and after the mammoth wait of over forty years, work finally commenced during the spring of 1890. The new route meant abandoning several miles of the original planned railway between Paddock Wood and Hope Mill at Goudhurst and a station in the centre of Cranbrook. A station at Horsmonden was provided in the centre of the village but this deviation required a tunnel, one of two provided, and extensive earthworks elsewhere. In the end the Hawkhurst branch line, as it became known, was far more heavily engineered than any of the original promoters had planned, and the terminal station was placed a long way from the village of Hawkhurst, as was indeed Cranbrook.

Remains of the Cranbrook & Paddock Wood Railway and how to get there

So what trace remains today of the ill-fated earthworks near Lamberhurst? Surprisingly, a short section of embankment still bears witness to the contractor Furness's efforts before being summarily whisked away by the SER to construct a railway on the Isle of Grain. It can be seen on the western side of the B2162 near Pullens Farm, opposite some farm buildings, postcode reference TN12 8ED. The height of the earthworks would indicate that the road would have been crossed on the level, emphasising some early confusion as to whether the line was to be a 'light railway' or not by avoiding the construction of a bridge. The embankment was constructed by spoil from rising ground on the eastern side of the road, thus creating a shallow cutting which has since been filled in. The line 'when finally built to Hawkhurst' had only two level crossings. Clearly William Courtenay Morland had planned this place for a station with goods yard and it would have been placed next to the level crossing, an area that is now occupied by farm buildings. No evidence can be traced as to what name the station would have carried, so one can only guess. The author's would be Lamberhurst Road, which is what the highway is known as today, but as the location is about half way between two villages, perhaps Lamberhurst & Horsmonden may have been the name chosen.

One needs to stand and contemplate on the site of the crossing at Pullens Farm when road traffic is quiet. This is the place where in former times an R or C Class locomotive hauling a rake of coaches may have come gently steaming through with an up train to Paddock Wood, pausing for a few moments to collect a handful of passengers on their way to the junction, while a down train waited to depart from the loop with some goods wagons destined for Goudhurst and Cranbrook. The dream never came true.

The end of the line as built still awaits a bridge to take the line on to Appledore.

Embankment at Pullens Farm in front of building.

CHAPTER 2

The Ouse Valley Railway

The London, Brighton & South Coast Railway (LB&SCR) was originally formed in 1846, at that time absorbing five companies, one of which had been responsible for constructing the main line from London Bridge to Brighton and an even earlier route to Shoreham Harbour.

In broad geographical terms, the company took in the whole of the Sussex coast and routes north to the metropolis and latterly with an extensive network of commuter lines in Surrey and the suburbs of London.

The company was confined to the east by the South Eastern Railway and to the west by the London & South Western Railway (L&SWR). This meant in effect that the LB&SCR operated roughly on a triangle of territory with London to the north.

Relationships with its neighbouring companies were often fraught when new railway routes were constructed, and in fact, there were early skirmishes at both Portsmouth in 1858 and Hastings in 1851. These were triggered by shared junctions where both companies quarrelled over access and train operation, leading in the extreme to track being removed to thwart rivals or even to threats of violence by railway staff.

Although incidents such as these were settled, the relationship with the SER was always tenuous and matters came to a head when the SER purchased the Reading, Guildford & Reigate Railway in 1849. The LB&SCR viewed this as a major incursion across its territory and promptly retaliated by threatening to restrict access between New Cross and Redhill. When the new routes from London Bridge to Dover and Brighton were constructed in the 1840s, both the SER and Brighton companies shared the tracks between New Cross and Redhill, which continually caused problems.

Thus it was in 1849 that the LB&SCR swiftly appointed a new Chairman, Samuel Laing (1812–1897), who was regarded as a capable pair of hands with a particular talent for negotiation. He quickly moved to form a positive relationship with the SER by drawing up a formal agreement which clearly defined the territories of both railway companies. This allowed the LB&SCR

free access to Hastings and London Bridge as well as other key places. In return the SER would have unrestricted access on the New Cross to Croydon line and receive revenue from intermediate stations. Laing's tenure was widely regarded as beneficial and he authorised several new lines, including those to Crystal Palace and the Three Bridges to East Grinstead Railway in 1855. At the end of that year he resigned and embarked on a career in politics.

The new Chairman, Leonard Schuster (1791–1871), was the German-born son of a cotton trader who married into British aristocracy and began his working life in 1820. He later formed the company Leo Schuster Bros. & Co., based in Manchester and trading there as well as in Bradford and Leeds. In common with other Jews in north west England at this time of rapid industrial growth, he converted to Unitarianism.

Samuel Laing – Chairman of the London, Brighton & South Coast Railway. (National Railway Museum)

Regarded as financially highly astute, he generated much personal wealth, so much that he moved to London in 1855 and formed his own merchant bank in Cannon Street: Schuster, Sons & Co. This was set up to finance railway schemes which at that time were attracting large investment opportunities. He was friendly with the former LB&SCR Chairman, Samuel Laing, who clearly was responsible for influencing Schuster's appointment as the new chairman of the company. They had both collaborated on the removal and reconstruction of Crystal Palace at Sydenham and connected that attraction by rail in 1854.

Schuster then embarked on a rapid expansion plan of new railways in South London, Sussex and Surrey. Some were financed by the LB&SCR, and additionally small companies were encouraged to construct lines in their localities which the Brighton railway intended to purchase upon completion. This shrewd decision at the time removed some risk from the LB&SCR

by passing financial hazards to these companies. Unfortunately for the LB&SCR, contractors still had to be paid for their work.

Leonard Schuster was clearly in need of a reliable civil engineer for the construction of the Brighton lines, and Frederick Banister (1823–1897) became involved with these.

At an early age Banister's family moved to Lancashire where he was educated at Preston Grammar school and later apprenticed to the civil engineering company, Charles Crawley, cutting his teeth in the burgeoning railway industry. Lines that Frederick surveyed and set out included the Irwell Valley, East Lancashire and extension routes of the Lancashire & Yorkshire railways. In 1846 following advice from his physician, who diagnosed a weakness of his lungs, Banister moved to the sunnier and drier climes of Brighton. He then worked on a variety of engineering contracts including the waterworks and various housing developments, setting up a civil engineering and architectural business in 1849.

By 1860 Banister, who was by then well known to the LB&SCR as a conscientious and reliable contractor, took the post of Chief Engineer at the LB&SCR with a brief to expand new railway routes throughout their areas of operation.

Working closely with smaller independent contractors and directly financed lines by the LB&SCR, under Schuster's direction, Banister undertook a major expansion of new railways, both in rural areas and the expanding commuter lines in South London. These included the development of Victoria station, Grosvenor Bridge, Battersea and the expansion of Clapham Junction. In rural areas, railways to Seaford, Groombridge, Pulborough, Ford, Bognor Regis, Littlehampton, Epsom and Leatherhead amongst others were constructed with his involvement. These projects and several more added a further 177 miles of route, the bulk of which were constructed after Banister's appointment.

This, the second period known as 'railway mania', could not be sustained and resulted in the sudden financial crash of 1866 when the LB&SCR's bankers, Overend, Gurney & Co., went bankrupt, immediately bringing to a sudden end the Brighton company's expansion plans.

The LB&SCR was close to insolvency and the powers of the company directors were suspended until a report into the financial affairs of the company was published. This did not make happy reading and made clear that the company had over extended itself with large capital projects, mainly sustained by passenger revenue. Several of their rural lines, such as Horsham to Guildford, and East Grinstead to Tunbridge Wells, were losing money and it would appear that the company was still planning to acquire and construct new lines that were of questionable viability.

In his defence, Schuster claimed that the LB&SCR was forced to defend its territory with new routes because of the threats of incursion from other companies, notably the SER and L&SWR.

As a result of this damning report the company agreed to abandon some imminent contracts and to form a closer working relationship with the SER.

Leonard Schuster and the company Secretary, Frederick Slight, resigned and the board of directors was able to persuade the previous chairman, Samuel Laing, to take charge. As a footnote it is worth recording that Schuster left an estate of half a million pounds on his death in 1871, an astonishingly large amount of money at that time.

The drastic predicament of the LB&SCR inevitably led to a severe curtailing of investment in new lines, one of which was partially constructed, the Ouse Valley Railway.

The background to this proposed railway was born out of events that were taking place in the east between Tunbridge Wells and Eastbourne. Under the renewed agreement of a closer arrangement between the LB&SCR and SER mentioned earlier, a proposed new line was approved in 1864 between Rotherfield (later re-named Crowborough & Jarvis Brook and not to be confused with a later station of the same name) to Eridge, Hailsham and Polegate, thus allowing access to the burgeoning seaside resort of Eastbourne. To the Act was added Section 27 which clearly stated that both companies were to work together between Tunbridge Wells and Eastbourne. A further schedule involved activity at Uckfield which at that time was regarded as a terminus and was later redesigned to allow for through working. In addition, in order to allow access to the SER railway station at Tunbridge Wells, a short tunnel was provided but not completed until 1867. Its status as a single-track tunnel rendered it a permanent bottle neck until closure. All this activity led to the provision of a complex junction at Eridge which ultimately served lines to Oxted, Tunbridge Wells, East Grinstead, Uckfield and Eastbourne.

One may wonder why the SER had gained such a swift advantage over the LB&SCR so it is worth noting that the Brighton company may well have had its eye off the ball as it was additionally being threatened by the London, Chatham & Dover Railway (LC&DR). This company, frequently at loggerheads with the SER, was free

THE OUSE VALLEY RAILWAY • 35

to exploit railways into the Sussex area as there was no signed mutual agreement with the LB&SCR. Thus unexpectedly in 1863 the LC&DR proposed a new line from Beckenham, Hayes, Limpsfield, Crowhurst, Lingfield, Sheffield Park, Lewes, Ovingdean/Rottingdean and terminating at Kemp Town near Brighton's sea front. The LC&DR had in effect drawn up a broadly parallel railway to the existing London to Brighton main line which would gravely threaten its main source of income. The Act was not passed and a second attempt in 1864 additionally resulted in failure. This, coupled with the LB&SCR revising fares more competitively on its main line, secured the abandonment of the LC&DR's plans. However, unlikely though it might seem, there is a legacy of this attempt to reach Brighton by the LC&DR. The company hurriedly changed its proposed route of the Mid-Kent Railway by creating a diversion south of New Beckenham via Clock House and Addiscombe. The line was then proposed to extend from Addiscombe and skirt around Croydon and make its way southwards to Brighton. These bold plans were snookered as described earlier by the double failure to obtain parliamentary approval and the impeding bankruptcy of the LC&DR in 1866. Just to be certain of killing off this incursion into their territory, the LB&SCR hammered the final nail into the coffin by constructing a branch line of its own from a point east of Brighton station to Kemptown, right in the proposed path of its rival, and opening in 1869. This railway, clearly a blocking tactic which never made a profit, closed for passengers in 1932.

Once the LC&DR had failed in its aims, it was clear that the SER gained advantage of this new arrangement by having full running rights over the new LB&SCR railway to Eastbourne. It was additionally apparent that the SER would have a much shorter route from Eastbourne to London, especially after their new line was constructed between Tonbridge and Sevenoaks, completed in 1868. Prior to this connection all trains took the Redhill line before turning north to London Bridge.

Thus the LB&SCR, spurred on by its victory over the LC&DR, realised the opportunity of providing a railway that would shorten the distance from Eastbourne and Hastings to London via Uckfield, the Ouse Valley and the Brighton main line to London.

The Ouse Valley Railway's (OVR) plan was to construct a railway commencing at the southern end of Balcombe's handsome viaduct on the London to Brighton line, designed by John Urpeth Rastrick (1780–1856). It would turn east and follow the Ouse valley

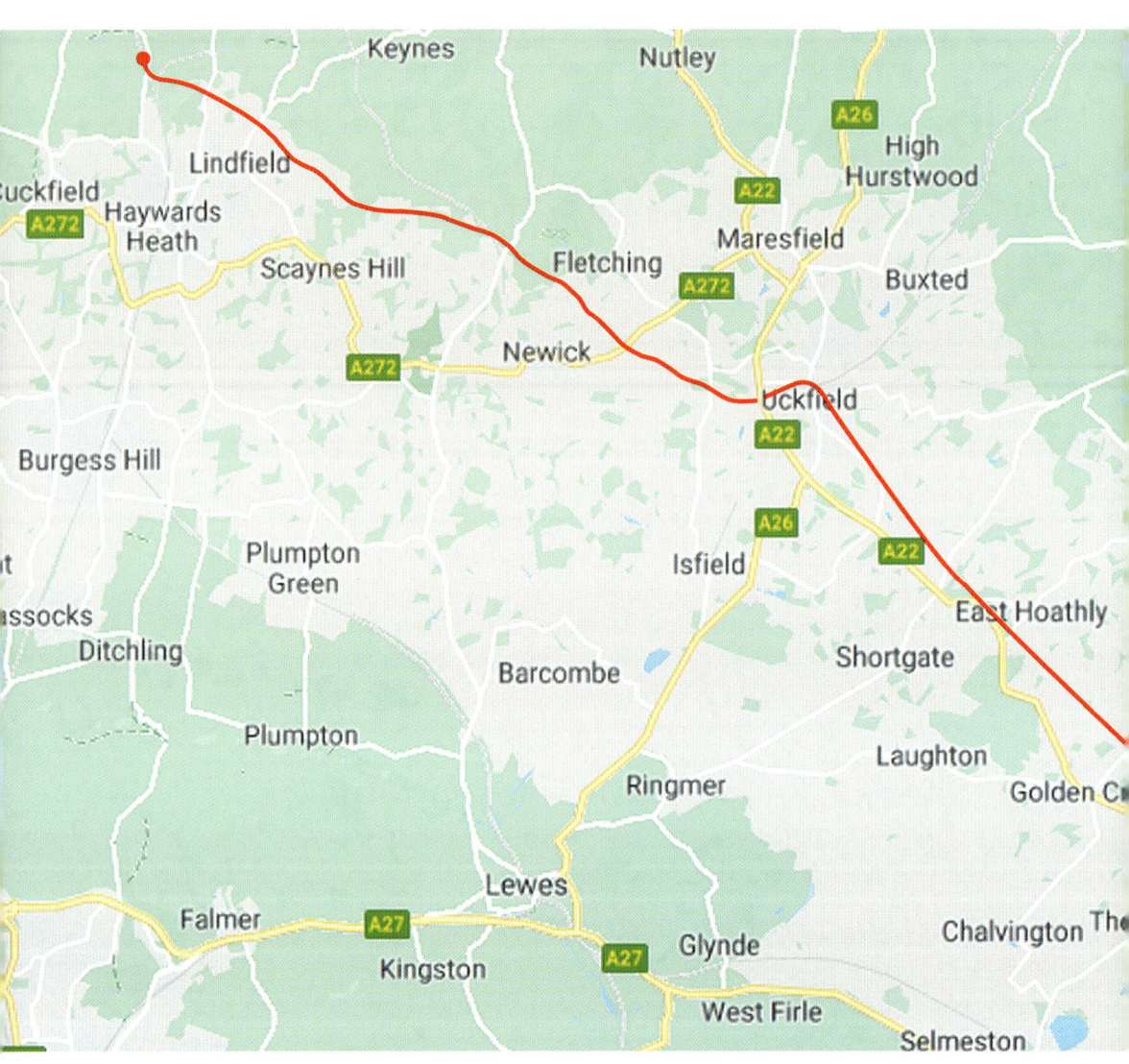

The Ouse Valley Railway Route as planned throughout. (Google. Map data ©2020. By Alex Griffin)

to Lindfield then to Sheffield Park, Newick, Uckfield, Framfield, Chiddingly, Lower Horsebridge, Hailsham, Polegate and Bexhill-on-Sea, connecting to the SER north of St Leonards station.

The Act of Parliament was received in 1864 and construction began in May 1866. This was swiftly followed in the same month by the collapse of Overand & Gurney's bank, a major investor in railway schemes, particularly the Brighton ones. As the Ouse Valley Railway was seen as vital to protect the LB&SCR's interest, work struggled until February 1867, but lack of finance and an unusually wet winter led to the abandonment of the works, which were never to be visited again.

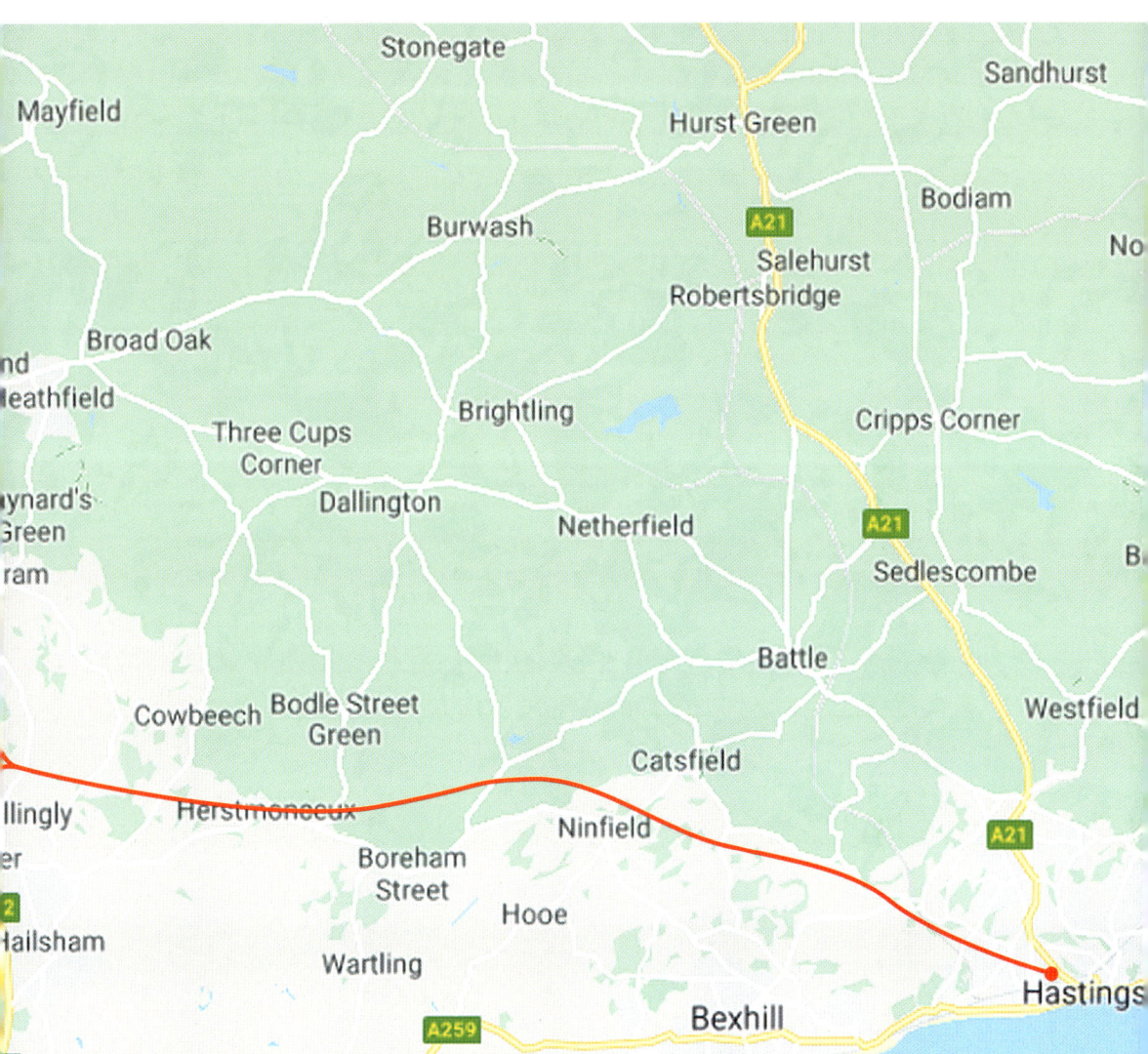

Surprisingly, there are several major remains of work carried out in spite of the rumour that the Brighton line worked slowly as a tactic of keeping out potential competitors. It is more likely that a simple lack of available finance hampered its progress.

Remains of the Ouse Valley Railway and how to get there

When one considers that this planned railway was abandoned over 150 years ago, it is surprising that several substantial earthworks are still clearly visible to this day.

Route of the planned Ouse Valley Railway from Haywards Heath to Uckfield, indicating extent of works undertaken. (Google. Imagery ©2021 Bluesky, Getmapping plc, Infoterra Ltd & Bluesky, Landsat / Copernicus, Maxar Technologies, Map data ©2021. By Alex Griffin)

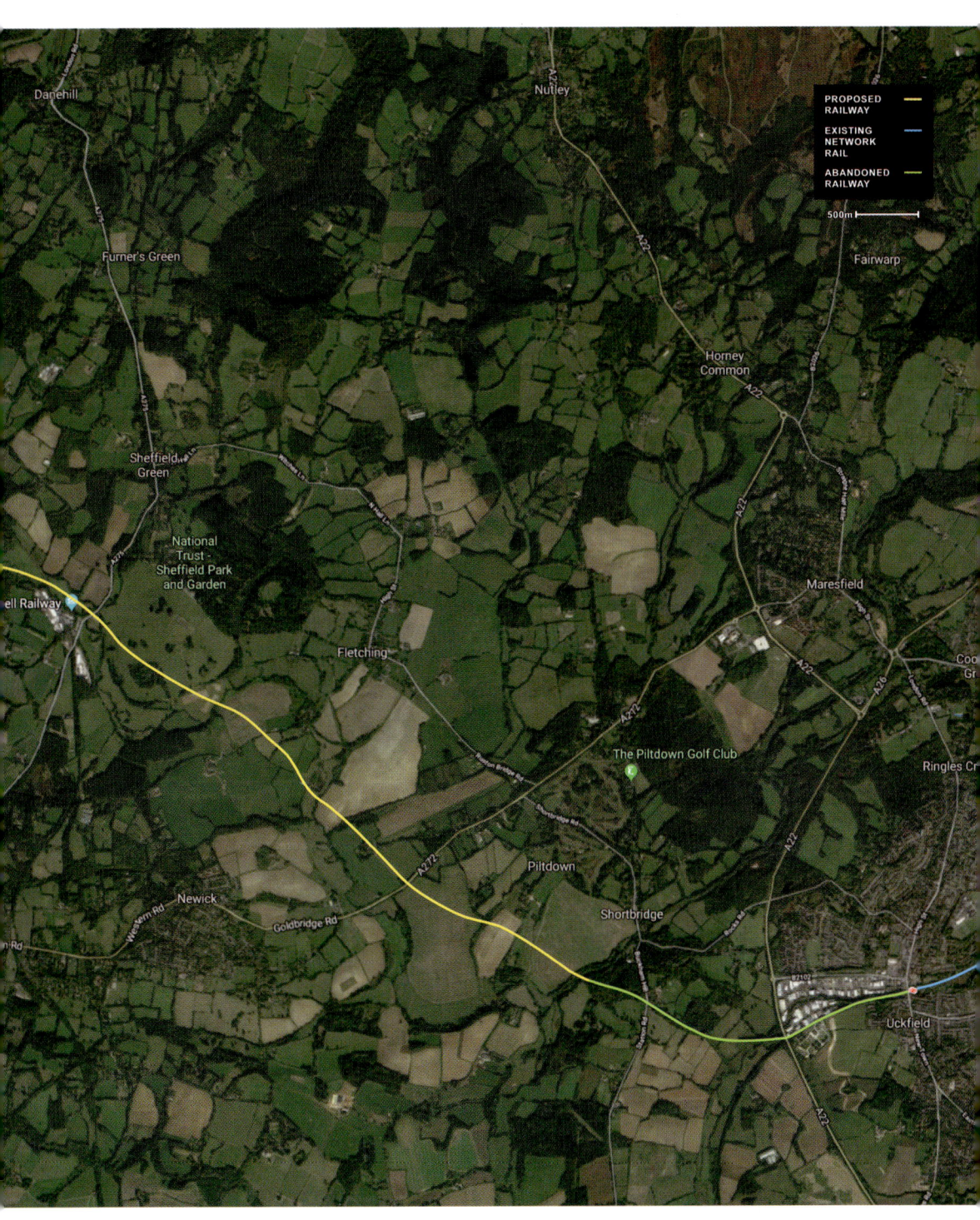

PROPOSED
RAILWAY

EXISTING
NETWORK
RAIL

ABANDONED
RAILWAY

500m

Much of the work was carried out on the western end, so we should start here where the proposed line turned east at the end of Rastrick's fine Ouse Viaduct.

The skew bridge at the proposed junction on the main Brighton to London line has partially survived, with substantial brickwork in evidence. From this structure, shortly after heading south east, the Haywards Heath to Horsted Keynes railway built in 1883 cuts across the OVR route at a right angle. These days the line, having lost its passenger service in 1963, carries aggregate traffic as far as Ardingly. Within 110 yards south of the line, the track bed is visible in woodland and continues until Copyhold Lane is reached. The route then takes a wide south easterly curve across Haywards Heath Golf Club before reaching High Beech Lane, which it crosses at a right angle. The track bed for a few hundred yards is now a footpath until it takes a straight course slightly south of Kenwards Farm where a tunnel was planned. Indeed, it is clear that construction was imminent as the access to the tunnel mouth has been excavated.

Ouse Valley
Viaduct.

Skew Bridge – At the western end of the OVR.

Buckham hill.

Hangman's Acre.

The line continues eastwards over a footpath and shortly after crosses the Lindfield to Ardingly road at right angles on a high embankment. Lindfield station was planned here on the eastern side of the road where the land had been levelled in readiness for the event. The brick bridge abutments were constructed on both sides of the road but were demolished recently as they were proving to be a hindrance to traffic flow. Allegedly these bricks were manufactured at a kiln on the Lindfield station site but there is no sign of this today.

Following the earthworks in an easterly direction, the flat ground then enters a cutting for a distance of about 200 yards. These excavations are of particular interest because the cutting has

Site of Lindfield station.

clearly not been completed. Evidence of navvy barrow runs can be seen and because the track bed drainage was never finished, there are several areas of flooded ponds, even when visited during dry summer months. This cutting comes to a sudden end at the road to Hangmans Acre Farm and it is clear that the road itself would have been excavated to accommodate an extension of the cutting for a further distance. From here there is no evidence of further workings eastwards.

However, it is clear that the LB&SCR carried out excavations west of Uckfield station. By working at both ends of the Balcombe junction to Uckfield station section of the railway, the company was able to demonstrate its determination to complete the works and at least operate trains on this part of the route before completing its planned extension to St Leonards in the east. Furthermore, completed excavations would enable the LB&SCR to bring in ballast, rail, sleepers and construction materials by train.

Work had commenced at the Uckfield end, possibly to keep faith with the populace that this railway would definitely be completed. Until the town's bypass was opened in the mid-1980s, the OVR earthworks could be seen heading west from a proposed junction on the Uckfield to Lewes line close to the present-day sewage works. The bypass made use of some of the railway's spoil for its embankment but in spite of this, remains of the route of the railway can still be seen. The line would then have crossed the lane north of Buckham Hill, entering Darville Wood, finally petering out close to the western end of this copse. There then follows a long cutting deepening towards Beeches Farm, currently very heavily overgrown with trees, and at this place the railway would have passed under the road between Beeches Farm and Buckham Hill. On the other side of this road a cutting has been excavated through Darvel Wood which peters out at its western end and there were no further workings beyond this point. The railway would have continued to Moons Farm and then Piltdown, famous for its 'missing link man' hoax of 1912, then passing between Fletching and Newick before reaching the southern part of Sheffield Park Gardens, a National Trust property. The line would then have crossed today's Bluebell Railway at a place north of Sheffield Park station. The present line, the Lewes & East Grinstead Railway, was not opened until 1882 and there is doubt as to whether it might have been constructed had the OVR been completed as planned. Having crossed the Bluebell line, the OVR would have run approximately parallel to Freshfield bridges, then Great Walstead Farm and then to Hangman's Acre, meeting with the western earthworks as previously described.

How to view the remains

There are three points of access by rail: Haywards Heath to the west, The Bluebell Railway at Sheffield Park Station and Uckfield to the east. Viewing the western abandoned works can best be seen north of Haywards Heath where it is recommended to travel by bicycle or by foot for the hardy. If an approach is made via Sheffield Park at the Bluebell Steam Railway, one must be prepared to walk or cycle some distance to view the remains both to the west and east, where all of the earthworks were originally made. However, taking a train from Network Rail's East Grinstead station, easily accessible from London, is a treat to brighten one's day. The earthworks at Uckfield are close enough to the town's railway station to be viewed by foot or bicycle.

Additional suggested western route walk

The East Sussex scenery is very unspoilt so a suggested route for visitors by train and car could be as follows: travel by car to Haywards Heath station car park then, armed with an ordnance survey map, walk to the abandoned skew bridge at the start of the proposed line to the north. Here one can view Rastrick's impressive viaduct before walking along Rivers Road, picking up the footpath 'The Ouse Valley Way'. Take this path to Lindfield, Little Walstead Farm, Nether Walstead, Costells, Freshfield, Wapsbourne Wood and Wapsbourne Gate. Take a short walk to Sheffield Park Station and take a train to East Grinstead. Change to the Network Rail platform and travel to East Croydon. There change to a train for Haywards Heath and collect your car.

The railway remains can be viewed at some locations by taking short walks from the Ouse Valley Way. Please be aware that some remains are on private land so care to avoid trespass without permission is recommended.

CHAPTER 3

The Mysterious Second Tunnel Portal near Cowden Station

Cowden station is to be found on the railway between London Bridge and Uckfield in East Sussex. This line, originally promoted as the Surrey & Sussex Junction Railway (S&SJR), has an interesting history in the annals of the London, Brighton & South Coast Railway, so we should begin by exploring its origins, which lay in the formation of these two companies.

On 6 July 1865, the Surrey & Sussex Junction Railway received an Act of Parliament to construct a line from a point just north of South Croydon station on the Brighton main line to Tunbridge Wells. It was to be laid via Oxted, crossing under the South Eastern Railway's line near Edenbridge before continuing to Hever, Cowden, Groombridge and Tunbridge Wells. This development upset the South Eastern Railway because it was in direct contravention of an agreement signed by both the LB&SCR and the SER less than one year earlier. Although the Brighton company did not own the S&SJR, it was obvious to the SER that the LB&SCR, with the direct connivance of its chairman Leo Schuster and several directors, were promoting its innovation. The 1864 agreement laid out proposals stating that neither company would construct railways in their respective territories and this development clearly was a major incursion.

Thus the wily South Eastern Railway chairman, Sir Edward Watkin, whose character is covered in chapter one in this book, ruthlessly sought to sabotage the S&SJR. The SER joined forces with its long-term rival, the London, Chatham & Dover Railway, to construct a directly competing railway between Beckenham, Lewes and Brighton. This was actually the LC&DR's third attempt to gain an Act of Parliament for such a railway, the first two having been refused in earlier years albeit on slightly altered geographical projections. Now with this revised route, the Act was passed on 6 August 1866. Had this railway ever been constructed, it would have commenced at a place near Kent House, passing through Hayes Common, Tatsfield, Limpsfield, Lingfield, Horsted Keynes, Sheffield Park, Barcombe, Lewes, Rottingdean and Brighton Steine.

It is interesting to speculate that a substantial portion of the line would have embraced most of the present Bluebell heritage railway, so who could predict that their fine collection of locomotives and rolling stock would be there today had this line ever been constructed?

Fortunately in one sense for the LB&SCR, the financial crash and bankruptcy on 11 May 1866 of Overend, Gurney & Co., heavily involved with financing railways, and with it the London, Chatham & Dover Railway, meant that this and other speculative plans would never see the light of day. However, in spite of the LB&SCR's relief at these events, it too was exposed to the bank's failure and was close to insolvency, its shares being suspended whilst an enquiry was undertaken.

In addition there were difficulties, both in the interpretation of both the companies' agreements and with unsatisfactory negotiations with landowners. The Duke of Richmond (1818–1903), regarded as a safe pair of hands, was asked to arbitrate, which resulted in the transfer of the S&SJR and its assets to the LB&SCR.

In spite of these difficulties the well-known contractors, Waring Brothers, were appointed to construct the railway and initially concentrated on the two tunnels at Edenbridge and Mark Beech near Cowden. The spelling of Markbeech is more commonly

Charles Henry Gordon-Lennox – the 6th Duke of Richmond.

spelt as Mark Beech. Tim Boyles in his history of the village, *Mark Beech – The Unknown Village*, agreed after some local pressure to spell the two words separately, which tends to be the modern way. However his research showed the word's origins to be correctly spelt as one word. Because of the need to avoid confusion, Mark Beech is shown as two words in this chapter.

Work commenced during December 1865 and was to continue to July 1867. Some £242,000 was spent on the project, £162,000 of which covered construction, and the remaining £80,000 for land purchases and compensation. At Mark Beech tunnel, substantial payments were made to the Meade-Waldos for land and disturbance to the north. The

Talbot landowners at the southern end were compensated for disturbance to their properties at Edells, Coldharbour and Wickens. In addition, Brook Farmhouse was to be razed as it lay on the proposed site of Cowden station.

From the start of railway construction, things went badly as the cost of works was greater than anticipated and they dropped seriously behind schedule. Warings later claimed that the engineering problems were more difficult than expected and further reported a shortage of labour. The board of directors of the LB&SCR became very alarmed at these developments as early as February 1866, which led to the formation of a new working arrangement with the S&SJR and its contractors. As noted earlier, a further agreement made on 18 May, subsequently ratified at the end of the month, indicated that the companies would merge, with the LB&SCR paying all the debts of the S&SJR and acquiring those shares which it did not already hold.

Co-incidentally, it was at this time that the contract was hit with a further calamity referred to earlier when on 11 May the brokers Overend, Gurney & Co. went bankrupt, sending shock waves throughout the British economy.

In spite of these developments, it was reported that tunnelling was underway from the northernmost ventilation shaft to meet excavation taking place near the portal at the London end. This excavation, which began in a 300 foot cutting at the north end, would drop about 50 feet through the tunnel before emerging at the bottom of Blower's Hill at the site of the proposed Cowden station. Three ventilation shafts would be built throughout its length of 1,341 yards.

This increased activity attracted hundreds of workers with their families and fellow travellers. Like so many similar schemes elsewhere on other railways, their presence posed problems with public health, food supply and lawless behaviour.

Between 700 and 1,000 navvies were employed on Mark Beech tunnel. Most were English and Irish, but French and Flemish speaking labourers from Belgium and Luxembourg were additionally recruited, including engineers and supervisors. These were provided by Waring Brothers through their long standing continental connections and rapidly increased in number, estimated to represent about half of all those involved with the contract.

Whether these employees were either replacing English navvies or being paid lower wages at around half or one third of the indigenous workforce, is not clear. However, it did lead to a toxic and explosive atmosphere which was likely to blow up at any time.

The Kent Constabulary had been formed by an Act of Parliament in 1856 and was well used to dealing with petty crime, which was particularly prevalent on the Mark Beech tunnel works.

On the 5 August 1866, Supt. Richard Dance from divisional headquarters at Tonbridge, accompanied by a sergeant and several constables, spent the day at Mark Beech following reports of heavy drinking at two local hostelries, one of which was the Kentish Horse, still there to this day. The threatening language he witnessed was so alarming that he ordered several policemen to return the following morning. They were too late because on the previous evening, in what was clearly a premeditated conspiracy at Mark Beech tunnel yard and Brook Farmhouse, English navvies invaded the site and assaulted French speaking workers as well as William Stanbrook, the inspector of masonry. They further smashed windows at the farmhouse which was being used for railway accommodation, before breaking into other huts nearby. The main senior occupant, John West, hastened to Cowden village to summon its two resident policemen, William Solly and George Bassett. They were hopelessly outnumbered by scores of taunting, aggressive and drunken English navvies, so Bassett rode to Tonbridge to get help while Solly remained at a safe distance and waited. Bassett returned the next day at 5am accompanied by Supt. Dance and twelve constables. Even these reinforcements proved to be inadequate and further help was requested by appealing to the Chief Constable Commander Ruxton.

Ruxton raced to Mark Beech and a company of infantry were placed on standby at Shorncliffe Barracks, Folkestone, enabling them to move rapidly by train to Edenbridge's South Eastern station via Ashford and Tonbridge, should they be required.

The immigrant workers had in the meantime fled north through Hever to Edenbridge, pursued by English navvies with the chief commander to the rear in his fly. The inhabitants of the village boarded up their windows as the foreign workers scurried up and down the High Street seeking sanctuary, mostly in vain. By the time that some 100 policemen arrived, the immigrants had congregated at the site of the uncompleted works of Edenbridge LB&SCR station where the English attackers were planning their final assault.

Cowden Station
was built on the site of Brook Farmhouse, which was latterly used to house navvies. (Ben Brooksbank)

The presence of so many policemen had a sobering effect on the English navvies, which led to the end of this ugly episode. For years stories about the riots of Mark Beech tunnel, which were reported to have allegedly led to deaths and serious injuries, were trumpeted by the press, and over time morphed into local culture. Whilst these stories were highly colourful, the truth is more prosaic. In fact the only two recorded deaths in relation to the tunnel were French or more likely Flemish speaking brothers named Schmidt who sadly died of cholera, and because of this, were buried in haste at Mark Beech church, the authorities recording that they resided locally. It is sad to reflect that they passed away so far from home with their families unaware of the fate that had befallen them.

On 9 August, following the disturbances, two magistrates at Edenbridge enrolled a large number of citizens and special constables in addition to the full-time police force. They visited the Mark Beech workings where they made arrests. Ten men were remanded and summonsed to Tonbridge Magistrates Court on 11 August and during October. Seven of those found guilty were sentenced to a year of imprisonment with hard labour.

Although this matter appeared to come to a satisfactory conclusion of sorts, the LB&SCR remained deeply dissatisfied with the contractors and rising costs. Although the line between East Grinstead, Groombridge and Tunbridge Wells had been completed on 27 February 1867, the cash-strapped company's directors decided to abandon further works between Hurst Green and Groombridge on 26 March that year because the costs of completion were estimated to be around £2 million. This action was refused by Parliament so the LB&SCR, in a desperate attempt to minimise its rocky financial position, agreed to pay a penalty of £50 per day with a limit set at £32,250, rather than continue the line's construction with ruinous costs.

In spite of this course of action, which followed all the trauma of riots, overspending and arbitration, there remains to this day the strange tale of Cowden station which, according to reliable records, was built some two years after the works were abandoned. The mystery as to why has never been resolved. We know that the station site was occupied by Brook Farmhouse, one of landowner Talbot's tenanted properties, and this was sold to the LB&SCR who razed it to provide the station platforms and buildings. Why these was constructed remains a mystery. The company was clearly short of money and much work remained to be completed on the railway, with no imminent prospect of providing a train service. Perhaps the Talbot family had drawn up a covenant insisting that their local station would have to be built as soon as the farmhouse had been demolished, thereby applying pressure on the LB&SCR to complete the line. After all, it is recorded that the family were to be granted special access when the line did finally open. Alternatively, was the contract to build the station drawn up earlier, a commitment that the company was unable to legally withdraw from? Perhaps one day the truth will be revealed.

So rather like closures in earlier times, this partially completed line took on the appearance of an abandoned railway during the Beeching era. Reports from witnesses indicated the growth of weeds and trees on the trackless formation and incomplete tunnels, with their timber supports gently rotting away. Most local people believed they would never get their railway and the only section of track laid appears on an ordnance survey map of 1872, indicating some 400 yards in the north near Selsdon station.

Finally, the LB&SCR, having regained financial stability, finished the line between Croydon to Oxted and East Grinstead before turning its attention to completing the S&SJR in 1889, some twenty years after abandonment.

The new contractors Firbank were engaged and prepared to finish the railway. Much of the work consisted of track laying, the construction of new stations in a similar architectural style to that at Cowden, and completion of the civil engineering works. Today's passengers who sit back and enjoy the view, would never guess that it had been only partially completed, lay derelict for twenty years and bore witness to drunken rioting all those years ago.

Except that is, Mark Beech Tunnel, which was only partially complete at the time of abandonment. When the LB&SCR returned

The original tunnel portal hiding in the trees at Cowden.

to finish the works, it was clear that one error needed to be rectified. This revealed that the tunnel was originally 20 yards short of its present length. Behind the present brick-built southern portal is an identical one hiding in trees to the north. Both tunnel portals measure 7 yards in width and there is no doubt that were the rear portal to be excavated, the brickwork including both wing walls would replicate its later replacement.

One can only speculate as to why the abandonment of the structure took place. It is the author's opinion, having thoroughly surveyed the site, that the presence of a bridle path serving Edells, a property to the east, and in addition a stream which flows profusely in periods of wet weather, are now both accommodated above the later extended tunnel. If this had not been lengthened, gushing water down a steep slope would have caused erosion on the railway embankment. As to the bridle path which would have crossed close to the portal, where the track inside the tunnel is laid on a curve with limited visibility, this represented an obvious danger to people and livestock which would have to have been addressed.

With skilled bricklayers on site, it was a simple matter to extend the tunnel by 20 yards, construct a new brick portal and accommodate the bridle path and stream in a new culvert, clearly visible to this day. At the same time the height of the tunnel was raised at its mouth as can be seen from the accompanying photograph. As the earlier portal could so easily have been demolished, we are fortunate that this small item of history has survived as a witness to the machinations of a late Victorian railway site that could so easily have been swept away.

How to get there

The best way of visiting Cowden station and Mark Beech tunnel is by rail as it is well served by an hourly train service from London Bridge and a similar one from Uckfield, the terminal station to the south. For added interest during the summer season, one can travel by steam train on the Spa Valley Railway from Tunbridge Wells West station to Eridge, changing platforms and taking a Southern train to Cowden. It is recommended that the heritage railway's timetable be consulted to calculate connections before travelling this way speculatively. If visiting by car, it is important to remember that the station car park is always more than filled to capacity on weekdays, so is best avoided at those times.

Some 22 yards within the Cowden Southern Tunnel Portal, the line of brickwork separating the new and old is clearly visible. (Adrian Backshall)

From the station car park, walk to the road, turn right and pass under the bridge that carries the railway. Immediately on the right take the public footpath and walk parallel to the railway for a distance of around 270 yards. Here the path divides so take the right turn and walk uphill which brings the walker above the tunnel. The abandoned portal can be found after 22 yards on the left.

CHAPTER 4

The Chessington to Leatherhead Railway

The county of Surrey in spite of its close proximity to London is still a beautiful area, particularly to the south. One of its main arterial roads since the early 1920s is the A3, which runs from the centre of London through Putney, Surbiton, Esher and Guildford, wending its way to Portsmouth.

Towards the north and west of this area, railway development during the Victorian era consisted of the main line from London to Kingston Town, later re-named Surbiton, which opened in 1863 and extended to Portsmouth. From the present town of Kingston-upon-Thames as far as Croydon to the west, lies a large tract of land that was ignored because few significant communities existed to attract railway development.

Ironically it was road development that stimulated population growth in this part of Surrey rather than the railway. The A3 was vitally important for the defence of the nation, and even in the 1700s, improvements were carried out to ensure speedier journeys by horse and carriage to the south coast ports.

Before the First World War, eminent figures such as Lord Montagu of Beaulieu campaigned for road improvements but to no avail. Eventually £500,000 was found, a large sum of money at the time, for a new 8.5 mile bypass which was constructed around Kingston and Surbiton to the outskirts of Esher. Work started in 1924 and the road was opened by the Prime Minister, the Rt. Hon. Stanley Baldwin MP (1867–1947), on 28 October 1927.

There then followed an early example of ribbon development, the haphazard building of unplanned housing, much of which was art deco or mock Tudor in appearance. Fortunately, later on an Act of Parliament, The Restriction of the Ribbon Development Act 1935, prevented further incursions such as these, unless planning permission was obtained. Other developments led to the construction of light industry and offices with still no sign of railway development.

It did not take long for Sir Herbert Ashcombe Walker (1868–1949), General Manager of the Southern Railway (SR), to observe that

Sir Herbert Ashcombe Walker – General Manager, Southern Railway.

traffic at Worcester Park Station on the Epsom to Raynes Park line was showing a marked increase directly as a result of these new developments.

By all accounts Walker was a 'born railwayman' who started life as an apprentice on the London & South Western, later the Southern Railway, at seventeen years old. He displayed a natural aptitude for remembering facts and figures as well as a broad knowledge of track and signal engineering. Popular with staff of all grades, he remembered their Christian names whenever they met.

Later in his career, he was well known for his grasp of third rail electrification and it's owing to his foresight that the Southern Railway invested heavily in this form of power, both on existing and new lines, until nationalisation in 1948. The company, very much embracing the art deco era, produced wonderful Southern Railway stations and posters which evocatively advertised south coast resorts, encouraging families to take their holidays by Southern Railway trains.

It is no surprise to learn that Walker's dedication, even when approaching retirement, was still to build new electrified lines, one of which would take advantage of the open space south of Raynes Park. The plan was to construct a new line from there to connect with Leatherhead in the south. In fact this venture was to be not only his final challenge, but also that of the Southern Railway before being nationalised after the Second World War.

The SR, taking advantage of traffic growth, was spurred on to construct two new stations on the Epsom to Raynes Park lines, at Motspur Park in 1925, and Stoneleigh in 1932. Walker's proposal at a Southern Railway Directors' board meeting held in 1929 that a new railway between Motspur Park, Chessington and Leatherhead be constructed was endorsed. This was sanctioned by Parliament in 1930 and after some delay, work started in 1934. So what caused this delay? Well, like all good stories, the truth can sometimes be stranger than fiction. The SR was counting on the development of large scale housing following the construction of the railway, particularly on land at Malden Rushett and to the north of Leatherhead. With large

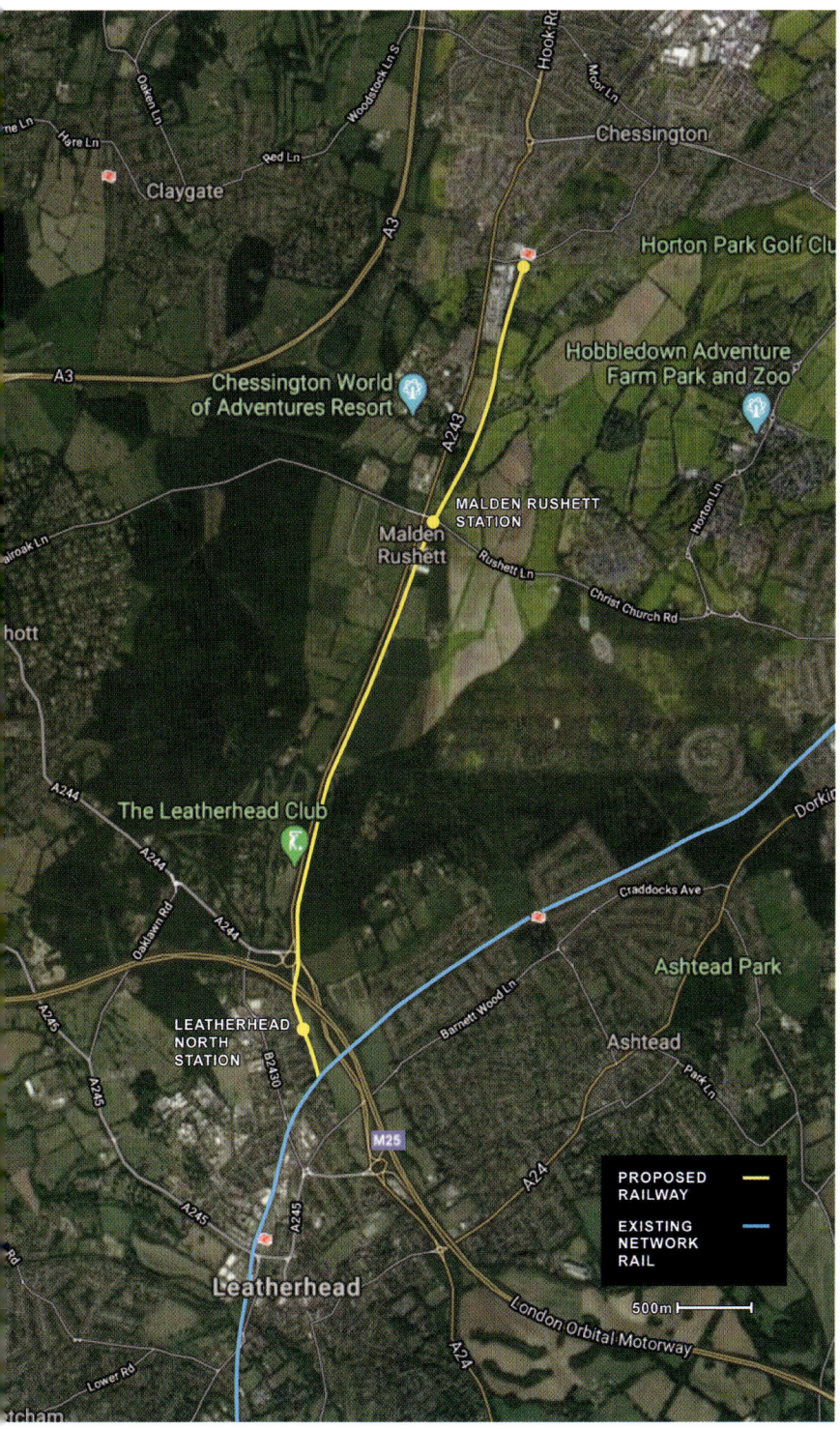

Route of planned railway from Chessington South to Leatherhead. (Google. Imagery ©2021 Bluesky, Getmapping plc, Infoterra Ltd & Bluesky, Landsat / Copernicus, Maxar Technologies, The GeoInformation Group, Map data ©2021. By Alex Griffin)

housing developments the need for sewage treatment and disposal of waste became paramount. It was clear that Surrey County Council was in the midst of the depression and not inclined to provide the necessary facilities as there was a squeeze on budgets, particularly on what was considered to be a speculative venture. It would appear that this difficulty was eventually overcome by negotiation, but the delay of four years before starting work lost the SR valuable time. It is interesting to speculate that had it not been for the lack of basic facilities for homes, the railway may well have been completed before the outbreak of the war.

The first stage after building Motspur Park Junction was to provide stations at Malden Manor and Tolworth, which were opened in 1938. In the second stage, the line was extended to Chessington North and Chessington South and opened a year later. It is interesting to note that the original station names were to be Chessington Court and Chessington Grange to the south, but these were changed to reflect the image of a clean, modern electric railway. As to the earthworks, these were constructed over

Malden Manor Station. (Nigel Thompson)

undulating land requiring a number of embankments and cuttings. Accounts at the time report that the acidic clay encountered was 'treacherous', requiring support for the track base and dry material added to the tops of cuttings. Extensive drainage was provided to prevent the movement of the soil. Stations were constructed in art deco style, designed by a Scotsman, James Robb Scott (1882–1965), the chief architect of the SR who additionally designed many other stations, including the Victory Arch at Waterloo Station. The railway was fitted with third rail electricity from the outset and early plans for providing island platforms were discarded, because of the risk of electrocution to foot passengers crossing live rails.

With the outbreak of war, work on extending the line from Chessington South to Malden Rushett and Leatherhead North stations came to a halt. The works by then had reached a short distance beyond Chessington South Station. As an army training exercise a substantial embankment was built by the Royal Engineers in the early 1940s, allegedly assisted by Italian prisoners of war. It was half a mile in length, with a temporary bridge provided over Chalky Lane, with work coming to an end at the edge of Chessington Wood. Spoil for this construction, apart from that provided by the Chessington railway, came from new works at Basingstoke West sidings, the widening of a cutting at Swanley Station as well as debris from bombing raids in London. Track that was laid on these new works used steam locomotive hauled works trains to build the branch and extension. In the early 1960s a goods depot was provided immediately beyond Chessington South, which closed twenty years later.

The railway's powers to extend the line to Leatherhead lapsed in 1962, but opposition to its construction had been gaining ground since the end of the Second World War. A new generation was growing up and the local population was vehemently opposed to this new line cutting a path through land which had become widely regarded as 'Green Belt'. It undoubtedly would attract large swathes of housing for which the railway was designed, so with these threatened developments a Protection Order was placed on Ashstead Common.

Furthermore, the newly nationalised British Railways made it clear that there was little enthusiasm to complete the line, which would not only be divisive but open to legal challenge. And if that were not enough, access to Leatherhead Station would prove to

**Chessington
Embankment**
1949. (Britain from
Above)

be tricky. Originally there were two stations close to each other on separate lines serving the town, one provided by the London & South Western Railway which closed in 1927, and the other still in use today, built by the London, Brighton & South Coast Railway. As BR wrestled with its options, the provision of a new second station to replace the old one which lay derelict in what had latterly become Leatherhead's goods yard was rejected. The obvious alternative was to use the surviving station and operate Chessington trains from a junction a mile to the north.

So the years drifted by and although powers to extend were technically active until 1962 they were formally abandoned shortly afterwards. History records that from time to time the matter of using the earthworks and reinstating the railway southwards had been raised. But these attempts were never taken seriously.

Remains of the Chessington to Leatherhead Railway and how to get there

The northern end of the Chessington extension is easy to follow because the embankment is still very much in evidence from a bridge carrying the road above the railway at Chessington South Station. The course of the route south crossing Chalky Lane runs parallel with A243 Kingston Road on a substantial embankment, much overgrown, with the earthworks ending at Chessington Wood. Continuing south in a straight line the railway would have passed over Rushett Lane to the planned site of Malden Rushett Station. It's worth exploring the common land south of here as the route continues to run alongside the A243. To those with sharp eyes, there are reputedly the remains of typical Southern Railway concrete fence posts, gently returning to nature.

As the A243 meets the A244 the proposed line would have crossed here bearing south near to a footbridge which is over the M25 motorway. From here the route would have followed south east at the rear of housing which to-day follows the curve of the proposed line to the east of Leatherhead Common. A junction with the main line was planned at the rear of Downsend Pre-Preparatory school and a station serving the common, which was then being further developed for housing, would have been provided here.

The stations along the section of line constructed are elegant, and unusually the canopies are unsupported by pillars which increase light to platforms. When freshly painted in white they look remarkably attractive. The licensee for the canopies, named Chisarc, was German, and in spite of the impending onset of war, not deterred by the SR contract. The British company's sole distributorship rights of Chisarc canopies in the United Kingdom was T.A. Chishom Ltd. whose products additionally spanned large buildings, including the cover of open spaces such as swimming pools and aircraft hangers.

Chessington South Station has two platforms constructed very much as a through station in mind but has only ever used its downside platform. The line is twin track, which allows trains to be stored adjacent to the up platform, thereby allowing a more frequent service to be provided when necessary. The up platform today has a mournful look and is showing its age through lack of use. This sad structure would have witnessed frequent electric trains from Leatherhead heading north to London, but it was never to be.

Although two platforms were provided at Chessington South, the only one used was on the down side, as shown here.

The obvious means of getting to the remains of the Chessington South branch is by one of the line's frequent electric trains from Waterloo Main railway station. Before taking the train out or on your return, try to take a look at Scott's First World War memorial as referred to earlier. It is recommended that a map or modern electronic equivalent be taken for the walk across the common where the earthworks, these days completely overgrown, can be viewed. The exploration from Leatherhead station is not recommended as it is built up all the way to Leatherhead Common with heavy road traffic.

CHAPTER 5

Kent's International Airport Railway

In the early days of commercial flight, the development of Britain's airports makes interesting reading. Names that feature internationally in the media often started life from local rural names. Few people would know that Heathrow Airport, for example, was developed from a row of agricultural cottages in a lane simply named Heath Row, now completely buried under a sea of concrete and tarmacadam, or that Gatwick airport gets its name from Goat Farm.

Apart from some early unofficial grass airstrips, the citizens of Kent were well served with a comprehensive railway system and a good choice of sea crossings to mainland Europe. As air travel in those days was deemed to be for the wealthy, the necessity of airports such as those of today was not judged to be a priority. Croydon International Airport 'on the A23 south of the town' had opened in 1920 and was at that time the only one of its size in the United Kingdom. For a while it was thought to be adequate for the London area but the opening of Heathrow rapidly proved to be the preferred airport, complete with rail connections and the A4 trunk road.

However, the Southern Railway, which had been formed by an amalgamation of several smaller companies in 1923, was forward looking and had already heavily invested in third rail electrification and stylish art deco buildings. The success of the opening of London's Airport at Croydon attracted the attention of the SR which saw commercial opportunities in the future of rail and air transport.

Why a new airport in Kent was considered is due to a series of unusual events. The site chosen was curious, and seemingly the main reason for its location was its close proximity to central London, at nineteen miles to the south east. The place was at Lullingstone in the Darenth Valley near Swanley, which is an outstandingly beautiful area to this day. The rolling hills with farms and woodland are best seen by rail between Swanley and Otford

Junction offering wonderful views from today's electric trains. It's hard to believe that during the 1930s, an airport would be proposed with apparently very little antagonism from the local community. However, before the Second World War little attention was paid to planning or Green Belt issues.

In addition, pressure was growing for commuter housing as London continued to expand and with this in mind the owners of Lullingstone Castle in 1935 sold 5,000 acres of their estate to the Kemp Town Brewery in Brighton which at that time was diversifying into property development. A new station was planned to serve houses and shops but strangely these plans were abandoned because, as often occurs in the housing market, a period of recession was being experienced. Then co-incidentally two further developments took place. Firstly, the brewery sold the land to Kent County Council, presumably with building in mind, and secondly, the SR expressed an interest in developing a new airport on part of the site. Thus in 1937, a Parliamentary Bill granted permission for a new airport to be built on 800 acres of land between Swanley and Eynsford. It was to provide three runways with two stations operating from six platforms. This was obviously going to be a grand affair for the SR and with great enthusiasm the plans were revealed. An early decision was to place the airport station close to the main line and the south portal of Eynsford tunnel. An art deco station based on the company's corporate style was designed by James Robb Scott, chief architect of the SR. It was to consist of two long precast concrete platforms with waiting rooms, brick chimneys, deep canopies and a footbridge. A second station was planned adjacent to the up line platform, similarly designed with a footbridge at the start of the railway spur to the airport.

Curiously this line from the main railway to the airport itself branched off to the north of the new station, which meant that trains from London could be routed directly to the airport. Passengers from the south would have to change trains on the new station and cross by footbridge to the first station on this short branch, which was planned to be three quarters of a mile long. As if four platforms were not enough, two further platforms were to be provided at the end of the double track branch in an underground station beneath the airport complex.

By now the Air Ministry was planning the provision of three further airports close to London, these being Heathrow, the redevelopment of Croydon, and Fairlop in East London to be served by the Central Line, and Lullingstone.

The planned layout of the Lullingstone airport and railway connection. (Google. Imagery ©2021 Bluesky, Getmapping plc, Infoterra Ltd & Bluesky, Landsat / Copernicus, Maxar Technologies, The GeoInformation Group, Map data ©2021. By Alex Griffin)

Lullingstone Station during demolition in 1955. (Sevenoaks Rail Travellers Association)

Construction of Lullingstone station commenced rapidly because the SR needed access for building materials, excavation equipment and the workforce. In those days transport would have been tricky with no main roads or administrative buildings, so the new station was planned to address these issues. So far so good, but once work got underway, local residents objected to the planned construction of new roads but not the airport itself.

These objections seemed to be the final straw because behind the scenes, the SR was having serious doubts about the viability of its venture. One of the problems was the refusal of Kent County Council or central government to contribute funds to offset the costs. Additionally the SR was alarmed by the expense of levelling the ground for the runways. Although at first glance the proposed airport terrain looked reasonably level at the top of the valley, on closer examination the ground was more challenging than first thought, so nothing happened. The planned opening date of 2 April 1939 came and went, with the imminent start of war beckoning. After hostilities ceased, green belt policies became a reality, finally burying the scheme forever, not under a sea of concrete but in the filing cabinets of government departments. However, in a curious twist of fate, the airport plan had not been entirely killed off. Kent was subject to severe bombing raids and aerial attacks by the

Luftwaffe, especially during the Battle of Britain, and the RAF, as part of its defence strategy, set up dummy 'Q' sites in various locations, including Lullingstone. These were to mislead the enemy into believing that these false airfields were actually real. They installed lights and inoperable dummy aircraft to lure attackers in, thereby reducing attacks on viable targets elsewhere.

Bishopstone station on the Seaford branch in East Sussex is identical to that planned at Lullingstone. (Johnh.eu)

Meanwhile, for ten years after peace was restored in Europe, the partially constructed station, nationalised in 1948 by British Railways, published the location of Lullingstone in its timetables. Between 1940 and 1955 the indication was that 'the opening would be on a date to be introduced'. It never happened.

And so Lullingstone station stood alone and unloved in the fields of the Darenth Valley until 1955, when the buildings and footbridge were finally demolished.

Stand here today and just imagine what might have been. A bustling terminal complete with multi-story car parks, taxis, roads and jet aircraft on aprons awaiting departure, with planes landing and taking off once a minute. The author is bound to record, even as a railway enthusiast, that the failure of this project does rather gladden his heart.

Remains of Kent's International Airport and how to get there

Although much of the original station has been lost, a visit to the Darenth Valley Park is recommended to take in the beautiful scenery with many footpaths and of course the remains of the station. Travel by train is recommended to Eynsford with a frequent service from London Victoria to the west and from the east from Dover, Ashford and Maidstone East. It is recommended that a large scale explorer footpath map be taken as this will allow visitors to explore the villages and public houses and all the other attractions, including the fine viaduct at Eynsford.

As to the remains today, Lullingstone's two platforms still survive in part although the coping stones and support posts have degenerated, so little remains of this once proud station. However, part of the approach road and adjacent pavement remain, albeit

Lullingstone Station approach road. (David Staines)

barricaded from prying eyes. These can be found a short distance from the southern portal of Eynsford tunnel in a shallow cutting just off Crockenhill Lane.

After demolition the canopy and its supports were despatched to Canterbury East station to replace their own.

The design of Lullingstone station can be appreciated elsewhere, particularly at Bishopstone station on the branch railway on the south coast between Lewes and Seaford. Although now unstaffed, the station is Grade 2 listed and served by a frequent train service and replicates that which partially survives at Lullingstone.

South Eastern train passing remains of platform. (David Staines)

Chapter 6

The First Channel Tunnel

England was separated from France some 10,000 years ago when polar ice started to melt at the end of the last Great Glaciation. With this global event, the sea level rose around 4,000 feet, flowing into what we know as the English Channel.

The rocks of the seabed are of course very much older, with geologists confirming that the earliest ones were laid down in the Triassic Period more than 200 million years ago. These rocks were then overlain by fossilferous rocks of the Jurassic and Cretaceous periods ending at the extinction of the dinosaurs 65 million years ago. During the upper cretaceous era vast quantities of marine organisms, of which Coccolithophorous plankton are the most important species, formed massive chalk beds hundreds of feet deep. Importantly the chalk, now covered by sea to a depth of 200 feet, is easily tunnelled. However, during the formation of the Alps at the Cretaceous Period, the channel beds were both folded and faulted which meant that in places, particularly on the French side, tunnelling was less predictable than geologists surmised.

The channel was in earlier times always a risky sea to cross because of lengthy tidal flows, treacherous currents, strong winds and thick fog. In taking these factors into account it was not surprising that alternatives to crossing by ship were being actively considered during the early part of the industrial revolution.

Apart from vague references to crossing by balloon and tunnel, the first serious proposal was promoted in 1802 by Albert Mathieu, a mining engineer from northern France. His plan was to dig a tunnel through the hard chalk seam with an artificial island in the centre on the Varne bank, which would allow ships to dock and passengers to take rest. The mode of travel would be by horse and carriage, with cast iron ventilation shafts sited at intervals designed to rise above sea level, and it would be lit throughout.

These plans were exhibited in Paris and in spite of much public interest, little action resulted. They were removed some years later, it is said by members of his family, never to be seen again.

Around three decades later a second French entrepreneur, Thomé de Gamond (1807–1876), a respected engineer who remembered much detail of Mathieu's plans, was able to reinvigorate the scheme in 1833, much along the details deposited in 1802.

Interest from representatives from the British and French governments varied widely during the following forty years, with political issues being the dominant factors. Many centuries of military conflict, and reservations by the British view of the world outside, would always be dominant in the thoughts of each country's leaders.

In Thomé de Gamond one sees a man obsessed by the project. He conducted endless surveys in boats, exploring the seabed weighed down by rocks, and was even witnessed diving with a homemade pig's bladder as an early form of aqualung which placed his life at risk. He claimed to have been attacked by monsters on the seabed, which were most likely from his description to have been conger eels.

In addition de Gamond proposed a cast iron tube lined with bricks, an iron bridge and jetties reaching out into the channel from both shores. These ideas, probably presented to keep a spotlight on the project, proved to be impractical as well as expensive and were quickly abandoned.

His final proposal, published in 1857, was detailed in addressing geological, technical and financial issues. Once again it featured a tunnel with an artificial island halfway at Varne bank, with access to a harbour and railway station. The route would have been from Cap Griz Nez in France to a place east of Dover where it was to have linked up with the South Eastern Railway's main line to London, and in France it would have joined the Boulogne, Amiens and Paris railway. Three ventilation shafts were deemed to be sufficient, one of which would have been on the island. It was to be gas lit throughout with the estimated cost at £8 million.

At first the responses to de Gamond's proposals were positive, but not for long. There was an attempt on Napoleon III's life in 1858 by an Italian named Orsini who lived in England and sailed to France with his bomb. This 'odious act', according to de Gamond, was planned to start a revolution but led the French to deport foreigners. The strained relationships between both countries led to the shelving of any attempt to develop the channel tunnel.

Little happened in the following ten years which led de Gamond to refer to the English as 'puerile' in view of their fear of a French

Above: **William Low**, the distinguished engineer. (wrexham-history.com)

Left: **Aimé Thomé** de Gamond.

invasion which he said, 'could be countered by flooding sea water into the tunnel in such an event'.

Meanwhile on the English side, interest in the project was gathering apace. William Low (1814–1886), a Scottish mining engineer, had studied de Gamond's plans and realised that he could improve some aspects, particularly the problem of ventilation. He devised up and down draft shafts incorporated into a twin tunnel system with connecting cross passages, which apart from providing a flow of air, would allow workmen and passengers to escape in the event of an emergency. In the early 1860s he presented his plans to Napoleon III who received them well, saying, 'I should like to see this (channel tunnel) done. As soon as your prospectus is ready, send it to me and I will lay it before my Minister and do all I can to support it'.

In a bid to develop the project, Low worked alongside de Gamond, who gladly provided all his studies in order to speed progress. Their cooperation allowed the plans to be taken up on national scale in both countries and Low recruited two engineers that he knew well, James Brunlees (1816–1892) and John Hawkshaw (1811–1891). They signed a report based upon Low's submission to Napoleon who granted an audience to the Anglo-French delegation in the summer of 1868. At its head were Lord Richard Grosvenor and on the French side, Senator Michel Chevalier. Amongst other members of the committee was the indefatigable de Gamond, still contributing to his lifelong dream. This time he was joined by powerful supporters, some ninety in number, including the Dukes of Sutherland and Argyll, members of Parliament, bankers, directors of railways, businessmen and the Archbishop of Canterbury.

This stage of proceedings is generally regarded as the 'Golden Age of the Tunnel'. Low's plans for a twin tunnel construction were accepted and because the problems of ventilation were successfully addressed, the idea of an island in the middle of the channel was dropped with de Gamond's approval. This was followed by a committee decision in 1868 to press ahead with the sinking of shafts on both shores with headings in the chalk seam out to sea.

Hawkshaw had already carried out his own survey with the eminent geologist, Hartsink Day, a year earlier. Borings were made at South Foreland east of Dover and a place three miles west of Calais. Their conclusion was that the proposed tunnel through the lower chalk stratum could be relied upon for stability from end to end.

In spite of technical progress, a request by the committee in 1869 for interest to be paid on the costs of capital required for exploratory works was refused. This was followed a year later by an application to the French government for a sole concession to build the tunnel, necessary of course to raise funds through share issues with official state backing.

Lord Clarendon, the British foreign secretary, was evasive and countered the request, citing the need to evaluate the project's viability with further studies to ascertain the attitude of the French government at that time.

But rather like in recent times when Prime Minister Harold MacMillan was asked what could knock the government off course, his cryptic reply was famously, 'Events dear boy, events'. And that was precisely what happened when the Franco–Prussian War broke out in 1870 leading to the unfortunate capture of Napoleon III. The Prussian King proclaimed himself the Emperor of Versailles and so for a while, any thoughts of constructing a channel tunnel were mothballed.

However, public opinion in England was on the side of the French, who had suffered badly at the hands of their enemy, and particularly as a powerful united Germany was a direct threat to Great Britain.

This led to the reinvigoration of the project in 1871 and a new application was submitted in the summer of that year, which was drawn up complete with costings by Hawkshaw, Low and Brunlees. De Gamond's name is conspicuously absent, indicating that early disagreements were taking place between the engineering team and that of the French engineer who was now backing Low's twin tunnel scheme, not Hawksworth's double track tunnel which he originally supported.

These were indeed sad days for de Gamond who had always been known as the 'Father of the Channel Tunnel'. Times had moved on and he was now being largely ignored by a younger team of British engineers with their own plans and it is likely that the committee was no longer paying his expenses.

In his final years he lived in penury, having spent all his working life and money on the project. His devoted daughter provided a minimal income by giving piano lessons and he died in 1876 some four years before the first serious attempt was made to excavate a tunnel. He would little realise that, not only would this fail but a successful connection under the sea would have to wait nearly 120 years, by which time the world would have entered the space age, with man walking on the moon.

Following the submission of the new application, the Anglo-French Channel Tunnel Committee formed a company to proceed with the project. Known as the Channel Tunnel Company Ltd, it was incorporated in London on 15 January 1872 with its articles and aims as follows: 'to construct an underground tunnel between the Straits of Dover, between England and France'. The company's capital was 30,000 pounds, divided into 1,500 shares each at twenty pounds.

During the extraordinary ebbs and flows of progress, things really started to move at the end of the decade. The Channel Tunnel Company Ltd wrote to the Board of Trade requesting permission to drive an experimental heading under the foreshore at a place to the east of Dover. The Board requested detailed plans but as engineer Hawkshaw had requested permission on behalf of the company from the address of his personal office, the Board wrongly sent its letter directly to him instead of the company's headquarters. Hawkshaw's response, posted without reference to his colleague Low, submitted a plan showing the tunnel commencing at St Margaret's Bay some distance east of Low's plans at a site near Shakespeare Cliff at Dover. This action led to a major row between the two engineers which had obviously been festering for some time as they both held trenchant views as to where the channel tunnel should commence. Lord Grosvenor, the company chairman, tried to mediate to persuade Low to accept Hawkshaw's proposal which he clearly felt was the best option. Low refused to have any further dealings with them and stormed out, taking his plans with him. This left the company with Hawkshaw's and Brunlee's plans for a single bore double track railway tunnel commencing from St Margaret's Bay. In the meantime the embittered Low formed his own company, The Anglo/French Submarine Railway Company.

On the other side of the channel during the strife taking place in England, the French government set up a commission of enquiry which Low attended at Arras in November of 1873. He presented his plans in direct opposition to the Channel Tunnel Company and whilst he was received politely, was only allowed to attend in the role of 'critic'. However, the commission did praise his plans presented earlier and reported that the Channel Tunnel Company's proposals were lacking in detail. The outcome of this enquiry was that much more geological work was needed before a concession could be granted. In addition the French wanted to know the level of support from the English government. The view stated the following year by the Board of Trade confirmed that the project would not be opposed 'providing that the English Government is not asked to make any gift, loan or guarantee'.

These actions triggered a wealth of positive correspondence between both governments, which led on 30 May 1876 to a protocol, signed by both sides as 'a basis of a Treaty to be Concluded Concerning the Submarine Tunnel'. With some rapidity the French pushed the project forward by granting a ninety-nine-year concession from 1881–1980. This was conditional on both the British and French tunnel companies forging an agreement before 1881. The French Tunnel Company had capital of two million gold francs (about £80,000) divided into 400 shares. The remainder of the required money was to be raised between the bank of Rothschild and the French money market.

This left the English side in something of a quandary as they clearly felt that the French had moved too quickly in supporting the scheme. Although it seemed logical to allow the concession on the English side to be granted to the Channel Tunnel Company, another player had entered the contest.

In spite of all the frenetic activities during the 1870s, conspicuous by its absence is any reference to the South Eastern Railway. After all, it was a company that would supply the track, signalling, stations, trains and rolling stock and more importantly, the connection with the tunnel whatever site was chosen.

There were in fact two railway companies which vied for access to the tunnel, the South Eastern and the London Chatham & Dover Railway companies. If the eastern portal favoured at that time was chosen, it would offer more benefit to the LC&DR than the SER. What did not help matters was the personal antagonism of each railway company's chairmen, Edward Watkins and James Staats Forbes. Their territorial wars in South East England were legendary and led to distractions such as constructing unnecessary lines to keep the other out and duplication of stations in key towns. The LC&DR was not in a strong position, having slowly recovered from bankruptcy in 1866. Thus the tunnel was not seriously considered for several years by either company until the scheme was well established in 'its golden age'.

William Low had not been idle after his falling out with Hawkshaw and the Channel Tunnel Company. His company, The Anglo/French Submarine Railway Company, was now defunct and unable to continue through lack of funds. However, the SER formed its own proposal which embraced Low's plans, thereby offering him the opportunity of continuing with his dream.

On 16 July 1874 the SER received the Royal Assent enabling it 'to afford pecuniary aid towards the construction of borings and other works in connection with a Tunnel under the English Channel'. This led to renewed conflict with Watkin's old adversary Forbes, Chairman of the LC&DR, and of course Lord Grosvenor.

With this seemingly intractable row remaining unresolved, Parliament empowered both companies to spend £20,000, separately or jointly on tunnel research. To his credit, Watkin indicated to Forbes that he was prepared to contribute his share and enter discussions. These talks quickly broke down particularly in regard to where the international station was to be built, a problem exacerbated by the famously high chalk cliffs each side of Dover. The French in the meantime could only wait and wonder which company would be chosen.

Within one month of the SER's assent the Channel Tunnel Company was granted its own on 2 August 1874 and without delay acquired land at St Margaret's Bay and sunk a shaft. Unfortunately, flooding from the sea rapidly engulfed the works, leading to them being abandoned, as clearly Hawkshaw's and Brunlee's calculations were seen to be wildly inaccurate. Low's reaction to this news is not recorded but a celebratory visit to a local hostelry should not be ruled out. The SER proceeded to advance their plans immediately.

On the face of it and according to exchanges of documentary evidence, the government had not intervened in the tunnel's progress. Now of course because it actually looked as though the tunnel just might be constructed, alarm was vocal and at the highest level. Queen Victoria made it known her abhorrence of this 'very objectionable project' and more importantly her perceived risk of a French invasion. In 1875 she wrote to Prime Minister Disraeli expressing her hope that 'The Government will do nothing to encourage the proposed tunnel which we think very objectionable.'

Meanwhile the Channel Tunnel Company, following its debacle at St Margaret's Bay, was facing financial problems. The company needed money to buy further land to enable a new shaft to be dug and this had to be raised within a year of the 1875 Act. Even with the support of its banker Rothschild and the company's own resources, it was still short by £40,000, the amount required to match the French counterparts. With what little funds it did have, some boring was carried out at Fan Hole on the coast between St Margaret's Bay and Dover, but was soon abandoned.

The French company had been very busy and spent much time and money with a paddle steamer, a naval hydrographer and other surveyors. Its detailed mapping of the seabed was complimented by the British geologist, William Topley: 'English geologists will be surprised at the extreme minuteness with which the French engineers have mapped out the bed of the channel.' He went on to report that in spite of the slight risk of inaccuracy of the chalk seam through which the tunnel would be bored, the French map could be regarded as generally correct. However it is important to note that at the time this report was written, all plans to connect with the works at St Margaret's Bay had been abandoned pending the excavation of a second shaft.

This did not seem to have discouraged the French at Sangatte, a short distance west of Calais near Coquelles where a shaft was sunk, and co-incidentally where the new Channel tunnel emerges today. By the late summer of 1877 a depth of 330 feet had been reached and the lower chalk seam had been penetrated. Water pumps and ventilation measures had been installed and a heading was being driven, considerably aided by the detailed plans drawn up earlier. Hopes were high in France and shares in the project were changing hands at increasing values.

The South Eastern Railway was now in a position to proceed, and following the collapse of its rivals, the Channel Tunnel Company and the LC &DR, preparatory work started in earnest in 1880.

Because land was already owned by the SER and there was a need to commence the first of the tunnels, Watkin arranged for Shaft No.1 to be dug at the base of Abbots Cliff between Folkestone and Dover. This was followed by the cutting of a horizontal gallery some 10 feet above sea level on a falling gradient and parallel to the Folkestone–Dover railway, the plan being to connect with the South Eastern Railway at Shakespeare Cliff. It is reported that around 800 yards had been excavated to a diameter of 7 feet, employing Welsh miners experienced in the skill of tunnelling. Work was discontinued when Shaft No. 2 was sunk near the western portal of the South Eastern Railway near Dover. Clearly, Watkin was either impatient to proceed on the main channel tunnel or felt that further work on Shaft No. 1 was no longer necessary at that time.

Shaft No. 2 commenced on the foreshore at the same time as the French were sinking their main shaft at 18 feet in diameter at Sangatte, near the place which William Low had previously recommended. Navvies from both sides started to excavate pilot tunnels of 7 feet in diameter with the intention of meeting halfway under the English Channel.

The initial Channel tunnel boring was to a diameter of 7 feet and is seen here between Shafts 1 and 2 at Dover. This would have been increased to the full width of 14 feet later in the construction process. (Nick Catford)

As ventilation was essential for the safety of the workforce and visitors, there was no question of using steam technology to bore the tunnels. Thus the tunnel boring machine, an invention by Edward Blackett Beaumont MP (1833–1899), was developed and employed to great effect. It was powered by compressed air which made the use of explosives redundant. It was capable of working three and a half times faster than manpower and was equipped with diamond rock-face cutting equipment.

Col. F.E.B. Beaumont MP RE had originally tested his boring machine with success at the Clifton Down Tunnel near

There were two rivals offering tunnel boring machines. F.E.B. Beaumont's version is illustrated and claimed to excavate the tunnel but it was the Thomas English machine that actually carried out the work. (Old Book Illustrations)

Bristol in 1874, which made his development the obvious choice for the channel tunnel. However, he had a competitor, another Royal Engineer, Captain Thomas English (1843–1935) from Dartford. He greatly improved Beaumont's design and received a patent in 1880. Some accounts of the first channel tunnel incorrectly credit Beaumont with providing his boring machine as used by the SER but in fact it was English's later invention that cut through the chalk seams near Dover to great effect. Records at the time indicate that a mile of tunnel could be achieved every two months.

At a shareholders' meeting in June 1881, an ebullient Watkin reported that the 7 foot pilot tunnel was estimated to be complete within five years, with a similar aim from the French Tunnel Company. The diameter would then be increased to full size once the tunnels met. Once again, because of objections from those in high places, the Board of Trade wobbled and passed the problem to the War Office, which not surprisingly, recommended that yet another commission of enquiry be set up in August of that year. Col. J.H. Smith RE, representing the army, and Vice Admiral Phillimore from the Royal Navy, sought views from the armed forces.

In the meantime Watkin was able to gain a new Parliamentary Act in 1881 empowering him to proceed with the tunnel as far as a pre-agreed limit near the shore line.

As he needed more money to continue the works, he applied to Joseph Chamberlain (1836–1914), President of the Board of Trade, for sufficient funds to allow the English and French tunnels to complete the remaining gap of eleven miles where they would meet in the centre of the English Channel. Chamberlain, still nervous about the speed of developments, refused the application. Never one to be thwarted, Watkin formed a new company in December 1881, The Submarine Continental Railway Company, with a capital of 25,000 pounds in one pound shares. It formally acquired the assets of the SER with works so far achieved and vigorously set out to achieve the company's aims by preparing two Bills to be placed before Parliament. The first was to formalise the new company's proposal and the second to excavate beyond the shoreline limit set by the Board of Trade earlier.

Unfortunately for Watkin the new commission's chief witness was Lieutenant General, later Field Marshal, Sir Garnet Wolseley (1833–1913), notably lampooned by the music composer Gilbert as 'a modern major general' in *The Pirates of Penzance* in 1880, and who was a severe critic of the tunnel project. He is on record as writing from the outset:

'No question of such vital importance has ever confronted the British nation. The hour when the scheme was definitely accepted would be calamitous for England. The abundance and intricacy of military precautions recommended for safeguarding the Tunnel mouth at Dover were, in themselves, the most convincing proof of the danger hanging over the island nation. No matter what fortifications and defences were built there would always be the peril of some continental enemy seizing the Tunnel exit by surprise, and all the commercial advantages of the Tunnel could not outweigh the risk.'

Wolseley had his critics, such as General Sir John Adye (1819–1900), Surveyor General of the Ordnance, who in 1882 reported to the commission:

'A French strategist who wanted to invade England would never regard the Tunnel as the answer to his problems. He would in any case have to mass his forces first on the French coast, and if Britain's intelligence service was of any consequence it would in good time give a warning of such troop concentrations so that adequate measures could be taken. But even if invading units started moving through the tunnel, a small force of infantry could destroy them with ease as they emerged at Dover.'

The outcome of the commission's report led to a typical British fudge. Clearly not supported by members of the military establishment, the scheme stuttered to a halt mainly because of irrational fears of the threat of invasion, its final stance being that agreement could not be reached. Thus another 'Military Committee' was formed under the Chairmanship of Major General Archibold Atkinson and a team mainly consisting of men with a military background. Other distinguished members of society such as Alfred Lord Tennyson, T.H. Huxley and Sir George Sitwell wrote vociferously against the proposal.

Spare a moment of sympathy for poor Watkin, the innocent party in all these disputes, because in addition to the negative reactions from the British armed forces, France was undergoing further political turmoil which resulted in a near coup d'etat. A trade war between the two countries led to the French government in 1878 cancelling the Anglo/French commercial treaty brokered some eighteen years earlier.

Field Marshal
Sir Garnet Wolseley, who stood solidly against the construction of the Channel Tunnel.

Watkin decided to act in a positive way by organising two VIP visits to the tunnel site, complete with press coverage, in 1882. By now the tunnel had progressed from Shakespeare Cliff for a distance of nearly 1,500 yards towards Admiralty Pier, and the French had progressed a similar distance at Sangatte. The *Illustrated London News* in its 4 March 1882 edition carried the following report complete with pictures, covering both visits thus:

'On Saturday, 18th February, Sir Edward Watkin conducted a party of thirty or forty gentlemen from London to inspect these works, the Lord Mayor of London being one of the party. They descended the shaft, walked a thousand yards under the sea, and admired the working of Col. Beaumont's compressed-air boring machine. They had electric light, by which the tunnel was illuminated from end to end. In anticipation of this visit Sir Edward had directed a luncheon to be prepared in the tunnel, which was undertaken of in a chamber cut to the side of the heading, tables and stools being set for the occasion.

'The Channel Tunnel was again opened to another party of London visitors on Tuesday of last week. Under the guidance of Mr Francis Brady, CE., engineer of the Channel Tunnel and Colonel Beaumont, RE., the visitors, six at a time, having put on rough overalls to save their clothes from dust, descended into the shaft by means of an iron cage, such as is used in coal-mines. The shaft is sunk in the chalk cliff at the foot of the 'Shakespeare Cliff' between Folkestone and Dover, and is about 160 feet in depth. The opening is circular, with boarded sides, and the descending apparatus is worked by a steam engine. At the bottom of this shaft is a square chamber dug in the grey chalk , the sides of which are protected by heavy beams; and in front is the experimental boring, a low-roofed circular tunnel about 7 feet in diameter, the floor of which is laid with a double line of tram-rails. This tunnel is admirably ventilated, and on visiting days is lighted with electric lamps, the steam power at the mouth of the shaft being sufficient for all purposes. The stratum through which the experimental borings have been made is the lower grey chalk. This material, while perfectly dry, and very easily worked, is sufficiently hard to dispel any apprehension of crumbling or falling in.

'The length of the Submarine Continental Railway Company's Tunnel, under the sea, from the English to the French shore, will be twenty-two miles; and, taking the shore approaches at four miles on each side, there will be a total length of thirty miles of tunnelling. The shaft goes down to the beginning of the tunnel, which is here 100 feet below the surface of the sea. A heading, now three quarters of a mile long, has been driven in the direction of the head of the Admiralty Pier (Dover), entirely in the grey chalk, near its base, and a few feet above the impermeable strata formed by the gault clay.

'The present heading is 7 feet in diameter. Machinery is being constructed by which this 7 feet hole can be enlarged to 14 feet by cutting an annular space, 3 feet 6 inches wide, around it. This will be done by machinery furnished with an upper bore-head. One machine will follow the other, at a proper interval; and the debris from the cutting by the first will be passed out through the second machine. The compressed air, likewise, which is necessary to work the advanced machine, will be similarly passed through the machine coming behind. Only two men are at present needed for each machine.

'At the end of the tunnel the visitors found one of the Beaumont compressed-air boring machines at work. The length of this machine from the borer to the tail end is about 33 feet. Its work is done by the cutting action of short steel cutters fixed in two revolving arms, seven cutters in each, the upper portion of the frame in which the borer is fixed moving forward 5-16ths of an inch with every complete revolution of the cutters. In this way a thin paring from the whole face of the chalk is cut away with every turn of the borer. A man in front shovels the crumbled debris into small buckets, which, travelling on an endless band, shoot the dirt into a 'skip' tended by another man. The skip when filled is run along a tramway to the mouth of the shaft. At present these trollies, each holding about one third of a cubic yard, are drawn by men, but before long it is hoped that small compressed air engines will be used for traction. The rate of progress is about one hundred yards per week, but will soon be much accelerated. As worked at present, the number of revolutions is two or three per minute, which amounts to being nearly an inch per minute while the machine is at work. But Colonel Beaumont anticipates no difficulty in making the machine cut its way at the rate of 3-8ths of an inch per revolution, and getting five revolutions which would give a rate of advance of two inches per minute.

'A very important question has been raised with the regard to the supply of compressed air. Carried in four-inch iron pipes, it now reaches the machine with a pressure of about 20 lb, the pressure at the compressor at the shaft mouth being from 30 lb to 35 lb; but by increasing the diameter of the supply pipe to eight inches the loss of working value by friction would be greatly diminished, if not rendered as appreciable. The boring has now advanced to the length of 1,250 yards and it is going on at the rate of three miles a year, which speed of working, as we said, will be increased. Simultaneous borings from the French side at the same rate would give six miles a year, or a complete tunnel underneath and across the Channel in three years and a half.

'The shape which the completed tunnel will assume will probably be a circle, 14 feet in diameter, but flattened at the bottom to receive the rails. It will be lined with two feet thickness of cement concrete; not that this is necessary to ensure the stability of the work, but to prevent accidental falls of chalk. The concrete will be made of shingle from Dungeness and cement formed from the grey chalk excavated from the tunnel itself. In this manner, the tunnel will form the means of its own lining at a cheap rate. The gradients will be 1 in 80, on each side, until the depth of 150 feet below the bottom of the sea is reached; after which the line may be said to be level, subject only to a very slight inclination from the centre outwards, to prevent the lodgings of water.

'The ventilation of the tunnel is, perhaps, the simplest matter in connection with it, but as some doubts have been expressed upon this, it be here shortly explained. During the construction of the tunnel, the air necessary for ventilation will be more than enough supplied by that used to drive the boring machines. When the tunnel is opened for traffic, the trains will run through by means of Beaumont compressed-air locomotives.

'The Channel Tunnel locomotive will weigh from sixty to seventy tons, and will be charged with 1,200 cubic feet of air, compressed to the density of seventy atmospheres, the equivalent of which is over 80,000 cubic feet of free air. This will give power sufficient to draw a train of 250 tons gross weight (including the engine) the distance of twenty-two miles under the sea. Assuming that the rate of travelling be 30 miles an hour, the air discharged by the engine would give a supply of free and pure air to the amount of 2,000 cubic feet, approximately, which will be far in excess of what is needed by the passengers in the train. Reservoirs will be placed at convenient intervals, so that the engines, should they need it, may be replenished with compressed air. It will, therefore, be seen that Colonel Beaumont's system of compressed air engines affords equal advantages with the ordinary steam locomotives, and with no increase in weight.

'The controversy now going on between different military authorities and politicians respecting the effect which the tunnel would have upon our insular safety from the risk of a foreign invasion has already been much noticed. In the *Nineteenth Century* for March, Colonel Beaumont replies to the arguments of Admiral Lord Dunsany and of a distinguished military man, understood to be Sir Garnet Wolseley, who disapprove of a tunnel upon this ground. Having been himself three years in the construction of the Dover fortifications, Colonel Beaumont is enabled to assure us that by the natural extent of the position, and by the powerful works erected there, Dover may be regarded as a 'first-class fortress, quite safe from any coup de main from without'. There will be arrangements, under control of the military for letting the water of the sea into the Tunnel; but these arrangements, which will be kept secret, will be of such a nature that they cannot be tampered with improperly, while they can be promptly put in operation without the existence of technical experts. The position of the inclined gallery, connecting the end of the tunnel with the main railway lines, will be such that the trains, on emerging from under the sea, must be lifted bodily, by suitable hydraulic apparatus, to the daylight surface; and without the aid of such hydraulic apparatus, the ends of the tunnel will be blocked. Hence it will be evident that, supposing a party of two thousand men could pass through the Tunnel by surprise, and could reach the bottom of the shaft at the Dover end, they could surely get no further.

'But Colonel Beaumont does not admit that it is possible for a surprise party of two thousand men, as imagined by Lord Dunsany and his military authority, to pass through the tunnel unobserved. They cannot come by trains as, irrespective of any suspicions on the part of the booking clerks, special train arrangements would have to be made to carry so large a number; they cannot march, as they would be run over by the trains, running as they will, at ten minute intervals, or oftener, without cessation, day or night. Beaumont thinks arrangements should also be made by which the ventilating engines, used for the ordinary purposes of the tunnel, could pump the smoke from their own furnaces into the Tunnel, in place of fresh air; this would soon produce an atmosphere through which no living being could pass. If we had lost command of the sea temporarily and the enemy had landed twenty or thirty thousand men on the coast, there would still be time for us to block or flood the tunnel, or to destroy its ventilation; at any rate, to destroy the hydraulic lifts, which would be done by firing a single charge of dynamite. It would appear, therefore, that the only time when, by any stretch of the imagination, the tunnel would be a source of danger, no invader could by any possibility make use of it.'

The words describing the tunnel and its military threat were circulated to the press, designed of course to apply as much pressure as possible to the establishment at the highest level. Further VIP tours were arranged, one of which was held at the Lord Warden Hotel in Dover some two weeks later. Lavish catering was provided to eminent guests, including the Prime Minister and Mrs Gladstone, the Prince and Princess of Wales, the Archbishop of Canterbury and Sir Garnet Wolseley. Although Sir Garnet was happy to accept the hospitality, he steadfastly refused to change his view on the military risk he felt the tunnel posed.

Some two months after the visits to the tunnel workings, the military committee reported on the defence procedures and the possible necessity of destroying the infrastructure in the event of attack by a foreign power. Its report recommended that the works on the surface should be provided with a fortress, mined at all times, with the addition of a portcullis designed to close the tunnel mouth. Measures should be taken to release poisonous gas with the provision of sluice gates. Explosive charges installed would enable flooding and the destruction of galleries, with additional mines designed to be activated both inland and from the newly built fortress.

These measures were not objected to by Watkin but in spite of the SER's acceptance of these conditions, for the two bills from both the Channel Tunnel Company and the SER placed before Parliament, the committee's deliverance was not recommended.

These were serious developments and if this decision was not bad enough, the final blow when it came was delivered by the Board of Trade. This came about in January 1883 when the Board advised Watkin of Section 77 of the South East Railway Act of 1881. This referred to the foreshore rights which forbade any tunnelling beyond the low water mark unless permission was explicitly granted. Some two months later the SER received a further letter from the Board reminding the company of their violation of the Crown's foreshore rights which meant that digging must cease at the three-mile limit. Watkin countered by claiming that he was driving the pilot tunnel under the sea and not infringing the Crown's rights because the land was owned by the Church of England. This indicated that Church land was subject to ancient rights which predated the establishment of the Crown.

The Board of Trade, whilst conceding the legal position to be correct in interpretation, nevertheless insisted that the Crown retained control over the water between high tide and the three-mile limit. It took the view that the SER had already reached the limit permitted by the 1881 Act and thus ordered work to cease immediately. The ever ebullient Watkin took no notice because the actual tunnel boring had reached around 1,500 yards at that stage.

The Board of Trade, aware that work was continuing, despatched a team to examine exactly what was going on. Although Watkin would have continued unabated, the Secretary of the Submarine Continental Railway Company, having been subjected to much pressure, agreed to stop construction with immediate effect. To buy more time Watkin then wrote on 9 April 1883 to Joseph Chamberlain, Chairman of the Board of Trade, to inform him that the boring machine had stopped and further reported that there were concerns over the atmosphere in the heading. Chamberlain suspected this to be a red herring but did give permission for work to continue should the workmen's health be at risk. He added that he would investigate whether there was any need for the workmen to remain in the Tunnel.

The Chief Inspector of Railways, Colonel Yolland RE, was then instructed to visit the works by the Board of Trade. Watkin countered that this would not be possible because the Duke of Edinburgh was due to visit on 18 April and thus no access could be made available for at least a week. Chamberlain, by now exceedingly irritated with these prevarications, demanded to know why a visit by the Duke should delay matters further. Watkin offered an olive branch by suggesting that Chamberlain visit the works for a personal tour but this was refused.

There then followed several months of obfuscation with the SER making excuses as to why the Board of Trade could not visit. Meanwhile English's boring machine was making relentless progress and influential visitors were encouraged to view the works in a desperate attempt by the company to present the scheme in a positive light.

The actions by the SER directors and Chairman led to a series of antagonistic letters which became increasingly acrimonious resulting in a complete impasse by both parties. Naturally this state of affairs could not continue and in July of that year, the High Court of Justice placed an injunction on the SER to allow access to the second shaft at Shakespeare Cliff. The ever defiant Watkin realised the game was up and further boring ceased. Colonel Yolland, instructed by the Board of Trade, visited the site on 18 July and measured the extent of the boring. He reported that over 600 yards of Crown property had been trespassed by the works and further confirmed that Watkins' claim of ventilation and other problems reported earlier were false. Yolland's report may additionally have been adversely coloured by his suffering a fall in the tunnel, sustaining injuries to his head on a rail. In spite of the pressure placed on the SER to cease working immediately, boring still continued when 'the coast was clear'.

There is written evidence of the final tranche of work recorded in 1882 which was discovered in the British Rail archives of 1972. This work sheet, an unlikely survivor from those early days, was entitled *Channel Tunnel Works – Experimental Boring (7 feet diameter) in an easterly direction from No. 2 Shaft, near the western end of Shakespeare Tunnel, Dover.*

The voluminous title of what was, after all, a mundane work sheet is interesting because it was clearly designed to prove that the tunnel was only of an experimental nature. Thus if the SER was challenged, documents such as these would be offered as evidence in its defence.

The dates, details of work and remarks make fascinating reading. The records begin on 20 April and finish three months later. It can be seen from the contents, that some delays were caused by visitors, which Watkin clearly felt was worth the price in his attempts to gain public support. As one would expect, work was additionally held up for essential repairs to what was early technology but in spite of this a further 500 yards were successfully bored at that time. It may be noted that the Beaumont Boring Machine was still not being credited to Major Thomas English even at this late stage.

Work effectively ceased at the end of July and Colonel Yolland paid a further visit in August having reacted to rumours of Watkin's continued defiance. He took measurements and reported to the Board of Trade that a further seventy yards had been dug since his last visit a month earlier. This resulted in a new court action against the Submarine Continental Railway Company which was vehemently contested by the company's chief engineer, Francis Brady who claimed that only ventilation work had been carried out to ensure the safety of Yolland. One further visit was made when Yolland admitted to the Board that he had been mistaken.

In the meantime the newly named French Societe Concessionaire du Tunnel sous la Manche stopped work having completed 1,840 metres, a similar distance to that on the English side. They were mystified as to why the Board of Trade continued to block progress and clearly thought that the cessation of work would be temporary. Thomas English's boring machine had been used on the French coast but the company experienced poorer geological conditions which hampered progress. It is interesting to note that similar problems occurred on the completion of the final project at the end of the following century.

Shortly after work had ceased towards the end of 1882, the two competing companies brought bills to Parliament to decide the future of railway connections on the English mainland.

Once again it was the President of the Board of Trade, Lord Chamberlain, who would have to pave the way forwards. He appointed a committee consisting of five Peers of the Realm and five from the commons. This was to be chaired by Lord Lansdowne and thereafter known as the 'Lansdowne Committee'.

Even before they formally met on 20 April 1883 conflict erupted, initiated by James Forbes, Chairman of the London, Chatham & Dover Railway, who submitted a petition claiming that the SER had infringed its rights and interests. He further 'humbly prayed that the SER's Bill will not pass into law as it now stands'. Conflict between both companies' Chairmen was well known because of continued internecine disputes over many years, with both parties equally to blame. Watkin countered by revealing correspondence between Grosvenor of the Channel Tunnel Company aided by Forbes, in which he accused the LC&DR of conspiring against his company in 1881 and 1882 and plotting to undermine the SER. Grosvenor wrote, 'Never having been able to obtain co-operation in any way (with the SER), I naturally turned to Mr Forbes.' The war of words continued when Watkin mocked Grosvenor's railway plan explaining 'that it merely showed a railway beginning at Fan Hole on the coast between St Margaret's Bay and Dover, where it was to end at Biggin Street without any link with the LC&DR or the SER line. You have deposited no plan nor made any money deposit for anything more'.

It was clear that the enmity between the two protagonists was intense but it should be noted that the Channel Tunnel Company over which Grosvenor presided was in a weak position in regard to the Lansdowne Committee. The inability to raise sufficient funds to sink another shaft after the first had flooded, apart from trial borings at Fan Hole, and the lack of a suitable rail connection, placed them very much in second place. That they were considered at all by the committee was because Grosvenor was part of the establishment and Watkin seen as 'not quite a gentleman and a nuisance to the establishment'.

The Lansdowne Committee completed its enquiries by 21 June, having sat for three months. Its task was 'to enquire whether it is expedient that Parliamentary sanction should be given to a submarine communication between England and France.'

Forty witnesses were summoned to which 5,396 questions were posed. Notable among those attending were Watkin, Grosvenor, Hawkshaw, Yolland, Beaumont, Forbes, the Duke of Cambridge (Commander-in-Chief of the army and cousin to Queen Victoria) and Sir Garnet Wolseley. There were other leading people who represented trade and industry.

When the report of the Select Committee was published, it not surprisingly came down heavily on the issues of defence of the realm, fear of an invasion being the main concern. Wolseley continued passionately to repeat all his earlier objections and then added his loathing of any commercial advantages by saying it would encourage 'mercantile activity, the hunt for riches by railway speculators and selfish cosmopolitans'. He then added 'it was ridiculous to save a few tourists from sea-sickness'.

Not surprisingly for a man in his position, he garnered a degree of support from his military colleagues but the remainder of the Committee regarded Wolseley as unhinged, never of course publicly stated, and so sought a more balanced report. In spite of this none of the peripheral proposals succeeded in achieving a sufficient majority.

Lord Lansdowne in his personal report wrote 'We have no course open to us except to recommend that this enterprise should not be prohibited on merely political grounds, and that it be allowed to proceed.' Unfortunately his view was in the minority and in spite of being Chairman, he was outnumbered by four to one. The report was sanctioned on 10 July 1883 concluding 'it is not expedient that Parliamentary sanction should be given to a Submarine Communication between England and France.'

Within a few weeks the Bills before Parliament were abandoned. However, the indefatigable Watkin introduced a new Bill on behalf of the SER and Submarine Continental Railways the following year. The Government opposed this and it too was defeated on 14 May 1884.

Two further bills were submitted in 1885 and 1886. The first was thrown out and the second withdrawn because of a pending General Election.

Later, on 8 July 1886, An Extraordinary General Meeting held in the board room at London Bridge Station by The Submarine Continental Railway Company, passed the following resolution.

'That the Capital of the Company be increased by the sum of 25 thousand pounds, in twenty thousand fully paid up shares of one pound each, for the special purpose of the purchase of all the rights and properties of the Channel Tunnel Company and its shareholders.'

It had been obvious for some time to both companies that mutual hostility was damaging the project. Discussions behind the scenes had been taking place and the logical solution was to merge both their interests. The more powerful of the two, The Submarine Continental Railway Company, was in a position to buy out The Channel Tunnel Company, its only asset being a derelict shaft and some land at St Margaret's Bay and Fan Hole. The name of the new company was to be known as The Channel Tunnel Company Ltd, shortly altered on 11 March 1887 to The Channel Tunnel Company. It was during these troubled times that the railway connection was finally agreed by the newly formed company.

Even though the SER's earlier plans successfully snookered the LC&DR by preventing any access to continental traffic, its own proposals were, when closely examined, flawed in several areas. Apart from the expense of the proposed international station in a massive chalk cavern at Shakespeare cliff, it was obvious that in spite of the undoubted SER's skills in hydraulic engineering, this method of lifting trains from the tunnel portal would be slow, cumbersome and considerably challenging in attempting to provide a ten-minute train service to and from France. As to the railway itself, the SER had only partially constructed one 7 foot tunnel between Shafts 1 and 2 with the need to increase its dimension to 14 feet. The necessity and cost of providing a second tunnel to allow for twin track operation would have to be addressed. Finally, should a significant increase in traffic occur, this would necessitate a four-track railway, causing inconvenience both at Martello tunnel and of course the twin track brick built Foord viaduct which crossed Folkestone at a height of 100 feet and was over 600 feet in length. Trains were destined to make their first arrival on English soil at Shorncliffe station so in 1880 the platforms were demolished and rebuilt further apart to accommodate four tracks. In 1881 Parliament disapproved of

The final proposed railway route from the Channel Tunnel with connections to London and Canterbury. As can be seen on the map the proposal named as 'Approach Railway No. 1' indicates the Channel Tunnel continuing on a long sweeping curve bearing north and east for about 2.5 miles before arriving at the international station. This would allow for a gradient of about 1:50 from Shaft No. 1 below sea level at Shakespeare Cliff to reach the station. The Tunnel would have passed beneath Round Down, then cross the route of the present Channel Tunnel, the B2011 near Farthingloe Close, Elms Wood and close to the South Eastern edge of Long Wood, the tunnel portal being reached after some 3 miles in a north easterly direction. The international station was to be constructed just before Noah's Ark Road and would be designed with an island platform to maintain security in regard to visitors from mainland Europe. Shortly after leaving the station the railway branched north eastwards on track named 'Approach Railway No. 3' to meet the LC&DR south of Buckland Junction. This short stretch of line would have had two short tunnels, one on rising ground to the south and the second to the north of this section. At the junction of No 3 Railway bearing south, the line known as 'Approach Railway No. 2' would have headed in a tunnel towards Clarendon Place and Western Heights on to the coast where the railway would link up with the SER about 50 yards east of Shakespeare tunnel. (Google. Imagery ©2021 CNES / Airbus, Getmapping plc, Infoterra Ltd & Bluesky, Landsat / Copernicus, Maxar Technologies, Map data ©2021. By Alex Griffin)

these developments which were unauthorised, but by then the new layout had been completed.

However, if the SER's plans proved to be expensive and impractical, the LC&DR's were dire. Its shaft at St Margaret's Bay had been flooded by sea water thus forcing the company to seek alternatives on a severely reduced budget. As some early borings were made at Fan Hole on the coast it was decided to route the railway through a tunnel from there to Biggin Street in Dover. Why the railway would have terminated so close to their line with Dover Priory station which was just a few hundred feet further west is something of a mystery. One can only surmise that this was a desperate attempt to demonstrate the company's credibility of the Channel Tunnel project. A more likely explanation was that difficulties had still not been resolved because Dover Priory is bounded by tunnels at both ends of the station. This rendered it practically impossible to design a suitable junction at that point. Any attempt to link with its Canterbury to Dover line further north, would require increased tunnelling and almost certainly the demolition of commercial and domestic buildings.

Following rejection of these plans, a new proposal was drawn up that would satisfy all parties.

Once all these details were agreed a new bill was presented to Parliament in August 1887 seeking permission to continue with experimental works on the tunnel at Shakespeare Cliff. Clearly the word 'experimental' was used to allay fears of the tunnel's construction actually progressing, thereby lessening antagonism from its many detractors. Simultaneously the company sought support from eminent citizens by way of a public petition, which was signed by almost fifty people across the political and commercial spectrum. The new Chairman was a London banker, Baron Frederick Emile d'Erlanger (1832–1911), previously on the board of the now defunct Channel Tunnel Company Ltd. A successful businessman of German descent, his appointment was seen to lend the scheme a degree of gravitas and financial security. Other members of the new board consisted of a group of talented people including Francis Brady, the leading engineer.

Meanwhile Watkin had fostered a close relationship with the Prime Minister, William Gladstone (1809–1898), spanning several years. Regarded as a stalwart of his time, having served as Prime Minister on four separate occasions, he was unusual in serving as a Tory (Whig) in his early career and later moving to the left with Liberal convictions. It was during his third period of office from 1886 to 1891 that coincided with all the difficulties experienced by the Channel Tunnel Company in attempting to gain support in Parliament. In earlier years Gladstone was firmly against the concept of an undersea connection with France, but, like his political change of views, he increasingly regarded his Tory colleagues as Luddites who did not want to encourage 'foreigners who might actually travel to Great Britain with great ease'.

By all accounts, Gladstone, who with his wife was one of the visitors to visit the tunnel works, clearly liked Watkin, which was aided by their holding the same political views. He is on record in 1887 as saying:

'Sir Edward Watkin is one of those men wicked enough to desire that a Tunnel should be built under the Channel to France and what is truly painful to me is that I am compelled to confess before you, and do it publicly, that I am one of those men who are wicked enough to agree with him.'

Sir William Gladstone.

Three years later he apologised to the French for all the delays as he continued to fight for the scheme in Parliament. He was particularly scathing of Britain's armed forces pointing out that, 'we have invaded France ten times compared with only one (against us by the French and they know we have a superior Navy). I believe this Channel Tunnel to be considerable measure and a useful measure'.

In spite of the Prime Minister's fulsome support, the bill was defeated by 81 votes and another application two years later was similarly voted down.

In 1898 the final blow to any hope of completing the works was delivered following a ruling by the Chancery Division of the High Court. In classic government speak devoid of any warmth it stated that the company was 'to be permanently restrained from any further boring beneath the seabed'.

This blunt statement belied all the drama witnessed in earlier years and concludes the dramatic story of the first Channel Tunnel. Watkin was getting on in years and retired as Chairman in 1894 stating ill health as the reason, but still had plans for future developments elsewhere. We can safely assume that the continuous rebuttals by Bills presented to Parliament would have tested the patience of a saint, so the scheme was allowed to die. The tunnel would eventually be constructed at the end of the next century which Watkin would have found inspirational, but that is another story.

However, as if all the challenges being experienced at Dover were not enough there is still one epitaph to this story. Watkin's ambitious plans for the project were dogged, as can be seen, but he saw the tunnel as only part of a greater enterprise. During his final years as Chairman of the Great Central Railway, England's last main line of the Victorian era was proposed and constructed between Marylebone and the north of England. Clearly, with the future of the Channel Tunnel in mind and in spite of repeated failures to gain Parliamentary approval, Watkin planned to connect northern England with France. His new railway was designed with minimal curvature and easy gradients, which allowed trains to travel at high speed. Watkin's adoption of the 'Berne Loading Gauge' would allow trains of a larger dimension, common in Europe, but still travelling on the standard rail width of 4 feet 8½ inches throughout. This obvious advantage would allow railway traffic from mainland Europe to haul goods and passengers through to Manchester without the need to change trains or tranship goods.

Furthermore, the route, which commenced in the north of England, crossed large towns such as Lutterworth, Leicester, Loughborough, Nottingham, Rugby and Sheffield. The final southern section was laid towards Marylebone early in the twentieth century but traffic never grew to expected levels. Today the space for extra platforms and two tunnels north of Marylebone on the westward side would never see traffic, although four ornamental portals survive for posterity. As these towns and cities were already separately served by the Midland Railway, continental traffic would not be crowded by local train services. In Manchester itself, the Central terminus would greet international trains when the line was complete. This station, nearly demolished in less enlightened times, is now the G-Mex exhibition centre which has hosted many conferences. What would Watkin have thought of that?

By the late 1960s, most of this fine railway was unceremoniously closed, deemed by politicians to be 'surplus to requirement'. Shortly after, most of the land was sold off and structures widely destroyed. One local landowner, the 9th Earl of Lanesborough Denis Butler, wrote bitterly to the *Daily Telegraph* in 1965 opposing the missed opportunity of 'the Great Central Railway forming a direct continental loading gauge from Sheffield and the North to Thames Valley and London for Dover and France'. Just one year earlier the governments of Great Britain and France planned once again to build the tunnel, so could not the route have been mothballed? Opinions vary but what is certain, modernising this recently built line would have been a miniscule sum of money compared to the over eighty billion pounds cost estimate in 2019 of the still unconstructed High Speed 2 route.

Watkin finally retired from the GCR in 1894 at the same time as the SER, citing poor health.

The possibility of building a Channel tunnel arose from time to time during the twentieth century, its greatest proponent being Winston Churchill, who raised the matter in 1920, 1924 and 1936. In the end, with support from Prime Minister Margaret Thatcher and financed by the private sector, construction of the tunnel was finally started in 1988, with it opening six years later.

Shortly after the Chancery Division of the High Court's permanent ruling of 1898, shaft numbers 1 and 2 were filled in and the tunnels at Abbotscliffe and Dover were abandoned, not to be revisited until 1974 when a new Channel tunnel was proposed.

Remains of the first Channel Tunnel

Initially in the early 1970s work was carried out at the base of Shakespeare Cliff because engineers were concerned that the original No. 2 Shaft or the tunnel was likely to be bisected by the new bore. In order to avoid blade damage by iron linings to the new boring machine, the shaft was fully excavated and the French bound tunnel drained. The shaft was found to be unlined down to solid rock and a circular steel ribbed and timber lining was installed. At its base the access chamber was found to be intact with the exception of some timber supports which had fractured due to pressure, and there were numerous chalk falls. The timber was replaced at the shaft base, a new sump installed and other works carried out to render the site safe. The circular bore of the tunnel was encountered some 40 feet from the base of the shaft. Once the water had been pumped out of the first section, it was discovered that the condition of this 1882 tunnel was poor, with numerous chalk collapses and broken ring linings. These were cleared, some linings repaired and colliery arches installed. As the tunnel continued to be examined further south east its condition improved but quantities of chalk in some places were evident to roof level, exposing large voids above. The debris was cleared to allow studies to progress. When access had reached 885 yards, a concrete bulkhead was constructed as the tunnel beyond this point was not lined and chalk falls were far more numerous. It is regrettable that the original tunnel boring machine could not be retrieved and now remains marooned beneath the seabed in perpetuity. Following these works, the shaft was once again filled in but in 1982 the 1882 tunnel was revisited by the eventual successful scheme. The boring machine bisected Watkin's tunnel beneath the shore of Shakespeare Cliff and history should record that at least one small section of the original tunnel space did ultimately serve its purpose.

The access to the easterly heading at Abbot's Cliff has been maintained under the auspices of Network Rail. This part of the Dover to Folkestone railway is notorious for flooding so a series of drainage adits have been driven from the base of the cliff to the line above. A drainage pipe meets the site of the shaft having traversed 76 yards under and beyond the London to Dover railway. At the junction with what is left of Shaft No. 1, there is a short timber lined tunnel to the left which once housed the tunnel boring machine. The machine-excavated tunnel to the right is initially in

Above left: **Tunnel inscription**. (Nick Catford)

Above right: **The place** where the old and new tunnels met, beneath Shakespeare Cliff. (Subterranea Britannica)

good condition with wooden boards on the floor. After 85 yards an inscription on the wall left by William Sharp, thought to be one of the Welsh miners, reads, 'This tunnel was begubnubnugn in 1880 – William Sharp'. His spelling mistake and effort at a correction is touching and survives to this day.

Beyond this point the tunnel begins a downward gradient towards Shaft No. 2 at Shakespeare Cliff. After a distance of 197 yards there is a large chalk fall which can be reached, although the tunnel is flooded by a yard or so of water. Beyond here the water reaches the level of the roof and no further exploration is possible.

Thus ends one of the most protracted battles of the Victorian railway era in which the establishment became the winner. There is no doubt that Queen Victoria's loathing of 'that most objectionable project' in the end, influenced her government 'to do the right thing'. You may judge which side was in the right.

Remains of the First Channel Tunnel and other sites

Samphire Hoe
Country Park where
Shaft No. 2 was
sunk.

Unusually for a book such as this, the reader will appreciate that it is impossible to visit the remains of the first channel tunnel workings because there is no access. It is to be hoped that it will suffice to know that they still exist for posterity.

Folkestone West.
Originally named
Shorncliffe, this
station was planned
to have handled
trains from France.

The remains of
Dungeness station
which would have
been the shingle
loading point
destined for the
cement lining of the
Channel Tunnel.

The remains of Shaft No.1 and adjacent tunnels are capped at ground level and can only be visited by Network Rail personnel. The site of the infilled Shaft No. 2, no longer visible, is at Samphire Hoe Country Park. The site itself is of particular interest because most of the park site consists of many tonnes of chalk excavated from the present channel tunnel.

Locations where activity took place in readiness for the ill-fated venture include Shorncliffe station, now Folkestone West, where the wide spaces between the platforms contained four tracks. Today with each platform carrying one set of rails with open space between, it is hard to imagine the hive of activity it might once have witnessed. Of additional interest is the place where the Elham Valley Railway ran to a bay platform on the western end of the down platform.

Elsewhere there is no doubt that the construction of the Dungeness line in 1881 was partially motivated by the plan to haul large trainloads of shingle to mix with cement to line the tunnels under the sea. This short line branching south of the Lydd to New Romney railway was not a success, but the remains of Dungeness station platform and some early fencing survives to tell the tale. The branch from Appledore that runs close to Dungeness is closed to passengers but regularly provides a freight service for the removal of nuclear waste from Dungeness power station.

How to get there

The Channel Tunnel sites. There is a very good train service to Dover Priory, Folkestone West and Folkestone Central from London and the south coast. It is recommended that a visit be made along the foot of the cliffs at The Warren to the east of Folkestone, made famous by Vera Lynn's nostalgic wartime song, 'there will be bluebirds over the White Cliffs of Dover'. Walking, biking or boat tours are the only means of travel from the track near Martello Tunnel to the east at the western end of Shakespeare Cliff. Access beyond this point is not possible unless by boat or swimming!

Samphire Hoe Country Park at Shakespeare Cliff is worth a visit and the easy way is by car from the A20 or by foot from Dover. This is where the site of Shaft No.2 was constructed and infilled during the 1970s. The old and new tunnel workings bisect near here and it is interesting to note that nearly all the park area is made up of chalk excavated from the latest Channel Tunnel workings.

The remaining site of interest is a trip to St Margaret's Bay to the east of Dover. For the healthy a bracing walk on the cliff top is recommended and on a clear day, the French coast is visible, but dog owners should be careful of exhilarated dogs running without a lead! The bay is accessible by car but care should be taken with tortuous bends down to the coast. The site of the first channel shaft engineered by Hawkshaw is to be found at the foot of the cliff to the west. Although long since filled in, even casual visitors must wonder at the folly of constructing a crucial shaft so close to the shore line on a shingle beach.

Dungeness. The remains of Dungeness station are best visited by the renowned narrow gauge Romney, Hythe & Dymchurch Railway, which operates between Hythe and Dungeness. Here one can witness wonderful small scale steam locomotives hauling rakes of covered passenger coaches. Access to the RH&DR is best

The site of the aborted St Margaret's Bay tunnel shaft.

achieved by bus to New Romney or Hythe and visitors with bicycles will appreciate the flat roads along this section of the south coast.

The Great Central Railway. Marylebone station is of interest because of its peripheral involvement in the proposed high speed railway from London to the north of England. Here the western side of the station was clearly planned for extra platforms and tracks which were never built.

Fortunately, part of the former Great Central route has survived between Leicester and Ruddington south of Nottingham and is one of Britain's leading heritage railways. With period main line steam locomotives operating on a fully restored double track formation, visitors can appreciate the minimal gradients and gentle curves that Watkin strived to achieve for his international trains. One striking feature is that all the stations were deliberately placed as island platforms. Thus had this main line proved to be an international success, two extra lines and buildings could be added without the necessity of demolishing the existing structures. This part of the Great Central Railway plc lives on at its base at Loughborough Central station and the best way is to travel by train to Loughborough Midland station – Watkin would have loved that!

Chapter 7

The Didcot, Newbury & Southampton Junction Railway

The origin of this rather grandly titled railway owes its birth to the era commonly known as 'railway mania' which took place during the decade leading up to the financial crash of 1850. At that time there were several schemes to connect the industrial midlands to Southampton, an area which was dominated by the London & South Western Railway. Its routes were generally provided from east to west and not in a northerly direction.

None of these schemes came to fruition and plans were not resurrected until the 1870s, when railways once again were being trusted, with memories of financial irregularities in earlier times being largely forgotten. That there was a need for improvements in railway routes was not in doubt and the emphasis now included coal traffic from South Wales. The Great Western Railway (GWR), which operated a broad track gauge railway of 7 feet ¼in, had a near monopoly of routes in South Wales, and this made the transport of coal circuitously expensive, involving standard gauge routes into England via the Forest of Dean. The only attempt by a relatively unknown company, the South Midland Railway, to construct an unwieldy standard gauge route via Lydney, Marlborough and Andover, collapsed ignominiously in Parliament in 1872 when the company failed to raise enough money for its deposit.

However, this effort did spark the idea of constructing cut-off lines to shorten distances which led to the birth of the Didcot, Newbury and Southampton Junction Railway (DN&SJR) by a Parliamentary Act of 1873.

In the meantime the GWR had already announced that it would gradually abandon its broad gauge lines, and indeed conversion to standard gauge had already begun, finally completing in 1892. This opened up the possibility of standard gauge short cut routes and so it was in 1873 that a bill was presented to Parliament outlining the aims of the DN&SJR. The railway was planned to commence east of Didcot and turn south, terminating at a junction with the London & South Western Railway (L&SWR) some two miles north of Micheldever station in Hampshire, a distance of 34 miles and 198 yards. Apart from the provision of a branch line to East Ilsley in the north, which was never built, a connection would additionally be provided at Whitchurch on the L&SWR between Basingstoke and Salisbury. At this stage the GWR had not been consulted so the problem of connecting with their broad gauge line at Newbury would be overcome by simply bridging the GWR route, thereby avoiding the need for a physical connection.

In spite of these grand plans there appeared to have been a distinct lack of interest by investors for the three-year period following the success of the Parliamentary bill. In order to prevent the project becoming moribund, an agreement was drawn up with the GWR which had recently re-gauged the rail to standard width on the Newbury line, allowing access to its station. In addition the GWR agreed to operate the service once constructed, although surviving records indicate that this was probably a defensive act to prevent the L&SWR from invading an area which was regarded as GWR territory.

The plans and finance were provided by William Statham, a solicitor from London who initially invested £30,000, a not inconsiderable sum of money in those times. Little is known of this shadowy figure except that his motives were certainly financial, in that he could sell his shares at a profit once the scheme began to prosper. But with a distinct lack of interest from further investors, Statham introduced a Parliamentary Bill in 1879 to abandon the railway. As the time approached for its third and final reading in the House of Lords, solicitors acting for Lord and Lady Carnarvon, the owners of Highclere Castle, announced that they had purchased the company and its powers. Undoubtedly the poor financial state of farming in Berkshire at that time inspired local landowners to subscribe to the project which would offer facilities for the transport of farm produce. In spite of this it was recognised that agricultural goods could not ensure the viability of the railway. Thus the emphasis remained on freight traffic between the Midlands and Southampton as a means of providing its main source of income. It's interesting to note that this railway would probably never have been built had it not been for the actions of a comparatively unknown solicitor from London.

Construction commenced during August 1879, following some minor route alterations. The contractors Falkiner & Tancred found the north to south terrain very challenging in spite of operating steam powered excavators to build the route through endless seams of undulating chalky soils. As the line was approaching completion at Newbury, a quarrel broke out between the GWR and the L&SWR over access to the south. The original agreement brokered during the 1860s indicated that neither company would build lines in their respective areas. Although this was still active, intense antagonism had erupted in the west of England where the L&SWR had constructed several directly competing railways in Devon and Cornwall.

A flurry of letters and meetings took place, the outcome of which was that the two larger companies agreed the row was not of their making and they collectively regarded the DN&SJR 'as an unmitigated nuisance'. This led to an uneasy truce which would allow the L&SWR to work the line from the south as far north as Whitchurch and the GWR would work the northern section from Didcot to Newbury. Who would work the line in the middle remained temporarily unresolved.

Aware of these discussions and arrangements, the leaders of Southampton City Council were stirring. They clearly had an entrenched dislike of the L&SWR and set about encouraging the DN&SJR to actively complete its railway, the Mayor quoting 'it is our desire to have a railway leading to the industrial heart of England, one that would bring increased trade and prosperity to the port'. In order to encourage the company in its endeavours, he offered to extend the sea front and give tracts of land on the foreshore, reinforced by the provision of financial support. The company accepted this offer and instructed their engineer to survey the site and works required, at the same time informing the L&SWR of these developments.

Predictably this led to an almighty row between both companies and the fragile peace brokered earlier now led to outright hostilities. Parliament became involved as the wrangling continued and the L&SWR produced various schemes to snooker the DN&SJR, all of which were rejected. The outcome of this expensive thirty-five-day battle was a decision favourable to the DN&SJR which received the Royal Assent in August 1882. This was to construct the line to Southampton terminating near the Royal Pier, with plans for the Micheldever section and Whitchurch loops to be suspended.

The L&SWR realised that outright opposition would be pointless as the DN&SJR had obtained Parliamentary approval which could not be retracted. They were reassured, correctly as it turned out, that

The original route envisaged of the Didcot, Newbury & Southampton Junction Railway. (Alex Griffin based on map from *The Didcot, Newbury & Southampton Railway* – T.B. Sands)

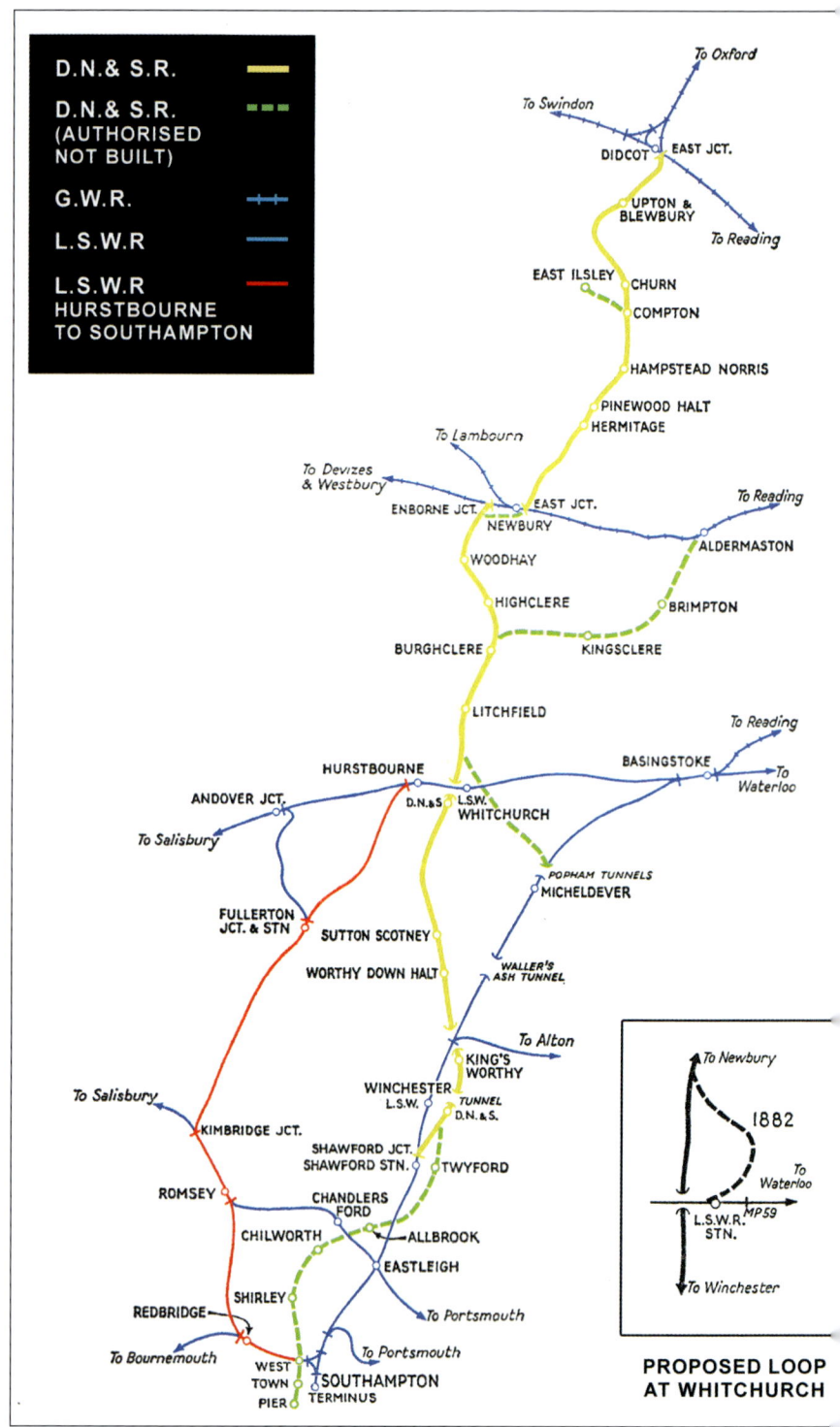

D.N.& S.R.	
D.N.& S.R. (AUTHORISED NOT BUILT)	
G.W.R.	
L.S.W.R	
L.S.W.R HURSTBOURNE TO SOUTHAMPTON	

To Oxford

To Swindon

DIDCOT — EAST JCT.

UPTON &
BLEWBURY

To Reading

EAST ILSLEY — CHURN

COMPTON

HAMPSTEAD NORRIS

PINEWOOD HALT

HERMITAGE

To Lambourn

To Devizes
& Westbury

To Reading

ENBORNE JCT. — EAST JCT.

NEWBURY

ALDERMASTON

WOODHAY

HIGHCLERE — BRIMPTON

BURGHCLERE — KINGSCLERE

LITCHFIELD

To Reading

BASINGSTOKE

To Waterloo

HURSTBOURNE

D.N.&S — L.S.W.
WHITCHURCH

ANDOVER JCT.

To Salisbury

POPHAM TUNNELS
MICHELDEVER

FULLERTON
JCT. & STN

SUTTON SCOTNEY

WORTHY DOWN HALT

WALLER'S
ASH TUNNEL

To Alton

KING'S
WORTHY

To Salisbury

WINCHESTER
L.S.W.

TUNNEL
D.N. &.S.

KIMBRIDGE JCT.

SHAWFORD JCT.
SHAWFORD STN. — TWYFORD

ROMSEY

CHANDLERS
FORD

CHILWORTH — ALLBROOK

EASTLEIGH

SHIRLEY

REDBRIDGE

To Bournemouth

WEST
TOWN — SOUTHAMPTON
PIER — TERMINUS

To Portsmouth

To Portsmouth

Inset, Proposed Loop at Whitchurch:

To Newbury

1882

To Waterloo

L.S.W.R.
STN.

MP59

To Winchester

**PROPOSED LOOP
AT WHITCHURCH**

funds would dry up because the final approach from Winchester to Southampton would prove to be expensive with a tunnel, viaduct and extensive earthworks planned. In addition the provision of stations at Southampton Pier, Town, West, Shirley, Chilworth, Allbrook and Twyford, would prove to be an indigestible final straw.

With this in mind the L&SWR took a decision to offer, through gritted teeth, an alternative to the DN&SJR's plans which they thought would be palatable. In 1865 the L&SWR had taken over the Andover and Redbridge (A&R) railway which ran between those towns on a broadly parallel route to Southampton as that planned by the DN&SJR further west.

Although the original promoters of this line had high hopes for its future, little money was generated and it lingered on as a single track railway with passing loops, providing local services. In 1885 its fortunes changed when the L&SWR doubled the line to accommodate the newly opened Midland & South West Junction route from Cheltenham. In addition a cut-off double track branch from Fullerton Junction via Longparish and Hurstbourne on the Basingstoke to Salisbury line was constructed, very much with the DN&SJR in mind. Simultaneously, east of Hurstbourne the L&SWR's Whitchurch station was enlarged by providing an island platform with a new building on the upside offering facilities for the main and loop lines. Once complete the DN&SJR was then invited to build a new line from the loop, passing under the Newbury Road where it would head north and west, connecting with its line thus enabling access from Southampton to Didcot with the promise of additional traffic from the L&SWR (see map). This speculative venture was rejected by the DN&SJR for several reasons. Firstly the mileage on this parallel route would increase which would put up its costs, secondly the line to Winchester south of Whitchurch would become redundant and finally, land ownership and the partially completed works in Southampton would have to be abandoned. In spite of the DN&SJR's refusal, it is interesting to note that construction of the loop at Whitchurch took place. Perhaps the thoughts at that time were 'you never know, just in case'.

However, in spite of the L&SWR's offer being refused, its newly constructed connection operated a service from Fullerton to Whitchurch, but as expected, was never profitable, with passenger services being withdrawn in 1931.

Success in those days seemed very tenuous. In Southampton when rumours abounded that the GWR and L&SWR had forged a new truce, local dignitaries smelt a rat which led to investment in the DN&SR, with its now simplified title omitting the word Junction, drying up. The crisis was compounded by a board of directors, most of whom had commitments elsewhere, and having to cope with the unexpected illness of its company Chairman, Sir Robert Loyd-Lindsay (1832–1901). It is clear from surviving records that he was a reluctant director, as several obituaries make little or no reference to his involvement with the railway. His military experience indicated great bravery, including his receiving a Victoria Cross during the Crimea war. He was heavily involved in local politics, serving as Member of Parliament for Berkshire from 1865 to 1885. As far as the DN&SR was concerned, he and his fellow directors admitted that 'they had not much experience in railway matters' and it was clear that they were reliant on their engineers for practical advice. Sir Robert resigned and moved abroad to aid his recovery.

Faced by intense financial difficulties, the now rudderless company recruited James Staats Forbes (1823–1904) as a director

Above left: **Sir Robert** Loyd-Lindsay – the reluctant Chairman of the DN&SR.

Above right: **James Staats** Forbes – Chairman.

with much experience in railways, particularly those in financial difficulty. Upon leaving school he joined the GWR in Isambard Kingdom Brunel's office as a draughtsman, then rising through the ranks to become goods manager, followed by employment at Dutch Railways as General Manager. Upon his return to England he joined two companies with financial problems, The London Chatham & Dover and the Metropolitan District railways, both in the role of director. Curiously and not explained was why at the time he turned down the key job of general manager of the GWR in favour of the DN&SR. He was a complex character and unusually for someone with hands on experience in railways, had a passion for fine art which he voraciously collected throughout his adult life.

Undoubtedly his credentials in preventing these companies from sliding into insolvency were legendary and his historic popularity with both the GWR and L&SWR would bode well during those unpredictable times. Although at first he was widely regarded as someone who was reliable and would continue to raise finance to complete the railway to Southampton, shareholders later realised that the opposite was the case. Some six months after joining the railway in 1883, he was voted in as Chairman and promptly revealed his true colours. His aims were to shut down all DN&SR railway development in Southampton and negotiate a new scheme with both the GWR and L&SWR over alternative running rights and routes. He was to remain with the company for the remainder of his working life to ensure that his plans were successful.

The DN&SR had spent about £100,000 in Southampton, most of which included the purchase of land, earthworks and a partially completed viaduct. Construction was temporarily suspended in October 1883, allowing a breathing space for Forbes, but was never recommenced in line with his long term plan.

But any thoughts of a peaceful conclusion to these events would later prove to be dashed. An early agreement was reached between the GWR and the L&SWR which recognised territories and sought to eliminate the building of competitive lines in the Southampton area. Both companies were at one in recognising that any progress in the DN&SR's aims would create severe problems, especially if the GWR operated the line directly to the port of Southampton. Thus at a meeting convened by Forbes in March 1884 the two larger companies later dismissed the efforts of the DN&SR saying 'that they did not consider the further construction of the railway to be an undertaking of great importance'. This unwise and dismissive

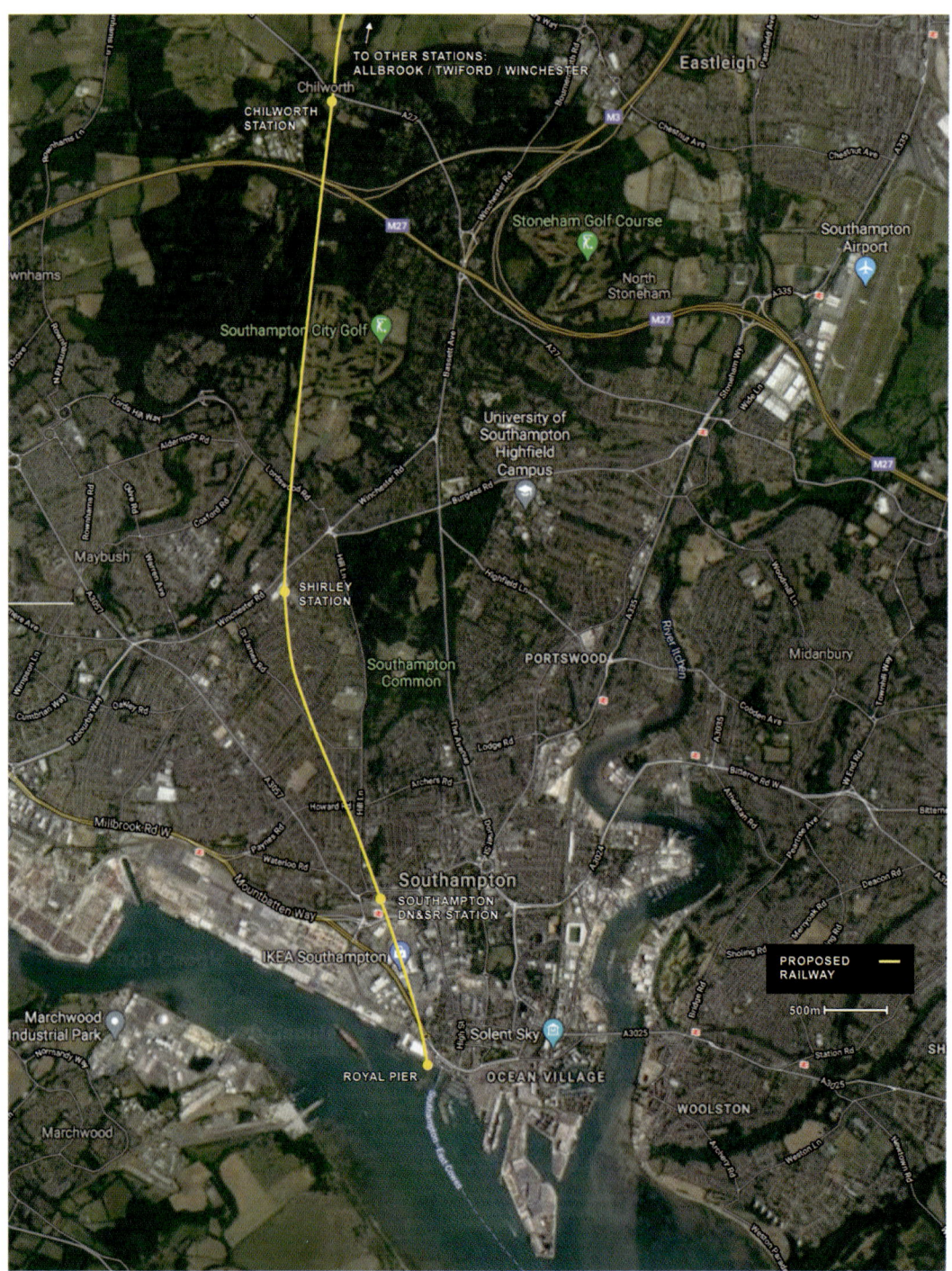

Detail of the Didcot, Newbury & Southampton Railway at the southern end. (Google. Imagery ©2021 Getmapping plc, Infoterra Ltd & Bluesky, Landsat / Copernicus, Maxar Technologies, The GeoInformation Group, Map data ©2021. By Alex Griffin)

statement enraged shareholders who promptly voted for a motion that would take the railway to the docks at Southampton. Forbes, in an attempt to broker a peaceful outcome, advised against this motion but was overruled. It should be borne in mind that at this stage of development the line was still languishing at Whitchurch 'several miles north of Winchester' and, as a result of the determination of the shareholders to fight on, all resources were ploughed into advancing the line to a new station to the west of the city. Known later as Winchester Chesil, this was to be worked northwards by the GWR and opened in 1885.

Lady Loyd-Lindsay's act of celebrating the line's opening ceremony was overshadowed by deep seated quarrels within the company as to how to proceed with their original aims. At least they were united in agreeing that a railway terminating at the edge of Winchester was unacceptable. Later a group of dissident shareholders met in London with the aim of unseating Forbes with a motion which concluded with the words, 'the services of Mr Forbes ought to be dispensed with'. This failed through lack of support.

Fundamentally as always, it was the lack of finance that severely limited options. Eventually after much wrangling with the L&SWR and amplified by angry shareholders, an agreement was struck at the end of 1884. They finally recognised that negotiating a deal with the L&SWR was their only option, so talks resumed. However, the success of this small majority led the general shareholders to believe that their trains would be allowed direct access to the port of Southampton, by which route was not made clear. How wrong they were!

Forbes' ability to manoeuvre was severely limited and his suggestion of a junction with the L&SWR north of Shawford station was met with outrage at a board meeting in August 1885. Later a small group of shareholders at a gathering in November narrowly voted in favour of this option. However, the L&SWR flatly refused access to Southampton, claiming that their line at Eastleigh was already operating close to full capacity and they would only permit the DN&SR to operate via the westerly route through Whitchurch, Hurstbourne and Fullerton Junction as previously suggested. Matters were not helped when Parliament 'after a lengthy session' refused the junction at Shawford anyway.

Fortunately for the DN&SR, it did have one final card to play. In 1882 the company had been granted permission to construct a junction north of Winchester at Alton Junction, giving direct access to the L&SWR railway between Winchester and Basingstoke (see map). These powers were never used and with time running out the DN&SR indicated that they would build the junction with immediate effect. This threat rattled the L&SWR who did not relish having to accommodate Great Western trains on its busy Winchester to Southampton route. Thus, recognising that the Shawford Junction plan was the lesser of two evils, the company agreed to it but insisted that any attempt to gain access to Southampton through an independent route was to be ruled out in perpetuity.

This truce led to a successful outcome. Two bills in 1888 and 1889 permitted the abandonment of the Southampton plans and an agreement for the construction of a junction between the two companies north of Shawford as previously outlined. A new railway 1.5 miles long would connect the two railways.

When it came to train operation, the GWR worked the northern route between Winchester and Didcot and the southern section from Southampton to Winchester, where the exchange of passengers and goods took place.

The line settled down to a peaceful life. Not surprisingly traffic never reached the level which would again strain relationships between the two companies. Goods traffic was moderate in spite of the railway's original aims and passenger services were always sparse. Severe pruning during the 1930s reduced its status to that of a cross country line of secondary importance.

However, as costs continued to be reduced and the railway severely rationalised, early promoters would have been proud to witness the large contribution the DN&SR made to the Second World War effort. During 1942 the track was doubled from Didcot to Newbury and on to Woodhay, which greatly increased the line's capacity. New passing loops were added or lengthened and others brought back into use having been earlier dismantled. The purpose of these rapid improvements, completed a year later, was preparation for the D-Day landings launched on 6 June 1944. Ammunition, stores and troops were encamped inland, much of these at Newbury racecourse, and it is recorded that 16,000 military trains travelled to Southampton in readiness for the invasion of Europe.

After the war was over in 1945, the line returned to its rustic existence and it was only a matter of time before closure took place, the final train running in 1964. Passenger trains had ceased to run two years earlier.

Today some of the route has been taken over by the A34 trunk road south of Newbury. It's strange to witness as one travels by car, the high chalk cuttings cut by navvies and steam excavators, where once steam trains plied their regular trade between the south coast and the industrial Midlands.

Remains of the Didcot, Newbury & Southampton – what to see and how to get there

Today the area through which these trains travelled remains remarkably unspoilt and well worth visiting. Parts of the line still retain structures of interest, particularly the viaduct south of Winchester, clearly visible from the M3, and tunnel to the north. An Ordnance survey explorer map identifies much of the route, which is surprising as the railway closed nearly 55 years ago. It is recommended that those who are fit and with a bicycle consider visiting these remains by rail. The DN&SR is served by Didcot to the north, and Newbury, Whitchurch, Winchester, Shawford and Southampton Central, offering flexibility of travel on railway transport.

When it comes to the remaining earthworks, these are to be found in Southampton.

As originally planned the DN&SR would have headed south from Winchester Cheshill station where Twyford station was to be provided west of Shawford. Shortly afterwards the line would cross the L&SWR at Allbrook Lock with a station of the same name, but without the word 'Lock', built here. Continuing south west, the railway would cross the Eastleigh to Romsey line at Oakmount Road close to Chandlers Ford. Then on a rising gradient the line would have passed under the present Leigh Road/Bournemouth Road Junction continuing to a tunnel which would have been constructed under the Chilworth Arms Public House. Chilworth station would have been placed on the south side of the tunnel before the line descended on a falling gradient through Lordswood and the present Sports Centre on the east side of Dale Valley. At this point the railway would have swung south east under the present Winchester Road and then passed through Shirley Junior School where Shirley station was planned. The route would then have run slightly to the south and west of Wilton Road before crossing to the east side of Hill Lane. It was to have headed south towards an intended bridge over the L&SWR and on to the Royal Pier where docks were to have been provided.

Part of an embankment still exists at the Dell football ground and Commercial Road, Milton Road near the place of the long demolished partially constructed viaduct. Two roads, appropriately called Didcot and Newbury, mark the place where the line would have been built in Shirley.

Part of the substantial embankment at 'The Dell', Southampton Football Club.

Overgrown bridge parapet east of Whitchurch station indicating the planned connection of the DN&SR to the north.

Further north at Whitchurch, the earthworks on the north side of the station indicate the remains of the loop line which was planned to connect the L&SWR with the DN&SR. Walk from the station to the former A34 trunk road, which now bypasses the town, turn north, cross over the present main railway and just beyond are two bridge parapets which mark the place where the line passed under to gain access to the DN&SR heading north. This was never completed.

Up platform of Whitchurch station, still an island platform without track.

CHAPTER 8

Edgware to Watford – Trains, Films and Military Planes

The London Underground railway system, or 'tube' as it is colloquially referred to, is actually a misnomer, as some three hundred miles of line operate at ground level. A glance at a London Underground map is interesting as it can be seen that most of this railway's historical development took place north of the Thames, with fewer lines to the south. This is because the Southern Railway, which was an early pioneer of third rail electrification, enabled the company to construct lines and take advantage of commuter trains into London which were free of smoke.

Tube railways to the north of London proliferated, most of which were constructed above ground or took over existing companies' traditional branch lines such as Chesham or Ongar.

One area of land north west of London known as the 'Northern Heights' was in Victorian times, rural in nature and traditionally farmed with few towns of interest to the newly developing railways.

A glance at a map shows that the London & Birmingham, later known as the London & North Western Railway, had comparatively easy gradients most of the way from Birmingham to London. It was forced to build an expensive 1,182 yard tunnel between Euston and Camden to gain height before tackling land west of the northern heights. In early days trains were hauled by cable powered stationary engines at Camden. Even that line required much in the way of embankments and cuttings further north so early proposals included routing into Paddington's Great Western Railway station, but these never bore fruit. Similarly the Great Northern Railway, whilst astutely avoiding the eastern flank of the northern heights, was still forced to construct a series of cuttings and embankments towards King's Cross. The Midland Railway to the north of St Pancras station was affected by having to tunnel under Lords Cricket Ground before avoiding the northern heights to the east. It should not be forgotten that locomotives manufactured in the 1830s and '40s relied on level surfaces to haul trains efficiently, quite unlike modern trains with multiple traction units which can climb gradients with greater ease than that of road vehicles. Therefore once the main lines were established, attention turned to the neglected tract of land which these companies had all avoided. Two notable towns, the citizens of which felt aggrieved at having been missed, were Finchley and Edgware. So finally in 1862 the Edgware, Highgate & London Railway Company received powers to construct a line which commenced at a junction just north of Seven Sisters Road, later named Finsbury Park station. The railway was 8.75 miles in length and once constructed was taken over by the Great Northern Railway (GNR) in 1867.

Soon after Parliamentary approval, several landowners on the northern heights were keen for their area to be connected to the railway network by an attempt at an act of their own, particularly as Edgware was situated on the southern edge of the northern heights. This proposal was to connect Edgware with Watford but suffered with the disadvantage of having to avoid Edgware station by diverting north from a junction to the south of the terminal station, Parliament having ruled that there was to be no extension from the terminus itself.

However, the proposal was now supported by the GNR whose manager Seymour Clark, under questioning from a Parliamentary Select Committee, explained that the original proposal had been provided by the Edgware, Highgate & London Railway which at that time had no intention of constructing a line north of Edgware because of a shortage of finance. It should be noted that had the GNR's new line ever been constructed, the extension to Watford would have made little sense. Trains from London to Watford via Edgware could only have been reached by complex shunting including running round carriages in and out of Edgware, not forgetting the necessity of using a turntable to enable the locomotive to run chimney first. Trains heading south from Watford would encounter similar difficulties.

Subsequently the GNR's enthusiasm for extending with the awkward junction at Edgware as previously described, rapidly faded, particularly as there was no desire to upset the L&NWR whose railway between Watford and London was well established. The final nail in the coffin was a lack of finance to construct the proposed railway and much protest from landowners, including the erudite proprietor of an art school on the outskirts of Bushey, Professor Hubert Herkomer, who described himself 'as an artist of Worldwide repute'. He objected to the railway coming within 110 yards of his house.

Hubert Herkomer
self-portrait.

Hubert Herkomer, later Sir Hubert (1849–1914), was a British artist of German origin who was known for his depictions of the lives of the poor. He founded the Herkomer Art School in Bushey in 1863 and continued to paint throughout his life, including a portrait of Queen Victoria which currently hangs in Osborne House on the Isle of Wight. He commissioned his own house, which served as a theatre, film studio and a facility for the composition of music. Designed by the prominent American architect Henry Hobson Richardson, it was based on a Romanesque style and constructed with Bavarian materials. Named Lululand after his deceased wife, it carried the nickname of 'The Bavarian Castle' by local residents.

This led to the GNR successfully promoting the abandonment of the Watford & Edgware Junction Railway in 1870.

Several proposals were made to extend lines from the Edgware branch over the years which came to nothing and the railway settled down to a peaceful rural existence as the twentieth century approached.

During all the proposals of the various schemes offered, Edgware had earlier been described by counsel for the L&NWR rather unkindly as 'the most decaying little country village that could be found in the neighbourhood of London'.

This churlish stab appeared to be the final blow to Edgware's plan to extend its railway northwards with a connection at Watford.

Meanwhile behind the scenes, there had been plans as early as 1893 to develop much of the land around Edgware with suburban housing but a lack of finance and poor transport links prevented progress. Finally on 3 December 1904 Metropolitan Electric Tramways Ltd opened a tram service between Cricklewood, Hendon and Edgware. This sudden development spurred new interest in connecting Edgware to the main London Underground network. However, the problem of finance continued to dog any proposal, so behind the scenes, two eminent Englishmen travelled to America to seek backing for the funding of lines north of London. Thomas Reeves and H.H. Montague Smith had made the journey in the forlorn hope that someone in the USA would back their schemes. They were in luck when they had a meeting with none other than Charles Tyson Yerkes (1837–1905) who had much experience in street car railway systems in Chicago and New York.

Of German origin, he is best described as a self-made entrepreneur who flaunted his wealth and lived opulently in a mansion on New York's Fifth Avenue. He developed a passion for fine art which he avidly collected thanks to the guidance of expert Sarah Hallowell (1846–1904).

He was brought up as a Quaker and began his career in banking and trading in bonds. Later whilst acting as a financial agent for the city of Philadelphia in 1865,

Charles Yerkes.

he risked public money on a large-scale stock speculation. Yerkes might have got away with it had it not been for the Great Chicago Fire of 1871 which killed 300 people and destroyed many buildings. When it came to the reconstruction of the city, much finance was needed both from their own resources and from across the USA. When the city of Philadelphia offered bonds to aid reconstruction, it was discovered that Yerkes had used them speculatively, thereby rendering himself insolvent. Later convicted of larceny, he was sentenced to thirty-three months in penitentiary. This was later reduced to seven months when it could be proved that others were additionally responsible.

After his release, the effervescent Yerkes had by 1886 considerably increased his wealth by promoting street car systems in Chicago and New York.

The timing of Reeves and Montague's visit was fortuitous. In 1889 Yerkes was bidding farewell to his employees as his railway interests had just been sold for several million dollars. He was contemplating life in retirement as a gentleman in his Fifth Avenue mansion and sailing his new yacht.

Suddenly he was presented with what seemed to be the opportunity of a lifetime. Here was a railway scheme in London, a city he had grown to love following several earlier visits. It was clear that as the city expanded, transport facilities within its boundaries were totally inadequate. The underground system was little more than the steam operated circle line and the streets above were heavily congested by horse drawn traffic, which was slowed down by endless queues.

Yerke's later career had developed in electric trains which he could introduce to the British market, thereby considerably increasing his wealth. Montague Smith outlined the history of the London to Hampstead Railway in Parliament and Reeves offered the Charing Cross to Hampstead Railway to Yerkes for £200,000.

He was hooked and in July 1900 arrived by train from Southampton to Waterloo as a great celebrity. The news had leaked of his coming and the press made much of his ability to revolutionise the London Underground system.

Wasting no time he purchased the Charing Cross, Euston & Hampstead Railway (CCE&HR) which included a terminus at Edgware, this being opened in 1906.

From the time of his arrival in London Yerkes became seriously involved with London Underground schemes, too many to outline here. There were challenges to his plans which in the main Yerkes fought successfully. All seemed to be going well until he had to return to the USA to resolve two court cases with his earlier American activities. Whilst this was proceeding he kept his head down by returning to London under the alias of Colonel Richards.

By now his health was failing but much of what he set out to achieve was becoming a reality. The existing tube lines were free of smoke as electric trains were being introduced and at that time the much maligned Chelsea Power Station supplied electricity. It is now known as Battersea and listed for posterity. He had worked at a frenetic pace and had more than his share of adversaries.

In June 1904 after returning from America, he was advised that he had eighteen months to live following diagnosis of nephritis (swelling of the kidneys) which were at an advanced stage. Refusing treatment in hospital, he remained at the Savoy Hotel being visited by doctors. Surprisingly he appeared to regain some of his vigour over a year later and went to France to recuperate. He was strong enough to return to London and chair a board meeting at the Underground Electric Railways Company in October 1905. He gave an ebullient report of the success of the company but realising that the end was near, gave one last interview before returning to

America. By the time the ship docked he was too weak to walk and was taken by stretcher to the Waldorf Astoria in preference to his home in Fifth Avenue where his long suffering estranged wife was in residence. Charles Tyson Yerkes died on 29 December 1905. In England he was widely feted by the media, the Westminster Press reporting that 'he became a street railway king in this respect not only in American cities but London as well'. He never witnessed the opening of his line to Edgware.

Once it was clear that the Edgware line was moving towards completion, a group of landowners on the northern heights once again revisited the plan to connect the line to Watford. The difference this time was to operate their railway from the new terminus of the CCE&HR and abandon all ideas of extending from that of the GNR terminus.

The railway would be 6 miles and 220 yards in length and twin track throughout. From Edgware it was planned to run parallel with the Watling Street Roman road and crossing that at Brockley Hill. A station was to be provided at Elstree which, it was claimed, would be no rival to the Midland Railway's, which was too far away from the village to be of any practical use. The line would then run south of the Aldenham reservoir, turning through Caldecott Hill, followed by the northern edge of Bushey. It was then to run south of The Avenue and Bushey Hall Road, passing under the bridge carrying the L&NWR, terminating on the Eastern side of Watford High Street.

As expected there were objections but most were of a transient nature and only two from local people, the vicar of Edgware and a local farmer, both of whom were later pacified. Even their by now elderly adversary Professor Herkomer was conspicuous by his absence on this occasion. It is likely that he regarded rumours of a tram system rife at this time, which he described as 'monstrous', a worse option than a railway.

It's important to note that at this stage the CCE&HR were reluctant to support this proposed new line, regarding it as unnecessary and 'would not serve any public need sufficient to justify the expenditure of £400,000 which its construction would prevail'. Part of this would be the necessity of remodelling the newly constructed terminus to allow for through running.

The Bill, by now amended, reached the Upper House of Parliament on 30 June 1903 and as all opposition had been removed, received the Royal Assent on 11 August. Construction was delayed until the

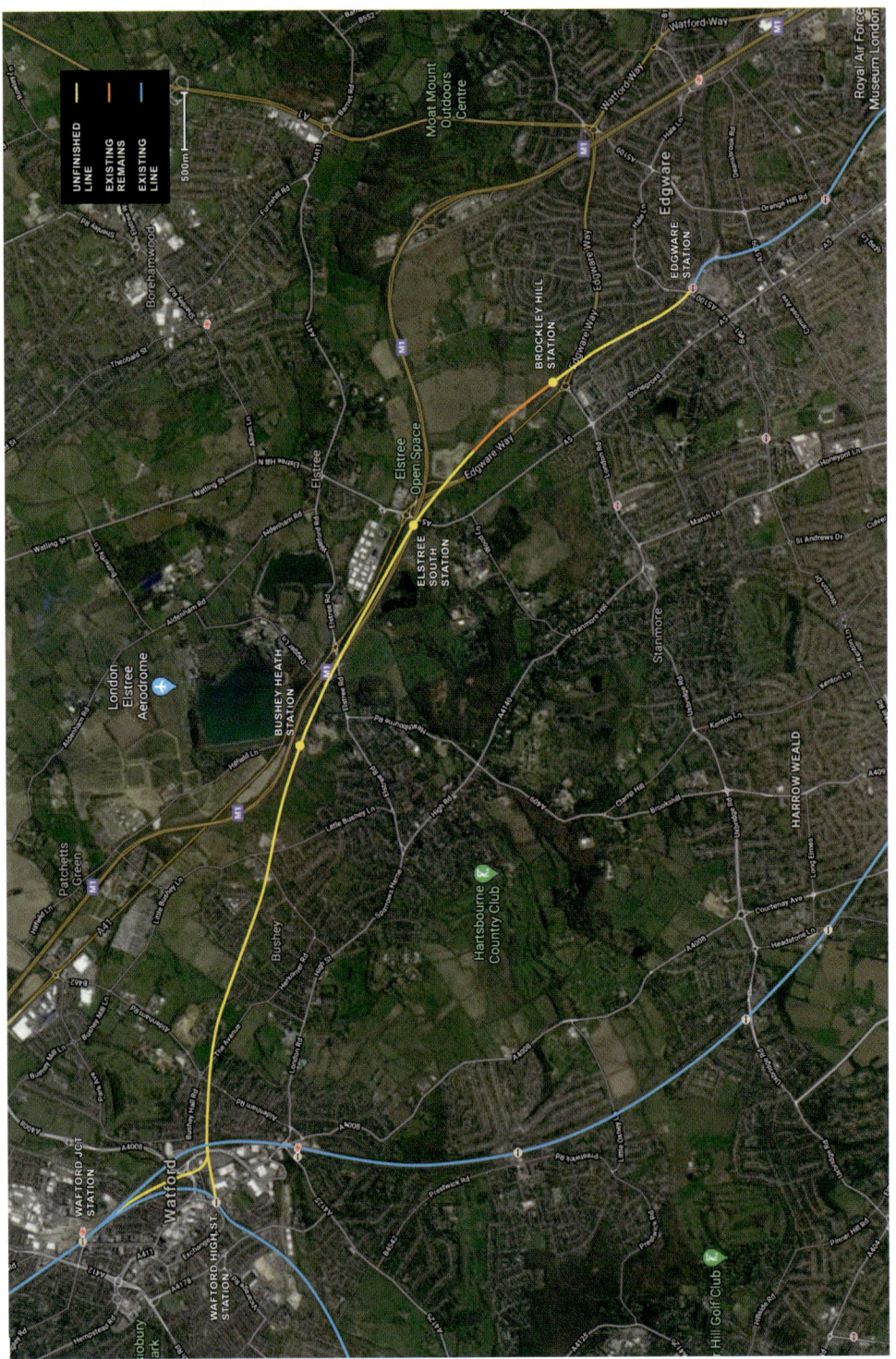

Planned route from Edgware to Watford. (Google. Imagery ©2021 Bluesky, Getmapping plc, Infoterra Ltd & Bluesky, Landsat / Copernicus, Maxar Technologies, The GeoInformation Group, Map data ©2021. By Alex Griffin)

completion of the CCE&HR from the south even though by now, the Watford extension was not being taken seriously because the terminus was not designed for through working.

Once these difficulties were ironed out, a serious proposal was presented to Parliament in 1925. This was for a line to continue beyond Edgware to Bushey where the railway would temporarily terminate. Bushey station would be built on a site owned by the Royal Masonic School which had entrances at the Avenue and Finch Lane. Further delays were then experienced owing to a landowner at Edgware demanding a high price for a strip of land and other problems, so by the end of the year all plans to build the extension were put on hold. The problem of land purchases continued to dog the scheme and even the estate of their old adversary, the late Professor Herkomer, was not finally acquired until 1927. In spite of progress, all plans to reach Watford were doomed, even though a series of starts and matters never envisaged tempted fate, as we shall see.

By 1930 the line from London to Edgware was running to capacity and The New Works and Improvements Committee voiced concerns that considerably expensive remodelling of Edgware station would be required if the Watford extension was ever to be constructed. Much argument continued and it was not until 1931 that a proposal to extend the line to Bushey was considered, which would later be extended to the newly built Watford bypass. It was at about this time that outside players were showing interest. Property prices were rising and the British film industry had already established studios at Borehamwood and Elstree. The promise of further investment in two new studios by American investors rendered the scheme viable, especially as they complained that the existing Elstree station on the Midland line was too remote. The London Passenger Transport Board, now showing interest in a new terminus at Borehamwood, was contacted by its vice-chairman Frank Pick. He and the proposers stressed the need for the extension, not only for the local community but particularly for those involved in the British film industry.

In spite of this the Borehamwood scheme was deferred and the plan to build a station at Bullbaiter's Farm placed on hold.

In 1936 after much correspondence in support of the railway, Pick forecasted failure, which happened later on that year.

After this latest setback new proposals were put forward suggesting, amongst other ideas, an extension to Watford from

Stanmore which would be longer and require a tunnel. One main advantage however was that Stanmore could cope with more capacity than Edgware, so talks continued. Another proposal was the development of empty land between Mill Hill, St Albans, Elstree, Radlett, Barnet and Potters Bar, making an area of about 36 square miles. Nothing came of this, so talks dragged on.

Life can sometimes throw up the unexpected such as that which would affect the Edgware to Watford railway. For decades the various schemes to accomplish this connection were thwarted. It was opposed by the L&NWR, local landowners, the terminus at Edgware which did not allow for through running, objections of several local government organisations and finally by the Northern Line which simply claimed 'it was full up'.

By 1936 the London Transport Bill's committee was urgently looking for extra space for depots and sidings, having realised that not only had space run out but that its Golders Green depot was too cramped to accommodate extra trains. This was exacerbated by the introduction of longer tube trains which could not fit and needed to negotiate access by dangerous point manoeuvres as well as having to be split to be accommodated in short sidings. In the London Passenger Transport Board's report of 1936, J.P. Thomas, General Manager (Railways), reported that with space for passenger and engineering trains being at near capacity, there was little room for an increase. He forecast that within 4–5 years extra housing north of London would require more depot capacity, particularly as 45 new train sets were to be provided.

Following this report the Board decided that land to the north west of Edgware station would be reserved because several attempts to find land elsewhere had not been successful. A report in March 1938 proposed an extension to Elstree for the provision of passenger services and a new depot.

Although yet more hurdles lay ahead the 1937 Bill to Parliament was submitted and broadly followed the route planned by the early proposals some thirty-four years earlier. One main change was the presence of the Watford bypass which had been built in 1927.

Finally, the Bill for the Elstree Extension was granted Royal Assent on 20 July 1937.

It was clear that the main motivating factor for extending the line was the need for a substantial depot at Aldenham near Elstree. But even now confusion continued. Some like the editor of *Modern Transport* reported trains on the line would only operate as shuttles, whilst others reported that to accommodate through trains, some would be routed via Edgware by sharing tracks with steam locomotives on the former GNR. Crucially the remodelling of Edgware station was of the greatest priority, including the provision of more space for the turning of buses.

In spite of the obvious need to increase capacity as a matter of some urgency, arguments continued back and forth on all manner of details. The problem was exacerbated by several bodies such as separate county and urban councils, objectors and disagreements within railway staff. There was even an intense debate about not only where stations on the extension were to be sited but what their place names should be called! Actually this was not unique as the residents of Finchley took exception to their station being named Finchley East End, which was subsequently dropped.

Finally, Parliamentary powers to construct the extension were granted in early October 1937 so that should have settled the matter. Even then, some two years before the outbreak of the Second World War, the government was making strategic plans for this event. Some minor details such as air raid precautions took place on the proposed extension but apart from that no contracts had been let, primarily because funds were not available.

Lord Ashfield (1874–1948), chairman of the railway, persistently pressed for funding through the Bank of England and finally achieved an agreement for a loan of over £1,000,000, enabling construction to commence.

Works were to be divided into two sections. Section one included long retaining walls as the line departed from Edgware station, a footbridge at Purcells Avenue and a 525 yard viaduct in length which included a five span section over Watford Way and a 55 ft span over the service road of Brockley Hill station. Section 2 consisted of earthworks on embankments and cuttings from the north end of the viaduct to the terminus and including the depot site. Included in this section were two 12 ft diameter tunnels two miles from Edgware.

Robert McAlpine & Sons successfully tendered for the works at £89,095 for Section 1 and £133,436 for Section 2. This company was founded by Robert in 1847 who at that time was an apprentice bricklayer. He single-handedly built up the business by himself in the housing market and before the age of thirty, was employing 1,000 men and owned two brickyards. After nearly going into liquidation by debts owed to him remaining unpaid, he went into railway contracting where he made his name. His most notable structure was the Glenfinnan viaduct on the Fort William to Mallaig railway in Scotland which was the first of its type to be made of concrete. This structure is regularly featured in films, such as the 'Harry Potter' series, and McAlpine earned the nickname, 'Concrete Bob' because of his development with this material in the building industry. He died in 1934 and his son, William, took over the business and was subsequently involved in the construction works on the Edgware extension. The contract was signed on the brink of the outbreak of the Second World War.

Just before the signing of McAlpine's contract in August 1939, Haymills (Contractors) Ltd, much experienced in building construction for London Underground, received the contract for providing the new train depot at Aldenham. With hostilities looming, the roof design was altered to better withstand air raids by removing the pitch glass roof with wired glass on the windows. Prior to both contracts being let, work had already started at Edgware station to allow through running and platform alterations. This involved excavating the covered way immediately north west of the station.

This was followed by removal of trees on the extension and the installation of culverts and drains under the embankments. The way between Edgware and Brockley Hill viaduct and the retaining walls near the station were completed. All the brick piers north of Watford bypass were complete up to arch springing level, with work commencing on three of them. On the southern side of the bypass the concrete base was laid in readiness for the six-arched viaduct. Between the northern viaduct and Elstree Hill, some work was carried out on the cutting leading up to the proposed tunnel and work on the first tube commenced shortly afterwards. A start was made on a sub-station near the site of Elstree South station. Foundation work was well advanced on the depot itself in spite of initial difficulties due to shortages of materials and labour following the outbreak of hostilities.

Unfortunately, not long after construction had started, the company board bowed to the inevitable, deciding that because of the need for building projects elsewhere, further work should be suspended until hostilities ceased.

However, as this decision was being made, in a report on 17 October 1939, it was noted that the underground carriage cleaning depot was nearing completion. It was clear that the building would not be completed until after hostilities, so Frank Pick let it be known that London Transport was open to suggestions for alternative uses. Coincidentally Frederick Handley Page, (later Sir Frederick CBE, 1885–1962) was alerted to the Aldenham depot which in the early part of the Second World War, was on the brink of the contract being cancelled.

Handley Page was an industrialist and pioneer in the aircraft industry and was notably regarded as the father of the heavy bomber. Shortly after a fortuitous meeting with Frank Pick and De Havilland, the aeroplane manufacturers, an agreement was forged whereby the two companies would join forces to produce the Halifax bomber. After much detailed planning the depot was adapted for the production of Halifax bomber fuselages in 1941 and by 1942 the addition of Mosquitos. At its peak the site employed nearly 1,000 production staff, many of whom had to be brought in by an intensive bus service.

The production of aircraft fuselages came to an end after the war and the site was vacated during the summer of 1945.

Sir Frederick
Handley Page.

When hostilities ceased, London Underground assumed that parts of its New Works Programme forged between 1935 and 1940 would be resumed. High on the list was the extension of the Edgware line, which was to be completed in 1947–1948 even though these dates were unlikely to be met. The pre-war figure of £40 million was, after fresh evaluation, later increased to £55 million. Confident of approval the London Transport Passenger Board deposited a Bill in Parliament for the re-siting of Bushey Heath station. There was deemed to be an urgent need to complete the works, mainly to avoid the decay of partially completed structures that had lain unused for several years.

It was correctly guessed that this application was likely to raise objections, the view being to get them out of the way before allocating any funds. The first to emerge were petitions from Hertfordshire and Middlesex County Councils who objected to the infringement of Green Belt policy, the digging up of important highways and provision of narrow bridges. In early 1947 the LPTB Bill was scrutinised by the Select Committee of the House of Commons by which time all the objections had been negotiated away with the exception of the Colne Valley Water Company. Percy Croom-Johnson, the railway's chief engineer, gave an undertaking to deviate the course of the line to avoid the reservoir and to clear the site of any wartime pollutants.

And as if nothing else could delay matters, the state ownership of railways, approved in 1947 and commenced on 1 January 1948, placed the line on hold for a further four years. In 1949 further discussions were held by the British Transport Commission and doubts were expressed. By now Green Belt land was highly prized and the lack of housing in the area west of Edgware placed doubts as to the extension's viability, in spite of spending £500,000 in earlier times. The presence of the depot at Aldenham was addressed and the BTC reported that land was available next to the Highgate and Morden depots which would adequately cope with current trains. The BTC recommended abandonment of the extension, which was approved by the Executive. The presence of the Aldenham depot presented a problem in that should the Green Belt rule be strictly applied, the land should be returned to agriculture. If the Town & Country Planning approval for alternative use was not approved, some £380,000 would be lost. At this time no public statement was made, without doubt because this had become a sensitive subject and the matter was not raised again until 1952. The committee of the House of Commons instructed that all maps which indicated a proposed extension be removed. The final public announcement of abandonment was made in February 1954. F.G. Maxwell, Operating Manager (Railways), cynically commented, 'it looks as though this supplies the final four screws for the coffin of this corpse as if it were not nailed down already!'

Haymills, the company responsible for constructing the depot at Aldenham, were commissioned for the demolition and alteration of buildings, work commencing before the official abandonment announcement.

Yerkes would have been astonished to learn that such a short extension of railway would have taken over fifty years to plan, only to be abandoned. As to the indefatigable Professor Herkomer with all his attempts to protect the tranquillity of Bushey, these would ultimately fail. The outward spread of London was relentless, as was the provision of transport links. Upon Herkomer's death in 1914 he fortuitously did not witness the First World War but would have been disappointed that his estate had later been broken up by being purchased by Bushey Council, apart from his 'Bavarian Castle'. This became derelict and a haunt of tramps and was demolished just before the Second World War.

What became abundantly clear was that new issues had come to light which did not trouble our Victorian ancestors. The Green Belt has since been strictly adhered to with 'no building' policies and much greater attention to the protection of wildlife. The advent of the Second World War prevented further progress, and with the provision of space for train depots provided elsewhere, it was clear that the depot at Aldenham could be dispensed with. Finally, it is obvious that in an attempt to be democratic in these matters, endless committees of many organisations had to have 'their say', thus ensuring that the brake on progress was permanently being applied.

What to see of the remains and how to get there

Most of the railway's construction took place between Edgware and Elstree and it is clear that had the Second World War not broken out, the extension to Bushey would have been completed. The earthworks of the line are clearly visible in fields to the north of Edgware parallel with the A41 between Brockley Grange and Edgwarebury Park. The M1 has obliterated part of the track bed further north and a hotel and housing estate occupy the place where wartime aircraft were once manufactured. Although all trace of Elstree tunnel has been obliterated, Edgware station's two short tunnels to the north bear witness to the plans to send trains through to Watford all those years ago.

The best way to view the remains is by London Underground to Edgware. It's hard to believe that this town was once, not that long ago, unkindly described as 'the most decaying village in the neighbourhood of London'. Readers can make up their own minds.

Trains await departure from Edgware Station.

The tunnel north serves as a fortified buffer stop.

CHAPTER 9

The Mid-Suffolk Light Railway

The county of Suffolk remains largely unspoilt to the present day and is known for its rich arable lands, wonderful historic Tudor houses and unspoilt coastline to the East. At this stage we can demolish one perennially inaccurate myth: the land is mostly gently undulating and not flat as frequently described, such as that to be found further north around the Wash at King's Lynn.

Suffolk and Norfolk get their names from an earlier Kingdom, East Anglia, which was settled by the Engels, a German tribe during the fifth century. In later years the two counties were formed and named 'Folk of the south' and Folk of the north', later to carry their present titles.

By all accounts the land was governed peacefully and even during the battles of the English Civil War in the mid-1600s, Suffolk remained staunchly Protestant as it does to this present day. In rural areas the Baptist faith is particularly widespread.

Agriculture has always been the county's prime activity and in Tudor times this was much more mixed with the advent of livestock as well as arable crops. In Reyce's *Breviary of Suffolk* written in 1618 he writes in glowing terms of the horses of Suffolk whose power and stamina on farms was legendary. Today the 'Suffolk Punch' is a much loved breed which can still occasionally be seen hauling brewery drays, much to the delight of tourists.

When the railway age made its appearance during the Victorian era, promoters concentrated on main lines to areas of large conurbations, with which East Anglia was not greatly blessed. Early railways connected Cambridge and Newmarket to London as they did to Colchester and Ipswich. A later entrepreneur, Samuel Morton Peto (1809–1899), developed lines to Norwich, Ely, Lowestoft and Yarmouth, making him exceedingly wealthy. He acquired Somerleyton Hall near Lowestoft as his 'baronial seat', only to lose all his wealth in later life, dying penniless in Pembury, Kent. But that is another story.

Apart from several branch lines such as Ipswich to Felixstowe, Wickham Market to Framlingham and Mellis to Eye, the central part of Suffolk was ignored by all the established railway companies throughout most of the nineteenth century. There simply was little incentive to serve a sparsely inhabited rural area which railway promoters regarded as a risky venture. For much of that time farming was suffering, with labour leaving the land and poor financial returns on agricultural produce, which contributed to the lack of interest.

It was clear to the government that incentives were needed to encourage improvement in transport links in areas such as this. This led the Government to sanction the Light Railways Act of 1896, which as its name implied, allowed for the construction of low-cost lines in areas which were devoid of railways. The main advantages to promoters were an allowance on gradients to avoid heavy earthworks, an absence of level crossing gates on minor roads, a simplification of signalling methods, a minimal provision of operational buildings and operational speeds of 25 miles per hour.

The first railway to be constructed under this act was the Rother Valley Railway, later re-named The Kent & East Sussex Railway, which ran between Robertsbridge and Headcorn across the boundary of both counties. Today 10.5 miles of this line has been restored between Bodiam and Tenterden and it is recommended that a journey be taken if you can. On quiet days, the atmosphere of a typical rural light railway is a memorable experience.

The Light Railways Act sowed the seeds of action to construct lines in the middle of Suffolk. A glance at a map indicates that railways operated in the west between Ipswich and Norwich, to the east between Ipswich and Lowestoft, to the north between Tivetshall and Beccles, and between Woodbridge to Stowmarket in the south.

The actions were commenced by H.L. Godden of Jeyes & Godden, civil engineering contractors in London, who contacted several parish councils and notable landowners in the Mid-Suffolk areas. The company indicated that with some financial support from the local community, extra support from outside could be made available for the construction of a Light Railway in their district. This letter was greeted with interest and a committee was formed in 1899 which met for the first time in Debenham and which took matters further.

This clearly went well and a further meeting was arranged in Laxfield, the centre of the proposed railway network, which was chaired by Dr Bider. It was revealed that if the local populace could raise half the money, the remaining amount would be supplied through a solicitor 'W.H. Smith' engaged by Jeyes & Godden, with city contacts who were willing to invest.

Shortly after this event the driving force behind the project became Francis Seymour Stevenson (1862–1938), described as a gentleman of leisure and Liberal Member of Parliament for the constituency of Ely, which included Mid-Suffolk, but more of him later. He was accompanied by Bernard Kilby who had some experience of Light Railway schemes in the Trent Valley.

The plans, when presented in 1898, were certainly grandiose, consisting of three lines which amounted to around fifty miles. These were for a railway between Haughley and Halesworth (27.75 miles), Westerfield to Kenton (13.5 miles), and Debenham to Needham Market (8 miles). Junctions would be provided with the Great Eastern Railway (GER) at Haughley, Halesworth and Westerfield. All the lines were to be of single track with passing loops.

Clearly the promoters had their eyes on a greater prize than that of the local district. Three junctions with the Great Eastern Railway, to destinations such as Ipswich, the East Coast and access to the industrial Midlands, had not gone unnoticed. The GER's co-operation should not have been taken for granted, because hardly had the print dried on the plans, the company lodged a formal objection. They had legitimate concerns about Mid-Suffolk Light Railway (MSLR) trains operating across their tracks and impeding the movement of their own trains and that they may have to allow access directly to Ipswich. Reassurances were rapidly provided when the MSLR indicated that each junction would be served by a separate station with no running connection with the GER. Mr C. Hutchinson, counsel for the GER, was reported as saying, 'It made us turn in our graves when we learned that they were planning on making connections with our railway, so that is why we opposed them'.

In general, however, the local landowners and farmers did support the scheme, with

Francis Seymour Stevenson, Chairman of the Mid-Suffolk Light Railway.

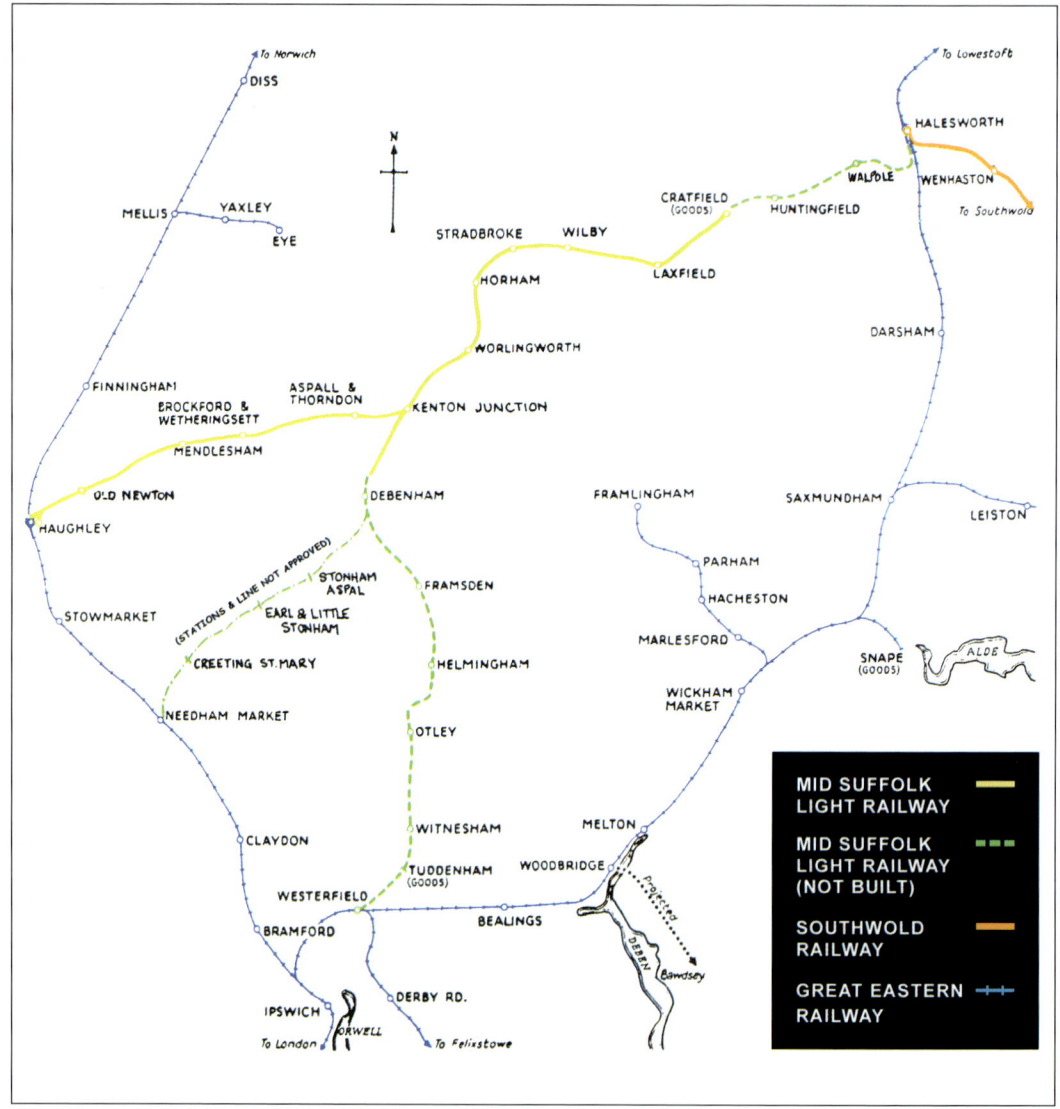

Original plan of the Mid-Suffolk Light Railway. (Alex Griffin (based on map from *The Mid-Suffolk Light Railway* – N.A. Comfort))

the single exception of those at Mendlesham who regarded the line as 'unnecessary' because of its close proximity to the GER. A certain Mr F. Robinson of Park Farm, a very prominent objector, claimed that 'trains would frighten his horses'. The fact that the pressure group was chaired by George Barnes, another antagonistic critic of the plans, ensured that this parish held sway.

Thus the MSLR took no chances and held a series of meetings at villages along the route in order to spell out the advantages and put the local residents' minds at rest.

The public enquiry was held on 6 July 1899, which generally was well received with some minor alterations requested, such as minor deviations and the re-positioning of Huntingfield and Witnesham stations south of Debenham. After hearing all the evidence, the Commissioners:

'…were of the opinion that an order from Westerfield to Halesworth could be made but that the company should reconsider the planned railway between Debenham and Needham Market. Constructing both lines would add little to revenue and add greatly to the MSLR's costs.'

The choice of one of these two routes was tenuous as the Needham Market line was certainly less expensive because it followed flat land along the Gipping Valley, requiring few earthworks, and serving three sizeable communities: Creeting St. Mary, Earl Stonham and Stonham Aspall. In the end the decision was taken to remove the Needham Market plans because it would appear that only one major landowner supported it for his own interests. Thus the complete proposed mileage was reduced to forty-two.

Signalling would be minimal and only present at passing loops and termini. There were to be 200 occupation crossings which did not require gates, and the track, if laid with 60 lb rail, would be subject to a locomotive axle weight of 12 tons. With the exception of one section, gradients would be to a maximum of 1:50 and the tightest curve 15 chains in radius.

Colonel Francis Marandin, an experienced railwayman who recommended the proposal to the Board of Trade, reported that, 'this was one of the best projects that had come to his notice'. On 5 April 1900 the Board of Trade granted the Light Railway Order.

Francis Stevenson and his colleagues immediately formed a company to bring the railway to reality. The initial directors were well chosen for their wealth and influence, consisting of the Earl of Stradbroke as Vice Chairman, Mr J.B. Chevalier of Aspall, Mr J.D. Cobbold of Ipswich and Mr J.D. Remnant of Wenhaston. Mr (later Sir) Daniel Goddard MP for Ipswich and Mr Kilby were two directors that took their seats on the board but resigned quite soon afterwards. History does not record their reasons but they were subsequently seen to be very wise in their moves. Those who did remain and invest were Cobbold and Remnant, who were to lose heavily within a few years.

The MSLR was empowered to raise £300,000 in debenture and preference shares, which would prove to be disastrous for the company. After some discussion with the Board of Trade which clarified matters, half its £225,000 capital would be in preference shares. The sting in the tail was that work could not commence until Stevenson, Remnant and Cobbold lodged securities of their own, to the sum of £10,617 between them.

New railways in Britain usually kicked off with the ceremonial 'cutting of the first sod' and this took place in a field to the north of Westerfield station on 3 May. Undoubtedly this somewhat hurried affair took place because of the mixed messages picked up by the press, with the *East Anglian Daily Times* seeing the line from Westerfield to Halesworth being the main route through Debenham. The Haughley to Kenton railway was regarded as purely a branch although it is obvious from historic records not picked up at the time of the ceremony, that contractors had already started work at Haughley anyway. The Duke of Cambridge, Master of Ceremonies and a grand senior figure of 83 years, made his speech and ended by saying, 'We are these too fond of rushing,' a very appropriate closing remark in regard to this particular venture.

The contractors, Jackson & Company at Doncaster, were appointed to build the line at £5,300 per mile and instructed to start work at both Haughley, where they were to construct a separate station, and Westerfield with the same arrangement. However it is clear that works at Westerfield were minimal and amounted to little more than clearing bushes and pegging out an access route to the GER's sidings. Track laying at Haughley consisted of 56 lb rail in 30 foot lengths laid on half-round sleepers.

At first reasonable progress was reported and the line had, by the middle of 1903, reached Horam and shortly afterwards Laxfield. Of course, the company had at this time sufficient funds for the project and, apart from some heavy earthworks east of Haughley at Mendlesham, was able to make considerable gains by following the contours of the landscape.

However, by now difficulties started to emerge. The remaining part of the railway to Halesworth amounted to 8.75 miles and it was not possible to follow the contours on this route and there were to be heavier earthworks on the way. A year earlier the company had been aware that the planned approach to Halesworth GER station was subject to marshy ground, the cost of which would be not only high but unachievable on a limited budget. Unfortunately this discovery had been clearly placed in the 'tackle this problem later' file, and the time to address it was now. The Mid-Suffolk applied for a Deviation Order which would take the railway north before encountering the marshland and gain access to Halesworth station in long loop before heading south *(see map)*. At a public enquiry in July 1903 held at Halesworth, the GER strongly objected to the MSLR shunting goods trains on a 1 in 70 gradient across both their running lines to gain access to sidings on the south eastern side of the station.

In spite of objections the Order was granted even though the earthworks were to be of a considerable nature on most of the remaining route. Work started on the loop in the north on the approach to Halesworth station. In the 1970s, the author recalls a conversation he had with a pensioner working on his allotment who indicated the place where a line of pegs had been put in the ground to the west of the town. He said he regretted not keeping one of them for posterity!

Obviously there was still much work to be done and the contractors were instructed 'to continue working at Halesworth and from Kenton Junction towards Debenham simultaneously'. This would appear to have been the final straw between the company and Jacksons the contractor. Money was ebbing away and rows broke out about changes of plan, lack of water supply for locomotives, fencing and many other petty grievances. In desperation the company wanted the Haughley to Laxfield section completed immediately in order for goods trains to run and the Kenton to Debenham section ready by the autumn of 1904.

Behind the scenes, in spite of ebullient reports from the Chairman, all was not well. The company had used up all its resources on a railway that was only half complete and even the deep cutting was not finished to the east of Mendlesham under the main Ipswich to Norwich road (the A140). This ruled out the operation of trains on the one piece of track that had been built. Legal action was considered against the contractor for failing to complete these works but it was clear that this would be throwing good money away on a fruitless cause. In desperation the MSLR approached East Suffolk County Council for a loan of £2,500 in order to enable works to be completed, but this was refused.

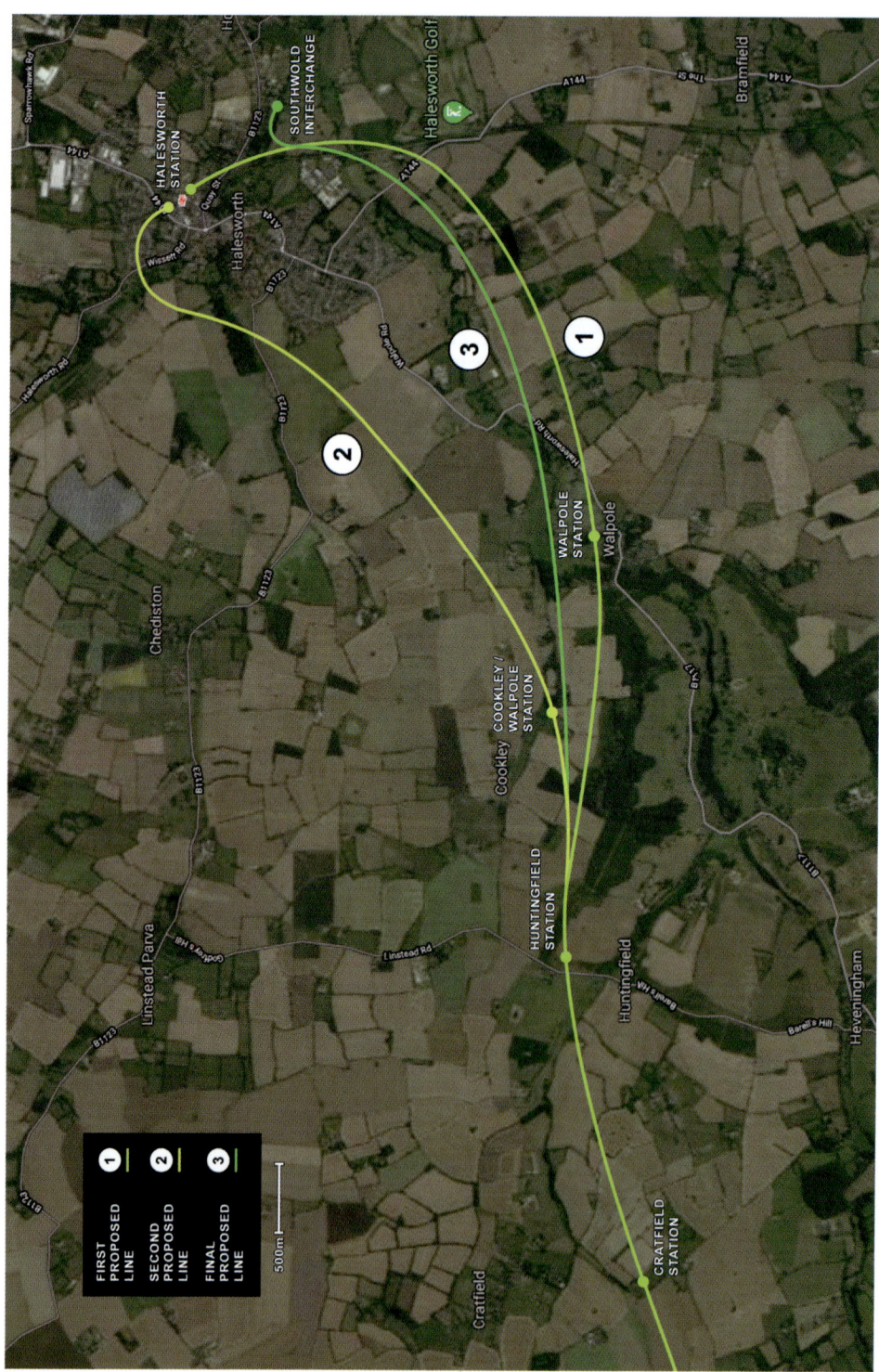

Three possible routes into Halesworth station were considered but never constructed. (Google. Imagery ©2021 CNES / Airbus, Getmapping plc, Infoterra Ltd & Bluesky, Landsat / Copernicus, Maxar Technologies, Map data ©2021. By Alex Griffin)

At the annual general meeting in July 1904 Mr Stevenson assured shareholders that the 'Laxfield to Debenham line would open in two months' time and in February 1905, the remaining section to Halesworth would shortly be ready for goods traffic'. Nothing was said about the line further south from Debenham to Westerfield because it was obvious that not only had the GER not agreed terms of access but more importantly, the money had run out.

Behind the scenes the company's only real choice was to throw what remained of its meagre resources into completing the cutting and providing a bridge under the A140 road at Mendlesham as mentioned earlier, thus enabling the start of a minimal goods service in 1905.

By now the rather unkind description 'Mad-Suffolk Railway' was somewhat justified when Hudswell Clarke of Leeds, who was supplying the 0-6-0 locomotive to operate the service, picked up rumours about the indebtedness of the company. As the engine had

Debenham Embankment.

The planned site of Debenham Station.

Aspall Road Bridge.

What is left of Laxfield station slumbers under the trees.

already been delivered to Haughley MSLR station in readiness for the commencement of services, it was chained to the track until the first instalment had been paid.

Finally trains did operate to Laxfield and unofficially to a point between Kenton Junction, a somewhat grand name for what it was, and Debenham shortly after the freeing of the locomotive, named *Haughley*, from its chains. Unfortunately trade did not live up to expectations but at least money was being banked. The ever-effervescent Stevenson reported at a staff meeting in February that 'optimism was the keynote', the same message being relayed to the press on a tour of the line later that day. At the Annual General Meeting that summer he reported that £5,000 was offered on loan to the company by Halesworth Council and backed by the Treasury for a similar amount in order to complete the works eastwards. However, alarmed by increasing indebtedness, the company's debenture holders blocked the proposal. This led to the spectacular downfall of the Mid-Suffolk Light Railway.

Stevenson hid the problems of the MSLR well but suspicions arose when he resigned as the constituency MP just after the 1906 election. A mere two months later he resigned as Chairman and director of the MSLR.

At the AGM in July of that year, the Earl of Stradbroke, having taken the role as Chairman, was solemn, playing down any suggestion of completing the line from Debenham to Westerfield. He further announced that the unofficial goods service to a siding north of Debenham would be withdrawn and all efforts would be made to get the railway to Halesworth. Simultaneously the company would apply for permission to operate passenger trains between Haughley and Laxfield. However, an inspecting officer found so many matters to be rectified that the company was forced to find a further £5,000 before the line could carry passengers. This was quite apart from the provision of carriages which they did not own.

Shortly afterwards the company decided to abandon the scheme to complete the approach into Halesworth from the north on the grounds of cost, despite works having been carried out near the station. Thus the third plan was to route the line (see map) south of the town and link up with the narrow gauge Southwold Railway at an interchange station on the eastern side of the town. Nobody found favour with this idea which was regarded as a desperate last ditch attempt, so not surprisingly it died on the vine with no progress being made. The GER was understandably relieved because the proposal would potentially have allowed the Midland Railway access to a port on the east coast which was firmly regarded as GER territory.

Shortly afterwards the Eagle Insurance Company, the MSLR's largest debenture holder, was clearly at the end of its tether and applied to the courts for a Receiver to be appointed to protect their interests.

The Receiver was called in before the details of the company's indebtedness was fully exposed, indicating some £30,000 for which creditors were demanding payment. It was obvious that a railwayman should take over the line and Major J.F.R. Daniel was chosen. He was used to managing railways on minimal budgets and had recently resigned from the Weston, Clevedon and Portishead Railway, another light railway which operated on a shoestring. Astonishingly he began employment at the MSLR at the age of 78 and remained in post until his death in 1918, never having formally retired. Although he successfully placed the company on a sound financial footing, he was forced to concede that any further extension eastwards was out of the question. Apart from some minor works, little else was done and the track was lifted at the outset of the First World War to provide steel for armaments.

Finally the MSLR opened for traffic at the end of September 1908 when the Board of Trade gave permission for trains to operate.

This chapter cannot be closed without examining the role of Stevenson who attempted to build a small railway empire but whose dreams were ultimately shattered.

Francis Seymour Stevenson MP was from the outset an enthusiastic supporter of the project and was Chairman until insolvency as described earlier. He was wealthy, having married well and largely lived on his wife's estate. Mary Kate Stevenson was directly related to the Joicey family who had profited directly from coal mining interests in Durham and lived in some opulence at Haltwhistle in Northumberland.

Stevenson was politically left of centre and cared deeply for his constituents who were suffering relative poverty in the agricultural community with low prices, made worse by an inability to deliver their goods efficiently to market. Obviously with hindsight Stevenson was totally unsuitable to deal with a venture that required astute business acumen. Apart from his activities as a Member of Parliament which in those days carried no salary, he had published several historical journals which are today, largely forgotten. So why, one might surmise, would this newly formed company choose such a man to become Chairman? Well clearly he was enthusiastic to the end and lived at Playford Mount, a substantial residence at Bealings near Woodbridge which is now a listed building. With his public school and Oxford University education, he did cut an impressive figure.

Whilst his motives were honourable, his financial and management skills were disastrous as he himself later admitted to creditors, saying, 'that he had never been in business and spent the greater part of his life in study and publishing academic works of little value'. Certainly, muddled instructions to contractors and continuous changes of plans additionally contributed to his downfall.

The end when it came was painful to witness. He had just been re-elected as Member of Parliament for the Eye constituency in January 1906 with no sign that the ship was rapidly sinking. As the General Election loomed in May he resigned without warning. In the ensuing public examination it was revealed that he had lost nearly £100,000 of his own money, a very substantial sum in those days and was towards the end, pawning his wife's jewellery in a desperate attempt to remain solvent. The presiding magistrate accused him of 'putting all his eggs in one basket and other peoples' as well'. Questions were raised about his motives in dealing with Midland Railway shares, further raising suspicions about double dealing against the interests of the Great Eastern Railway. His houses, including one in London, and their contents were sold and he was further humiliated by his wife's family, the Joiceys, who later settled his debts. Even then Stevenson's pain was worsened when his total indebtedness was revealed as being about £248,000. He retired to Felixstowe a broken man.

So was the MSLR project doomed from the beginning? Well hindsight is easy particularly from the perspective of the modern world. The story of Stevenson and the company's actions make tragic reading which would well apply to historians seeking to make sense of the shenanigans described here.

Clearly it is easy for us to speculate how things could have been done very differently. Let's start with the scheme itself. Yes it was over ambitious and the LRO commissioners were wise to recommend removal of the Needham Market extension from the MSLR's plans. But that still left a lot of railway to be constructed. Certainly there was clear need for goods traffic, which generated a fair income as indicated after opening. That the company's financial position was majorly flawed from the outset is obvious. To rely heavily on preference and debenture shareholders to provide the necessary capital proved to be disastrous. However, one could be legitimately critical of local businesses, landowners and individuals residing in the area, who in the main either bought few shares or did not make good on their promises of support.

It would be fair to say that the budget of £5,300 per mile for construction was a woefully inadequate estimate for a project of this nature. Other conventional railways at that time estimated their costs at ten times that amount. There is no doubt that building the line by following contours contributed to its low cost, but several parts of the projected railway would require much in the way of embankments, cuttings and bridges. Additionally one must remember this figure did not include the construction of stations and the purchase of locomotives and rolling stock.

This brings up the matter of project management. A scheme to build a railway of nearly 43 miles in length should certainly have been managed by an experienced railwayman who could prioritise the work and deal firmly with contractors. By all accounts decisions in this area were dealt with directly by the board of directors, probably in the main by Stevenson. Needless to say bad tempered disputes at board meetings regularly took place as the company's affairs sank between the waves. As described earlier he admitted that in the affairs of business, he had no experience. Matters were worsened by undertaking work in no less than three places simultaneously, thereby diluting the contractor's efforts to complete the project. This was done to demonstrate to shareholders and the press that the project was progressing well when the opposite was the case.

As to the matter of the original survey, the MSLR was badly advised. The company was forced to increase the gradient between Haughley and Mendlesham from 1:50 to 1:40, creating continuing problems of slipping on wet rails. More seriously the approach to Halesworth had been completely misjudged by surveyors who had not taken into account the marshland on the approaches to the town. This error was unforgivable, as historic records from the Eastern Counties Railway (later the Great Eastern Railway), indicated that their earlier works in 1859 to bring the railway into Halesworth, had proved to be expensive and troublesome.

Viewing the project in the fullness of time, might it have been a more productive decision to have commenced the railway north from Needham Market and abandon the Haughley to Kenton and Debenham to Westerfield lines? As the map shows, the route from Needham Market to Debenham, a substantial community, was on comparatively level ground with three villages in between. This would then pick up the route as constructed as far as Cratfield, leaving the remainder to be financed, taking the northern route into Halesworth.

In the opinion of the author this may have been possible providing the contractors worked solely on this route and avoided other distractions. It would have provided a relatively straight route directly south to north across the centre of Mid-Suffolk. The only significant works requiring earthworks and bridges would then have been concentrated in the Halesworth area. There is no doubt that the line if completed in this manner would have been a classically attractive light railway with fifteen stations and connections with main lines at each end. And at considerably lower cost. The reader is invited to draw his or her own conclusions.

It appears that the Stevensons remained betrothed and Mary Kate Stevenson remained living locally. The only mention of her later in life was when land held in trust by her and her husband that could not be seized, was made available after her death in 1934 for the benefit of the village hall at Playford.

As for the unfortunate Stevenson, little seems to be recorded as he sank into obscurity. He died in 1938 and is buried in St Mary Church, Playford, but no mention of him is made on his wife's grave. Parish records indicate GPR (grave penetrating radar) and number 192121 lists him as the husband of M.K. Stevenson.

After opening without ceremony the MSLR continued to operate in receivership until 1923 when it was taken into the ownership of the London & North Eastern Railway under the grouping act of that year. Apart from moving the junction station into a bay platform at Haughley station, which would have been preferable from the outset, little appears to have changed. The railway continued to operate peacefully throughout the Second World War, being nationalised in 1948 and finally succumbing to the inevitable axe in 1952.

Today the casual traveller needs to look diligently to find any trace of this railway that once endured such trial and tribulations. As most of the route followed contours across the landscape, farmers, who in many cases had witnessed the opening of the railway, simply removed fences and returned the track bed to the plough with all signs of the route vanishing without trace. It is worth pausing for a few moments at say, the platform at Laxfield, now covered in vegetation, to imagine what it would have been all those years ago.

Remains of the unused parts of the Mid-Suffolk Railway

As one would expect, the best place to view the remains of the MSLR is at Debenham.

The two prominent features are the bridge abutments which carried the railway over the B1077. Construction is of red brick and the deck has been removed. From there the most extensive earthworks on the line are still prominent. Passing through a cutting, an embankment continued down to the west of the village where work had stopped just before the road to Stonham Aspell. Here was the place where a temporary siding was provided. Debenham station was to be built on this side of the road.

KENTON JUNCTION
STATION

ASPALL &
THORNDON
STATION

KENTON JUNCTION

Kenton

B1077

Aspall

ASPELL ROAD
BRIDGE

Aspall Rd

Mon

END OF TRACK
GOODS 1903-1906

Debenham

DEBENHAM
STATION

High St

Ashfield

JUNCTION

Winston Rd

Winston

B1077

A1120

M.S.L.R
RAILWAY

CONSTRUCTED
(NOT OFFICIALLY
USED)

PROPOSED
RAILWAY

A Mill PHW

1km

A1120

Aspal

A1120

Pettaugh

The Mid-Suffolk Railway in the Debenham area. (Google. Imagery ©2021 CNES / Airbus, Getmapping plc, Infoterra Ltd & Bluesky, Landsat / Copernicus, Maxar Technologies, Map data ©2021. By Alex Griffin)

Work did commence on Railway No. 2 at the north west of Halesworth station but has completely disappeared in road and housing development during the 1970s.

With little remaining of this once iconic railway, it is well worth visiting other attractions which have been revived in spite of the railway having been closed for nearly seventy years.

The first of these is the Mid-Suffolk Railway, an award-winning museum where one finds a very impressive restoration of Brockford & Wetheringsett station as it would have appeared in early days. It is here that one can soak up the flavour of those times, enjoying the museum, shop, refreshment room, model railway and real ale bar. Use is made of an original platform and there is a range of locomotives and rolling stock which offer journeys at various times throughout the year. Currently trains run eastwards for 500 yards but plans have been approved to extend the railway to Aspall & Thorndon.

Restored Brockford & Wetheringsett Station, at the museum of the Mid-Suffolk Light Railway. (Ashley Dace)

Laxfield and Horam station buildings were rescued by the Mangapps Railway Museum near Burnham-on-Crouch in Essex. The museum has restored these buildings, which stand proudly on its operating line, allowing the visitor to dream of earlier times when trains go ambling through.

Finally, in regard to attractions, a visit to the area would not be complete without a visit to the newly revived Southwold Railway where its headquarters are in the town at Blyth Road. This fascinating 3 foot gauge railway which ran between Halesworth and Southwold, opened in 1879 and closed in 1929. It was 8.75 miles in length and it is the preservationists' aim to restore as much of the railway as possible. As described earlier, the MSLR, in a desperate third and final attempt to bring its line into Halesworth, offered a deal to the Southwold. This was to provide interchange facilities with the Southwold Railway at their station in Halesworth, where a goods shed still survives. Not surprisingly this was not warmly received and this crucially contributed to the final demise of the completion of the MSLR.

How to get there

For supporters of rail transport and keen cyclists, the best way of viewing the uncompleted works is by train. Stations offering access to the former Mid-Suffolk Railway are at Halesworth, Westerfield and Needham Market. Travelling on quiet roads is a joy and pre-arranging accommodation at historic inns and farm houses can be tailored to the energy of the cyclist. The Southwold Railway and Debenham remains can reached by bus services from Stowmarket or Ipswich and the former from Halesworth. The Mangapps Farm Museum is a half hour walk from Burnham-on-Crouch station and has a wealth of GER memorabilia in addition to the restored Mid-Suffolk stations. The single track branch line from Wickford to Southminster is in itself a very attractive journey across unspoilt South Essex and the journey can be commenced from London Liverpool Street station.

For those who want to tour by car, the Mid-Suffolk roads are quiet and not greatly different to what would have been witnessed all those years ago. Enjoy the tour and dream of what might have been.

CHAPTER 10

The South Devon Atmospheric Railway

Unless one is a railway enthusiast, you could be forgiven for not knowing what atmospheric railways were. Fairly recently a clever and rather amusing poster from a well-known heritage railway advertised itself as an atmospheric railway, deliberately carrying an ambiguous message and increasing interest in what was on offer.

Actually, the concept of atmospheric railways was invented a long time ago during the 1840s, not long after the dawn of the railway age some twenty years earlier than that. Astonishingly they were revolutionary in that they offered silent, speedy trains, free of grime and soot associated with slow steam-hauled locomotives. Compared to today's modern trains they would not have looked that much out of place.

In essence trains operated on conventional track and the power was provided from pumping stations sited strategically at two to three mile intervals beside the line. With some slight variation in design, cast iron tubes around 15 inches in diameter were placed on feet screwed to sleepers between the rails and joined continuously in lengths of 10 feet. At the top of the tube was a 2 inch wide slot sealed almost permanently by a complex valve mechanism and strip of ox hide. This was only opened briefly by the passing of a train and immediately re-sealed by a jockey wheel attached to the underside of the carriage. Into this slot was a connecting rod fixed to a piston similar to that of a modern car.

The steam operated engine houses were equipped with large air pumps which exhausted air from the tubes. This action forced the train forwards, at incredibly for those days, speeds of up to 60 miles an hour or faster. For the driver who stood at the front of the train equipped with little more than a crude braking system and pressure gauge, this would have been a frightening experience.

By all accounts for passengers waiting beside the line, this was an incredible experience. The first they saw was a smokeless train with the driver standing at the front of the leading carriage with his hand on the brake handle. All that was heard was a hissing noise upon

Early construction of the atmospheric railway at Dawlish, with engine house to the right. ('ikbrunel')

arrival and departure. To the uninitiated, there would have been no clue as to how the mechanism of this new-fangled invention worked.

The concept of using air pressure as a means of transport was being explored as long ago as 1800 and several engineers spent much time on the project, in some cases almost ruinously. Some that deserve mention include George Medhurst, John Valance, John Hague, Frederick Bramwell and Henry Pinkus. They should not be forgotten even though their efforts have faded into history.

However the true disciples of atmospheric railway development can be attributed to Samuel Clegg (1781–1861), a prominent engineer who in early life developed the use of gas at the dawn of that new industry. Certainly his knowledge heavily contributed to his interest in atmospheric railways, and in addition Jacob Samuda (1811–1844) and his younger brother Joseph (1813–1885) completed the team. The Samudas were originally involved in the manufacture of marine engines and later as their mutual interest in atmospheric power grew, agreed that all patented developments would be for the benefit of the three trustees. Clegg initially carried out research in France in 1838 but was accused by John Herapath of poaching the ideas of Pinkus. Herapath (1790–1868), then part owner of *Railway Magazine,* not to be confused with today's publication that was later re-named, was continually a vociferous critic of the atmospheric system, much to the irritation of its main supporters. The fact that he was later proved to be right did not improve relationships with those who had supported the scheme. By all accounts, Herapath was belligerent, aggressive, self-opinioned and not helped by being homophobic, once referring to someone he knew as 'he does not like the ladies!'

However, it did not escape the notice of railway builders that the costs of construction were one quarter of that of a conventional main line, which was at that time about £42,000 a mile. Operating costs were also different, at £1,246 for the atmospheric system to the alternative of £4,174. In addition the claims of fewer earthworks, light rails, reduced fuel costs and faster speeds rendered this form of transport a very attractive option. After several demonstrations, in spite of Herapath's acid comments, other reports were broadly favourable. In addition the witnessing of 40 mph trains by Prince Albert sealed its acceptance, which rapidly moved matters forward.

Thus the Atmosphere Railway Company was incorporated by an Act of Parliament with a capital of £400,000 with Clegg and Joseph Samuda as engineers. The company's objectives were to contract with railway companies in terms of haulage traffic with options for them to purchase these by negotiation. By now the Samuda brothers wanted to directly become involved with the construction and operation of a 'real atmospheric railway' and they got their chance on the newly constructed London & Croydon Railway (L&C) which had been suffering with problems with gradients of 1:100 near New Cross station. At that time, steam locomotives suffered with wheel slippage on even mild slopes such as these. The Samudas contacted W.A. Wilkinson, the Chairman of the L&C, suggesting that the annual running cost of their atmospheric system placed on the gradient would be less than half of the L&C's present figure at that time of £5,500. They would provide all means of atmospheric infrastructure and provide sixty-ton trains that would run at a frequency of fifteen minutes.

This offer was too attractive to resist, particularly as the existing lines into London were becoming seriously overcrowded, By an Act of Parliament granted in 1844, permission was given for an atmospheric railway system to be developed between London

Bridge and Epsom. Much was achieved for the following three years but this is a complex historical story and outside the remit of this chapter. But if nothing else the company was able to prove, in spite of much trial and tribulation, that the atmospheric railway could work very effectively.

The legendary figure of Isambard Kingdom Brunel (1806–1859) had successfully completed the broad gauge Great Western Railway between London, Bristol and Exeter in 1844. He was now contemplating extensions westwards into Devon and Cornwall and reliant on the South Devon Railway (SDR) to plan the route and raise the necessary funds. Naturally the line would be of 7 foot ¼ inch gauge, the same as that on the Great Western Railway at the time, and would almost certainly be purchased by the GWR upon completion.

The SDR planned initially to take the line to Plymouth and was faced with two fundamental options. One would be to meander inland and the other to take a direct route from Exeter

Isambard Kingdom Brunel.

via Newton (later Newton Abbot). The second option was made easier for the company when Parliament rejected the inland proposal anyway, which was sparsely populated, and approved the more expensive line through Dawlish in 1844.

Work at the eastern end was comparatively easy from Exeter, Newton and Totnes. Brunel in his role of engineering director at the SDR relished the task, particularly in blasting a series of tunnels through Dawlish Warren. The track, a little above sea level, offers to this day wonderful panoramic views of the coast on its westward journey.

In modern times Brunel is frequently blamed for choosing a route which would allow him to 'show off his skills', with little care of sea invasion at Dawlish where storms regularly tear out the track and undermine the sea wall. We have all seen pictures of tracks festooned above the waves and requiring expensive repairs. So spare some sympathy for

Brunel by remembering that Parliament approved this route many years ago after the SDR failed with its earlier proposal.

The line, including several tunnels, was opened in stages to Newton in 1846 and completed to Plymouth in 1849.

Meanwhile behind the scenes, much discussion was taking place on the question of motive power, and the atmospheric railway system was top of the list. Following experiments in 1840 on the trial atmospheric railway at Wormwood Scrubs in London, Brunel was an early visitor who reported that he found 'the atmospheric pipe and valve laid down did produce very fair results as to the power of traction' and that 'a moderate exhaustion of the pipe was easily attained. The working of the valve appeared to be sufficiently satisfactory at that time and might work (better) after further improvements in construction'. However, he was deeply involved with the construction of the GWR between London and Bristol at the time, so did not explore the system further. In 1844 his interests were reawakened after several trips to Ireland where he took great interest in the Kingstown & Dalkey Atmospheric Railway (K&DR) near Dublin, which had recently opened. Six months later in July, the board of the SDR met and soon after, the Samuda brothers made their approach, no doubt instigated by Brunel who set out in glowing terms the advantages of their atmospheric system. By then Thomas Gill, Chairman, and directors of the SDR had made a visit to the K&DR in Ireland and were by all accounts 'most impressed'. Brunel, picking his moment, produced his (here edited) report to the board of the SDR as follows:

'I assume that stationary power is free from the weight and friction as alternatives such as rope and particularly locomotive. The atmospheric system is a good and economic mode of travel and the loss of vacuum by leaking or friction was small enough to not be taken into consideration. By having a single atmospheric line instead of double track, increasing gradients, reducing the radius of curves and providing single line structures, £270,000 could be saved. And in addition a further £50,000 on locomotive costs and their shed would be saved'.

He then went on to reveal the advantage of atmospheric propulsion:

'...which would be 40–50mph up gradients and around curves, nearly twice as fast as a conventional locomotive and frequent operation of trains.'

He finished his presentation by saying:

'I have no hesitation in taking upon myself the full and certain responsibility of recommending the adoption of the Atmospheric System on the South Devon Railway, and of recommending as a consequence that the line and works should be constructed for a single line only.'

Such was the board's faith in Brunel that they voted for his proposal unanimously and later at a shareholders' meeting a month later. They confirmed a broad gauge line of single track with some double track sections on inclines, from Exeter via Totnes and Newton Abbot to Plymouth, a distance of fifty-two miles. The matter of then extending the railway into Cornwall was wisely deferred, as most of the directors felt that the system should be fully tested before proceeding further.

In March 1845, Brunel signed an agreement with the Samuda brothers in which the South Devon Railway would pay £250 per mile upon opening and a further £250 per mile one year later. The limit would not exceed £25,000. In April, construction of the engine houses was started at Exeter, Countess Weir, Turf, Starcross, Dawlish, Teignmouth, Summerhouse and Newton. Each was provided with two large and two small engines and reservoirs filled with water.

Finally at the end of May 1846, the line opened between Exeter and Teignmouth, completing the distance in 40 minutes. Behind the scenes though, all was not well. In spite of reassuring reports from the Samuda brothers that the atmospheric railway was operating successfully, this was not the case. Brunel was well aware of this and his scarcity of attendance at SDR board meetings led his fellow directors to probe matters further, particularly on the Croydon line. They soon discovered that there was significant valve trouble and were very troubled by this news.

Brunel took steps to reassure the board at a meeting in September 1846 when it was reported that the SDR was carrying 10,000 passengers a week and that technical problems relating to valves had been resolved. Clearly the board was reassured because they had approved an extension of the Cornwall railway and a branch line to Torquay, with atmospheric trains operating as far as Torre, the then terminus north of the town.

In spite of reassuring reports about the imminent opening to Newton, problems were being experienced with depressing

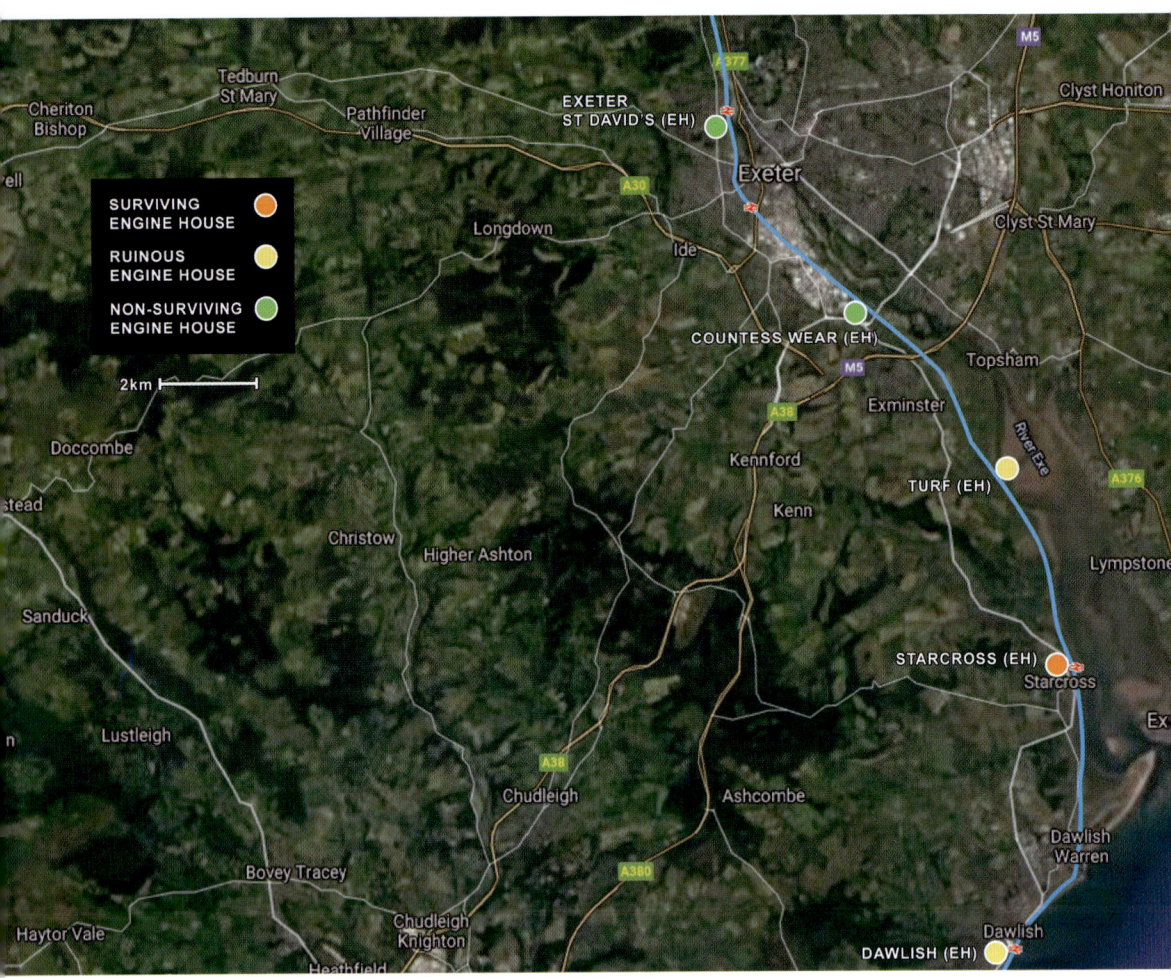

SURVIVING ENGINE HOUSE ●

RUINOUS ENGINE HOUSE ◐

NON-SURVIVING ENGINE HOUSE ●

2km

Cheriton Bishop
Tedburn St Mary
Pathfinder Village
EXETER ST DAVID'S (EH)
Exeter
Clyst Honiton
ell
A377
M5
Longdown
A30
Ide
Clyst St Mary
Doccombe
COUNTESS WEAR (EH)
Topsham
M5
stead
Exminster
A38
Kennford
TURF (EH)
River Exe
A376
Kenn
Christow
Higher Ashton
Lympstone
Sanduck
STARCROSS (EH)
n
Lustleigh
Starcross
Ex
A38
Chudleigh
Ashcombe
Dawlish Warren
Bovey Tracey
A380
Haytor Vale
Chudleigh Knighton
Dawlish
Heathfield
DAWLISH (EH)

Location of engine houses on the South Devon Atmospheric railway. (Google. Imagery ©2021 TerraMetrics, Map data ©2021. By Alex Griffin)

regularity. Test trains were used to clear debris from the tubes which regularly silted up, the engine houses were far from complete so trains were expected to draw power from the few that were actually working. Time was running out in the purchase of land for the construction of the recently authorised line to Torre. Strangely the construction of an engine shed took place here without the route being fully agreed.

As if these problems were not enough, the SDR discovered that the London & Croydon atmospheric line had closed completely in May 1847, shattering confidence in a system they truly believed would revolutionise travel on the SDR. Hurriedly Joseph Samuda,

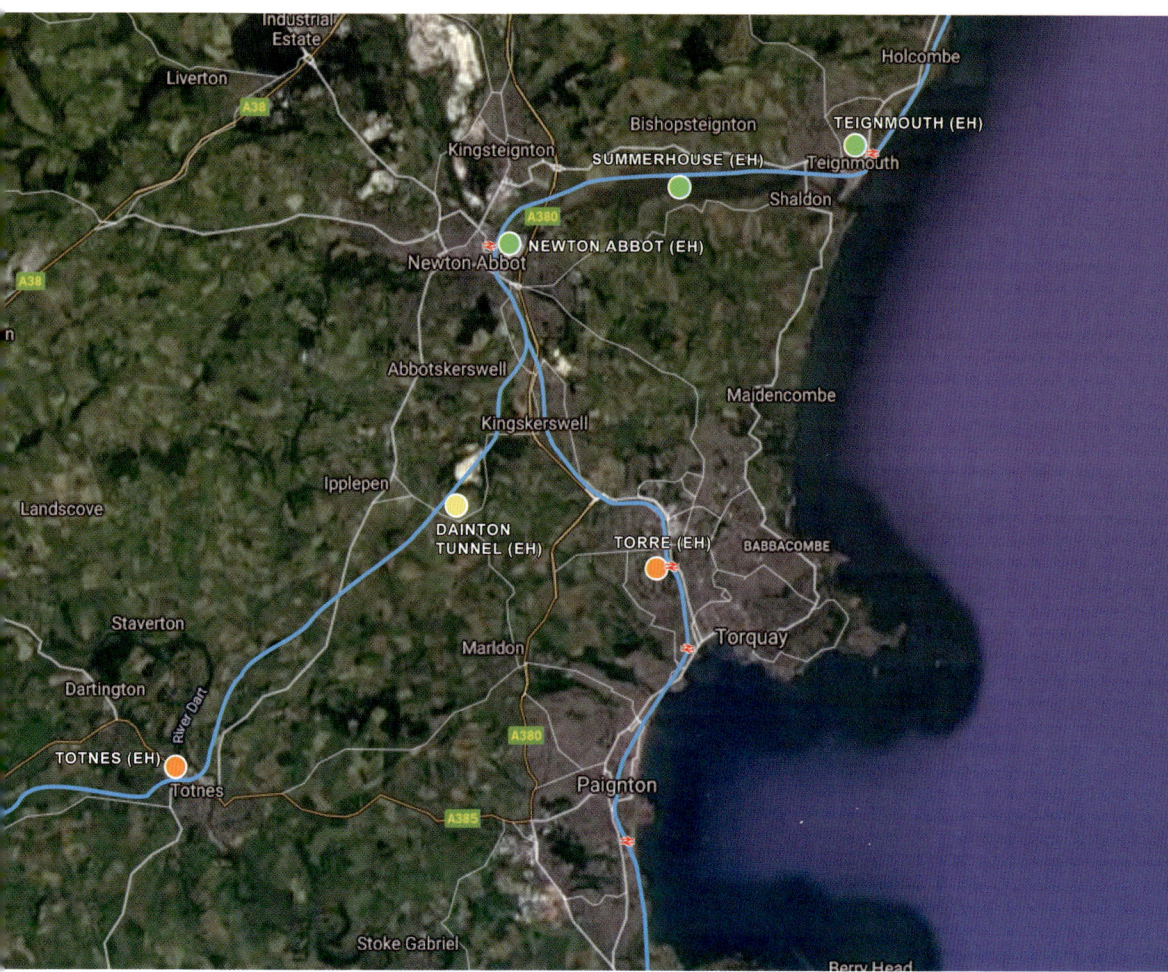

(his brother Jacob had died in 1844), clearly embarrassed by events at Croydon, reassured the directors of the SDR that successful progress had been made and that trains would operate successfully within a few weeks. The board quite wisely chose to suspend any atmospheric working beyond Totnes 'for the time being'. In spite of this decision Brunel continued some development on the engine houses near Dainton tunnel, Totnes, Rattery, Wrangaton and Torre.

Later at a shareholders' meeting in May 1847 the Chairman sought to calm nerves by explaining that the Croydon's two systems were incompatible, with both interfering with the other. This was reported as the reason why the atmospheric railway had been abandoned. He went on to explain that the SDR was different and tests had been carried out successfully between Exeter and

Dawlish using different weights and speeds of up to 70 mph so that, to cheers, 'we have no doubts in our own minds that our atmospheric system will be shortly extended to Teignmouth and to Newton in three months' time'.

In spite of these warm words, troubles continued to dog the company, with failures of pistons, valves and air pressure. Obviously unaware of these problems the Railway Commissioners authorised the opening of the line to Totnes for conventional locomotives. They questioned why the gradients had been altered from 1:52 to 1:42. Brunel explained that this was a temporary problem because he anticipated that the atmospheric system would be shortly introduced and the matter of gradients would resolve itself. Later generations of steam-hauled train crews would curse this decision as they toiled up this gradient. However, today railway enthusiasts and photographers flock to witness the occasional fine heavy working of steam trains, little realising that they owe their witnessing of hard-working locomotives to Brunel and his atmospheric system.

In a somewhat defensive report in early 1847, Brunel sought to blame others for the troubles of the new system. In particular he singled out the lack of deliveries of steam engines for the engine houses, which he claimed had seriously retarded progress. The response to this accusation was swift from one of the suppliers, G. & J. Rennie, who wrote:

'In reply to that part of your letter of yesterday's date complaining that you are waiting for our engines, we beg to say that these engines were ready for delivery agreeably to our contract nearly two years since, and that subsequently we have met with such repeated interruptions for want of engine houses, and other preparations being ready to receive them, that it has been impossible to proceed with them faster.'

Brunel's problems were not over. Shortly after this acrimonious exchange, George Hudson (1800–1871), the later infamous railway baron, and several other Midland Railway directors who were now sitting on the SDR board, demanded the cessation of atmospheric works immediately. A further proposal was that detailed tests be carried out between Exeter and Totnes to ensure the reliability of the system. This was met with a stony response but a compromise was agreed whereby the board agreed to make no further progress west of Totnes pending satisfactory working of the existing line.

Later at a shareholders' meeting on 29 August, Gill, the SDR Chairman, was still seeking support for the line between Exeter and Totnes to be successfully proved, particularly on the gradients referred to earlier. He went on to say:

'...that he regretted and for the company he represented had got itself in to an expensive system. This was attributed to the public and inventor who wished to see this successfully constructed. It was therefore important that it should be fairly and properly tried.'

The shareholders cheered and turned their ire on Hudson who was described as destroying the Croydon system by continuous spying and rumour mongering, 'just as he was now doing here'.

Finally and probably for the first time in the SDR's life, a celebratory ball was held at Sea Lawn House, Dawlish, on 7 September 1847. James Powell, the owner of this property, had passed away a year earlier, which was probably just as well because he was about as hostile to the railway coming as it was possible to be. He had moved from the Midlands after the London & Birmingham Railway had blighted his property there and was looking forward to a peaceful retirement on the south coast with direct access to the beach. The coming of the SDR destroyed his dream, as the railway passed within a few feet of his house. The only consolation would have been the prospect that at least the atmospheric trains were to be considerably quieter than steam trains. Evidently his widow was more forgiving and allowed the celebrations for the SDR to go ahead.

By all accounts the ball was a great success with Mr and Mrs Samuda and Mrs Brunel mingling with local dignitaries, and demonstration trains running successfully. All boded well for the future.

Within three days, final test trains did begin to operate on 10 September 1847. These carried a dynamometer coach and six coach trains operating to 52 mph with loads of 60 tons. The inventor was satisfied and with gasps of sheer relief a full public service opened a further three days after that. On 25 September Brunel and Samuda carried out a non-stop test trial between Exeter and Teignmouth, which was timed at seventeen minutes. A local reporter recorded, 'lightning itself looks not half so mysterious as did this string of carriages, flying, without any cause attached'.

At that time trains for Newton Abbot were complemented by conventional locomotive haulage. Initially a full service of nine atmospheric trains ran reliably well for the remainder of the month and the public at large was favourable with their comments.

But ominously passengers saw many sections of old valve abandoned beside the line, witness to the continued unreliability of the mechanism and its ox hide. In order to maintain a reliable train service, behind the scenes a host of men was constantly at work rubbing grease against the valves. Another problem was the leakage of rain and condensation which collected in the base of the tube overnight, necessitating the running of a piston locomotive to clear the system before trains of the day commenced. During the winter of 1847 and 1848, very cold weather was experienced and frost caused widespread delays, and even the SDR's supporters were forced to be critical.

In spite of this the directors reported that out of running 884 atmospheric trains, 790 were on time and the remainder only mildly delayed. In the light of these results they were persuaded to continue construction of the atmospheric system to Plymouth.

But trouble was brewing and at the shareholders' meeting the Midland Railway faction, headed of course by Hudson, was insisting that the atmospheric system should not proceed beyond Totnes. Brunel, who was present at the meeting, brushed these comments to one side by providing a positive report on progress. As if to prove his assessment was accurate, through the remainder of 1848 and the spring of 1849 the train service had markedly improved, with Brunel reporting, 'that certain mechanical difficulties had been overcome'.

In May 1849, the railway was completed to Laira just short of Plymouth, which allowed a train service from Exeter, albeit with a change of locomotives at Newton. But all was not well on the atmospheric front. The engine house pumps were providing insufficient power on gradients west of Newton and the continuing failure of the leather on the valves was so serious that they were tearing when trains were passing. This had not been experienced on other atmospheric systems, so the reasons for these problems would have to be resolved quickly. There is no doubt that the cost of men and materials needed to carry out constant repairs ate heavily in to the profits of the company.

The atmospheric system was financially bleeding to death so Brunel and Samuda asked for more time to resolve the existing problems and gained support from Gill, the SDR's Chairman.

Unfortunately he was unable to get a seconder to his proposal for continuing the works. A further resolution was made to close the atmospheric system completely in August 1849, which was passed.

Apart from a later chaotic shareholders' meeting in September, blame was apportioned to the promoters by those investors who not long earlier, had cheered them from the rooftops. Was it ever thus? After closure *The Western Times* which had always supported the aims of the SDR reported:

'The engine houses already present a melancholy aspect, they are dark at night and silent by day. The change did not occur without an expression of deep regret on the part of a large number of persons who have been accustomed to the atmospheric traction.'

Within a few years all the assets of the atmospheric railway were sold and put to various uses and the players in this story went on to lead other lives. In the case of Hudson he proved to be fraudulent in his railway dealings and was sent to prison for three months after the stock market crash in 1850, never to regain his reputation. Joseph Samuda, who had always maintained a good relationship with the SDR, went on to build equipment and coal trucks for them, although the loss of the atmospheric system must have been a major blow to his reputation. Thomas Gill was forced to retire as Chairman at the age of sixty-one shortly after what was regarded as a fiasco.

As to Brunel, his lasting epitaph should come from the words of Daniel Gooch, the Great Western Railway's Superintendent of Locomotives, who commented on the atmospheric system, 'I could not understand how Mr Brunel could be so misled. He had so much faith in his being able to improve it, that he shut his eyes to the consequences of failure.' However Brunel's overall reputation did survive this debacle partially because his son Henry, upon inheriting his father's records after his death, destroyed all references to the atmospheric era. Brunel continued to lead a very prosperous, albeit short life with further railways and the construction of ships. But those are separate stories.

Before closing this chapter and with the advantage of hindsight, it is worth examining in some detail of what led to the failure of the SDR's atmospheric system.

At that time, steam locomotives were underpowered and early technology was fraught with problems. Railways had to be constructed with easy gradients because those any greater than 1:100 caused great difficulty, leading to a loss of power and slipping. This meant the cost of constructing routes was high, involving tunnels and major earthworks. When the atmospheric railways were demonstrated it would have been seen to be a complete marvel, almost comparable to the space age of today. To witness silent trains gliding as if by magic in a clean environment at speeds of 60 mph or more would have been a sight to behold.

Unfortunately in all the excitement, the case for this form of travel was never really made. Factors that should have been addressed were things such as changing tracks and shunting, especially of goods trains, and primarily the use of technology that should have been proven to actually work. By all accounts the SDR resorted to manhandling coaches and trucks to form trains at stations, something of a comedown when one has experienced the wonders of modern high speed travel. To be fair, research was being carried out on the hoof whereas unlike railways of today, formal scientific testing procedures were not available. Brunel did discover late in the day that the slotted pipes did not allow for the provision of sufficient power, particularly on gradients, and he partially converted the diameter of the tubes from 15 to 22 inches to compensate. This involved the SDR in major expense with new pipes and engines to provide an increase in power.

The one place where trials could be observed was at the Samuda brothers' test track at Wormwood Scrubs in London, but the conditions there were greatly different to those in Devon. Most of the route from Exeter to Teignmouth and beyond is near the sea where it was observed that salt spray and mechanical plant proved to be incompatible bedfellows. In hot weather, tube expansion led to air leaks at the joints so more power was needed to compensate. Rust was a major factor, which interfered with the smooth running of the pistons, and as to the pumping engines, these were supplied by companies with sound reputations to specific requirements. In this case blame must be apportioned to Brunel and Samuda who were responsible for the detailed, and more importantly, underpowered specifications, even though in particular, Brunel subsequently attempted to avoid any personal blame.

And now we get to the matter of the leather strip used to seal the top of the pipe. Rumour persists to this day that it failed because of rats chewing the vital part of this mechanism. No doubt this made the story read well in the press at the time and because ox hide had some calorific value, rats may well have gnawed it, but this is certainly not the reason why it failed. In simple terms, leather was not suitable for this level of advanced technology. A frequent service of fast trains placed too much strain on the valve mechanism, which is why large gangs of workmen spent an inordinate amount of time carrying out expensive repairs.

In the end, the sheer cost, which Brunel had initially estimated to be around £190,000 for the whole line to Plymouth, with engine stations complete with equipment at £5,100 each and tubes at £3,300 per mile, proved to be very much higher. In spite of later revising these figures upwards, the SDR clearly could not support a scheme where this estimated figure had only got the atmospheric railway to work as far as Teignmouth.

There is no doubt that the directors of the company made the right decision to abandon the project. They could not stand by and allow expenditure to rise to astronomical levels and even then, not be certain of success.

Today the railway through Dawlish Warren is the high point of the journey, with spectacular views along the coast between Paddington and the west, and it has certainly witnessed its share of dramas. Once the atmospheric system had been abandoned, broad gauge locomotive hauled trains took over on double tracks. The SDR was sold to the Great Western Railway in 1876 and by the end of the Victorian era the broad gauge system itself had been converted to the standard rail width of 4 feet 8½ inches, which was adopted throughout most of Europe, the United States and much of the Commonwealth.

What remains can be seen on the South Devon Railway and how to get there

Surprisingly, in consideration of the long period of time that the atmospheric system has been abandoned, there are several remains, some almost complete, of the engine houses that were sited beside the railway.

To explore the engine houses, it is suggested that the reader takes a local train from Exeter St Davids to Totnes and then back via Newton Abbot and Torre. The sites of the engine houses are indicated as mileposts and chains radiating from London.

At Exeter the remains of the engine house could until recently have been seen on the upside of the railway at the station, mile post 193, but today no trace remains. As the train pulls out it is not long before Exeter St Thomas comes into view on a low viaduct. Originally this was built for a single track railway but was doubled in size when traffic increased in later years.

Our journey continues south where Countess Wear engine house stood on the upside at approximately milepost 196, but today no remains can be identified.

The next item of interest is Turf where the remains of the engine house do survive at milepost 199 53ch. A substantial reservoir was excavated to provide water for the pump and there are footings which indicate where the engine house stood. As the train does not stop here, it is later worth taking time to explore the remnants which to this day can be seen on the down side of the line. This remote place can be visited by bicycle or for the hardy on foot as well as the car, its approximate postcode being EX6 8EE.

Note that the square mound surrounded by trees on the riverside was where the engine house water reservoir was provided. Just to the south of this feature, the foundations of the building exist.

Remains of Turf Engine House.

The engine house was demolished in 1860 and the stone used for construction on a nearby farm.

As your journey continues, the train passes through the remains of Exminster station, where the building exists to this day. It was opened in 1852, after the atmospheric era, and closed in 1964.

As we approach Starcross at milepost 202 36ch, the most widely recognised engine house on the line comes in to view. It actively saw service during the year that the railway operated and is situated on the landward side of the line at the southern end of Starcross station. Constructed in heavytree, a coarse sandstone excavated in Exeter, it is dressed with Bath stone with the addition of a Romanesque tiled roof, which was replaced in 1980. The ornate tower and chimney was reduced in the Victorian era for safety reasons. This engine house unlike those elsewhere, has not weathered well owing to the choice of sandstone as its main constituent. Inside the building, several features survive to indicate its primary use. Ducts that carried smoke, a recess in the wall to house a flywheel, and the west block which housed the steam engines can clearly be identified.

Starcross engine house.

After closure, the building was put to several uses, including the conversion to a Wesleyan Chapel in 1869, which closed in 1950. From then until 1981 the building lay derelict, when British Rail sold it and an atmospheric museum was established shortly afterwards. Recently it was occupied by the local Starcross Fishing and Cruising Club and of particular interest is the recently discovered reservoir which had remained hidden for many years.

After pausing briefly at Dawlish Warren, which was built in 1905, we reach Dawlish at milepost 206 07ch. This station and its surroundings have the dubious honour of being featured in the media every time sea storms batter that part of the coastline, causing much damage. The engine house, sited on the up side of the line, was largely demolished after the closure of the atmospheric system. However, to those with sharp eyes, part of the remaining engine house wall with bricked up windows still exists and it can be seen at the back of Dawlish station car park.

At Teignmouth milepost 208 70ch, our next stop, has had several structural alterations over the years and there are no remains of the engine house which was built on the up side and slightly east of the present station.

The rear wall of Dawlish Engine House in the station car park is its only remaining feature.

We continue our journey to Summerhouse engine house at milepost 212 10ch, which was constructed on the downside, but today there is no evidence to indicate where it stood.

Our next stop is Newton Abbot at milepost 215 09ch. Recent modernisation of the station has completely altered its Great Western flavour and it is certain that Brunel would not recognise it today. The engine house was built on the down side at the junction where the branch line to Torquay commenced to the south, but today there are no remains, as they were swallowed up by the modern A380 trunk road.

Our train now travels west towards Plymouth and tackles some severe gradients as it approaches Dainton tunnel. At the western portal at milepost 217 76ch, the next engine house was partially built on the down side of the line.

Now after travelling on through stunning unspoilt Devon scenery, we arrive at the bustling traditional market town of Totnes.

The engine house here at milepost 222 66ch is largely intact but was never used by atmospheric trains. The building consists of two blocks: the engine and boiler houses, which are placed at right angles to the east end of Totnes station up platform. They are composed in an Italianate style constructed with course limestone square blocks with red sandstone dressings and a pitch slate roof.

The south east gable end of the house has an opening to the ground floor and a large arched opening with rusticated voussoirs and a metal framed window above. A sandstone band at sill level continues through the south gable wall of the attached former boiler house and there are four arched openings to the ground floor of the boiler house, but two are hidden by modern additions. There is a central keyed circular opening in the gable above. The projecting eaves to the south east gable ends are supported by brackets, which are in turn supported on stone corbels. The south west elevation of the engine house consists of five bays, and historic photographs indicate that it consisted of five round-headed openings. These are now blocked and the wall plastered. The north west gable to the rear of the engine house has a similar opening to that of its opposite number but is plainer. Its campanile chimney was demolished some years ago, probably for safety reasons.

The interior of the engine house was originally constructed to provide a single space which would accommodate a beam engine, and in later years was sub-divided with the provision of a mezzanine floor.

Although boilers were installed, the house was never fitted with a steam engine, thus never fulfilling the purpose for which it was originally designed. After the demise of the atmospheric system it was abandoned, and featured again nearly a century later when Dawes Creameries occupied the building for processing dairy products in 1934, finally closing in 2007.

Some miles further west, Brunel reported that Rattery and Wrangton engine houses 'were under construction' but no remains can be seen. It is interesting to note that the distance between engine houses from Newton Abbot were increased from three to five miles. Brunel had invested in larger diameter tubes on this section, clearly believing that sufficient power could be provided over greater distances. This theory was never put to the test.

We now cross over the lines to the up platform at Totnes and return to Newton Abbot where we will change trains for Torquay. Our journey south passes through the remains of Kinkerswell station, which was closed in 1964, before arriving at Torre milepost 219 12ch.

Torquay (Torre) engine house was abandoned shortly before the SDR board had made its decision to shut down the atmospheric system totally. Ironically, against the odds it can claim to be the most complete of all the engine houses. Sited north of the present

Totnes Engine House.

Torre station on the up side of the line to Newton Abbot, it is constructed in local limestone rubble with red sandstone brick dressings. Currently it carries a gable ended corrugated asbestos roof, completed with a campanile chimney. Two parallel adjoining blocks roofed on a north to south axis were probably intended to contain the boilers and beam engine. Viewed from the outside the east block is single storey, part floored with a 3:2 window end elevation. The chimney is placed in the centre of the right hand side block. The left hand block has three high set windows in the gable end and the central plastered window is round-headed with a key block. The right hand block has two round-headed windows with proud architraves with a modern opening beneath, and the left return of the western block has a chamfered string course. Here there are two large square-headed windows with proud architraves which are almost certainly original.

On the inside the roof on the western block is concealed. However, the eastern one contains timber tie beam trusses with purling held on cleats.

Having built a grand engine house such as this, the SDR was so short of cash they allowed the building to be used for victims of families with cholera.

Torre Engine
House.

Atmospheric railway pipes on display at Didcot Railway Centre. (Chris Allen)

As to the final place to visit, it is recommended that a journey to Didcot by train be made to the Great Western Society's museum, which is next to the main line railway station. Here the visitor will find a well-crafted display of broad gauge track, one of which is fitted with a section of atmospheric pipe.

This faithfully recreates that which was originally built near Dainton Tunnel at its steepest gradient of 1:36. The three sections of pipe were discovered being used as a drain at Goodrington Sands in Devon and were rescued by the society, to which a considerable debt of thanks is owed.

How to get there

The Didcot Railway Centre, www.didcotrailwaycentre.org.uk, is easily reached by train on Brunel's original route between London Paddington to Bristol and trains are fast and frequent. There is a wealth of Great Western Railway equipment, locomotives and rolling stock, so do enjoy your visit.

CHAPTER 11

George Hudson's Virgin Viaduct at Tadcaster

There were two periods in the Victorian era which could be referred to as 'railway mania', the first of which was in 1850 when after much ill-judged speculation, the market spectacularly crashed. Of course man's greed is littered with similar events in history, the most recent scheme being the Ponzi episode of 2008 when Bernard Madoff Investments, colourfully termed as 'made off with our money', went spectacularly bankrupt in a similar manner. In essence he was able to accumulate huge personal wealth and pay healthy dividends to shareholders as long as new investors kept buying into his schemes. But of course, once the markets wobbled and the income dried up, his house of cards came tumbling down. So what, the reader may ask, has all this to do with a mysterious viaduct at Tadcaster in Yorkshire?

To answer this question it is necessary to address the first period of 'railway mania'. By 1845 the United Kingdom had largely been connected by railways between its principal cities, with London at its hub. Lines radiated out like the spokes of a wheel with several large companies making healthy profits and investors more than happy with their returns. In spite of this, there was a need for additional railways to fill cross-country routes and complete remaining main lines. It was into this void that entrepreneurs sought to make their fortunes.

Thus during the mid to late 1840s the great British public were encouraged to invest in new railways, which of course many of them did. Well, why wouldn't they? After all, returns on railway shares had always been healthy, so why not continue to support them? By 1846 over 272 Acts of Parliament enabled new companies to construct extra lines amounting to 9,500 miles of railway. Around one third of these were never built because either the promoting companies were underfunded or fundamentally fraudulent.

One such character was the larger than life George Hudson (1800–1871), who emerged in the Victorian era when the railways were at the dawn of their expansion. Born the son of farming stock

George Hudson.

in Yorkshire, Hudson left home to initially work for a millinery company in York, later marrying in to the family. By a stroke of good fortune, when the owner of the business died, he left around £30,000 to Hudson in his will. Clearly uninterested in continuing the business and spotting a means to make money, he became involved in the development of railways as well as pursuing a career in politics. At this time the north east of England was lacking sufficient cross-country lines and still did not have a direct line from York to London or Scotland, so Hudson set about developing railways in the region. One of his first successes was to knock down a part of York's medieval wall so that the railway could terminate in the city centre, an unimaginable act in today's world.

Hudson continued to expand his empire, becoming directly involved with the burgeoning Midland and Eastern Counties railways, with interest in lines far away as Devon. (*See Chapter 10.*) In addition, by linking up with George Stephenson, known as 'the father of railways', at the height of his career, he pioneered the main east coast main line to Scotland and south to London. In addition Hudson surreptitiously leased the 31 mile Hull and Selby Railway, which prevented his competitors from gaining access to this significant port. He accrued great personal wealth, including the acquisition of two large estates in East Yorkshire, further preventing competition, and was active in serving as a Tory in Parliament.

By all accounts, Hudson was outspoken, bellicose and aggressive, regarded as impolite by those who dealt in business matters with him. He was feared as a serious adversary and was often able to buy his way out of obstacles in order to further his ambitions. Well aware of his roots, he sent both his sons to Harrow school to enhance his reputation. Unfortunately for Hudson, he was regularly lampooned in the press and unkindly looked down on as 'nouveau riche', often by those who directly benefitted from his business dealings.

The railway relevant to this chapter was a proposal to directly link York with Leeds. At the time York, like all cities, needed coal for industrial and domestic use, and the area around the city was rich in farmland, unlike the West Riding of Yorkshire. Although Hudson's grip on new railways was solid, it did not deter others from planning their own. In this febrile climate the Manchester & Leeds Railway (M&LR) planned to open a new route from its industrial heartlands to Hull via York. This would simultaneously haul coal and finished cotton goods eastwards and raw cotton westwards from Hull on the same route.

Understandably Hudson (the 'Railway King') took against these proposals by planning two new routes of his own which were intended to block any incursion from outside. The first, actually surveyed by Hudson's friend George Stephenson, ran from Church Fenton to Harrogate via Tadcaster and was opened in 1847. The station at Tadcaster was a fine example of Victorian splendour, having been designed by G.T. Andrews (1804–1855), a distinguished architect who provided similar drawings for many of Hudson's stations on the North Midland Railway. It is sad to record that this and many other stations were not listed for posterity and later demolished.

During the frenetic plotting and devious tactics, particularly the continuing threat from the Manchester & Leeds Railway, Hudson cemented his position by purchasing large tracts of land east of York, including the Londesborough Estate which was then owned by the Duke of Devonshire. This enabled Hudson to block any railway routes towards the east coast. In spite of these extravagant measures, the M&LR remained determined to achieve its aims, which were to establish a line between Liverpool and Hull via York, thereby offering a direct connection between two major ports. Although Hudson poured scorn on his rival's scheme, describing it as a 'a mere bubble, not worth notice', he was privately rattled, crucially as the route between Leeds and York would be 6.5 miles shorter than his own, the Y&NMR.

In due course, an Act of Parliament was passed in 1846 which authorised Hudson to open a new cut-off section of railway, thereby considerably shortening the route between York and Leeds.

The railway was planned to divert from the York to Church Fenton line south of Copmanthorpe station and then run to Tadcaster, before continuing south west, joining the Selby to Leeds line at Cross Gates.

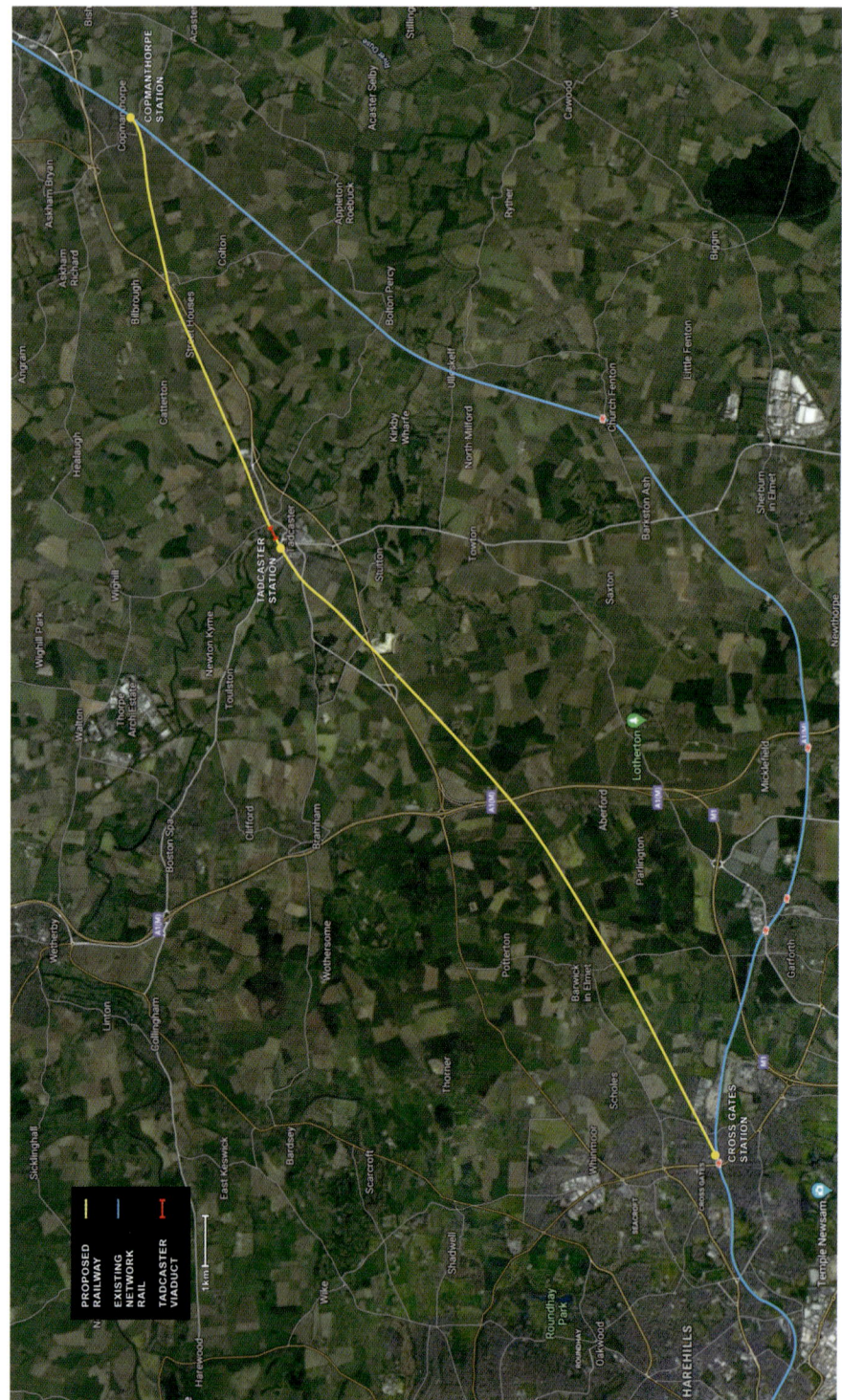

Hudson's cut-off route between Copmanthorpe and Cross Gates stations. (Google. Imagery ©2021 TerraMetrics, Map data ©2021. By Alex Griffin)

By now Hudson's activities were receiving much widespread attention, not all complimentary, including for example, a surviving letter from the distinguished author Charlotte Brontë, who wrote to a Miss Wooler as follows:

'The York and North Midland is, as you say, a very good line, yet I confess to you I should wish for my part to be wise in time. I cannot think that even the best lines will continue for many years at their premiums and I have been most anxious for us to sell our shares ere it be too late to secure the proceeds in some safer, if for the present less profitable investment.'

History records that she and her family did not sell their shares in spite of their doubts, a good example of not paying attention to one's instincts.

In spite of this and many other warnings, Hudson pressed ahead with the Y&NMR by initiating the construction of a fine viaduct over the River Wharfe at Tadcaster in 1848, as if to demonstrate to his critics that all was well. However, at a shareholders' meeting in early 1848 he reported that due to the depression, dividends would be lower than expected both on the Midland and Eastern Counties railways. To be fair Hudson did offer to resign but was cheered with shouts of 'No!' from the floor. Clearly his shareholders still remained loyal to their king.

Behind the scenes all was not well and by the end of the year Arthur Smith, a railway author of note with an astute knowledge of stock market dealings, published a damning indictment on Hudson's malfeasance. His pamphlet entitled *The Bubble of the Age. The fallacies of Railway Investment and Railway Accounts and Dividends,* raised legitimate concerns about the management of Hudson's companies and in particular the Y&NMR and the Eastern Counties Railways. It led decisively to the accusation that the two companies had paid dividends out of capital which should have been provided from revenue. Smith concluded by reporting, 'then it must be clear to every honest man, that an enquiry should be instituted'.

In spite of ebullient reports in Hudson's *Gazette* which predictably praised the viability of the accounts, they were countered by John Duncan, the editor of *The Yorkshireman* newspaper, who savagely reported that 'Mr Hudson must either believe he is dealing with simpletons or he is laughing in the face of shareholders.'

Hudson, now sensing danger, opened up dealings with the Great Northern Railway by offering access to York and the route to Scotland. But this led to divided loyalties and was all too little too late, and by the dawn of 1849, Hudson's reputation was severely damaged with dividends tumbling. By all accounts his half yearly shareholders' meeting in February was stormy, not only due to falling income but equally the question of Hudson's morality.

Some while later, Hudson announced a somewhat lower dividend on the Y&NMR, which was reluctantly accepted by its shareholders who continued to support him. However, it was not for long when it was revealed that rails destined for the new cut-off line had been overcharged, netting the sum of £9,000 which was paid personally to Hudson. George Jennings, a director of the company who was taking part in the enquiry in to Hudson's affairs and in particular the overcharging of rails, asked, 'Now Mr Hudson, here are three thousand tons for which we seem to have paid you £3 per ton more than we ought, so how do you account for that?' Under intense pressure Hudson agreed that he had and justified his action by saying, 'I thought I had done so much for the company, that I had a right to be paid'. During this sorry tale, it was revealed that Jennings and his co-directors had, with Hudson's connivance, awarded themselves nine hundred shares between themselves which were quickly sold after purchase, netting a large profit! In spite of the pot calling the kettle black, the final straw as far as the Y&NMR directors were concerned was the undoubtedly scandalous affair of the sale of land from the Landesborough estate to allow construction to commence. Hudson had bought the Duke of Devonshire's estate for £40 pounds per acre and proceeded to sell the Y&NMR 50 acres at ten times that amount, netting him a personal profit of £18,000.

After much humiliation, the demise of Hudson continued into 1851 with his having to pay debts and face other enquiries. The land that he had sold to the Y&NMR was later purchased by Sir Albert Denison, the Whig MP for Canterbury, and any hopes of the railway to be built between Copmanthorpe and Cross Gates were dashed. The calamity of Hudson, his poverty and imprisonment is another story. But what is clear from this sorry tale was that others around Hudson were ready to make money on the back of his activities and just as quickly turn against him later when the tide turned. In spite of all his travails, he was physically tough and lived to be seventy-one years old. He should be credited with the construction of attractive stations, scenic railways and the attractive Tadcaster viaduct which have stood the test of time.

Remains of the York & North Midland Railway at Tadcaster

The viaduct fortunately has been listed as a Grade 2 monument since 1985 and although occasionally damaged by flooding, is sympathetically restored as protected by its status.

As to who designed this elegant structure, information appears to be scarce. However, it would seem that one of the leading Y&NMRY engineers, J.C. Burkinshaw, was responsible for its construction. The materials used consist of rough-faced magnesium limestone with vermiculated millstone grit dressings and orange brick soffits. There are eleven arches, seven of which are land based and the remaining four are two to the east and two to the west. Two wider segmented arches span the river, rising from cutwaters which support paired pilasters. These are rounded to the north and flat to the south. The land based arches support paired pilasters and the finishing touches include Millstone grit voussoirs with chisel draughted margins and coping stones on the parapet.

Tadcaster Viaduct. (Andrew Whale)

(Alison Stamp)

Although never used as a double track railway for which it was intended, a single line was eventually laid from Tadcaster Station in 1883, which served as a siding to Ingleby's steam powered corn mill. This was demolished and replaced by a coal fired steam generating station for John Smith's Brewery just before the First World War and continued in use until 1959 when the track was lifted.

By all accounts the track bed continued for a further distance before petering out in fields towards Copmanthorpe. However, Hudson has not been forgotten, as there is a road named after him known as Hudson's Way. Although the western end is inaccurate, the eastern one clearly follows the route of the railway that was planned and never completed.

Visitors may pause and wonder at this monument to one man's ambition and reflect on the politics and dramas of the period all those years ago.

How to get there
Nothing would please the author more than to direct visitors by rail and take in the view of Tadcaster's attractive station, which is now on the site of an inevitable industrial estate. Its closure in 1964 has meant that visitors must now seek alternative ways of getting there. By public transport a bus from York is recommended because visitors can take in the National Rail Museum and Hudson's house at 44 Monkgate, which are part of the history of this chapter. For those inclined to walk or cycle, the viaduct is about three miles from Church Fenton station on the York to Leeds railway, which offers a frequent train service.

The Birmingham &
Oxford Junction Railway

The history of this railway is complex and involves personalities
and early competition over routes to the prosperous West Midlands.

Two great rivals in those days were the Grand Junction (GJR),
London & Birmingham (L&BR) and Great Western railways (GWR),
all determined to exploit the heavily populated city of Birmingham
and its industrial surroundings. The GJR was already established
there, having built its main line from Manchester and Liverpool
in the north and opening in 1837. To the south the L&BR was
forging ahead to complete its line from Euston in order to provide
a connection at Birmingham. This was opened in 1838, and six years
later the two companies merged to become known as the London &
North Western Railway.

Meanwhile, the Great Western Railway had not been idle. Having
constructed its broad gauge main line from Paddington station to
Bristol in 1841, and forever colloquially known as Brunel's 'God's
Wonderful Railway', the company set its sights on constructing a
line to Birmingham and then to continue from there to the north
west. A start was made at Didcot when a group of GWR directors
independently funded and built a branch line from there to Oxford
which opened in 1844, whereupon it was purchased by the GWR.
This was Oxford's first station, which was sited at the corner
of Marlborough and Western Roads. At the time it was cheaply
constructed in timber because, although the GWR realised it was
an unsuitable site for a terminus, this was the best the GWR could
achieve. Continuous antagonism from the great and good in the
city and its universities, thwarted the plans by objecting to this
'monstrous' undertaking with numerous comments such as 'it might
encourage the lower orders who may be tempted to move about'.

Later, plans were laid by the Oxford & Rugby Railway to extend
their line northwards, by which time the city of Oxford would appear
to have overcome its aversion to steam trains and from all accounts,
was making use of them. A new station was built on its present site
before extending to Banbury and Rugby. The Parliamentary Act was

Grandpont, Oxford's first railway station. (Oxford County Council)

granted in 1845 and construction commenced towards Banbury, and a place some four miles north of Fenny Compton. History reports that progress was slow, particularly north of Banbury, with contractors working lethargically and farmers proving to be reticent in parting with their land. The partially completed works languished for several years with the GWR losing interest, especially when they realised that their junction at Rugby would face London and not Birmingham, thus necessitating excessive shunting of through trains. In addition, the route was clearly a dog's leg and whilst traffic would be gained at Rugby, it was certainly a long-winded way of reaching the West Midlands.

Meanwhile, any hopes of dealing amicably with Brunel and the L&NWR were fading. There was considerable personal antagonism at senior level between the ever stoic George Stephenson (1781–1848), who regarded himself as the 'father of railways', aided by his son Robert (1803–1859). These dour northerners took against the flamboyance of Brunel, who was fêted by others overwhelmed by his grandly designed buildings, bridges and tunnels. But what really came between them was the question of the Great Western's broad gauge of 7 feet ¼ inches and what was fast becoming the standard gauge of 4 feet 8½ inches in many other areas of the United Kingdom. These differences in track width caused great difficulties in transferring goods at jointly worked junctions, which all had to be manually handled. Where the different track gauges had to be intertwined, the point work was complex and inevitably increased the risk of derailments.

As if these complications were not enough, Parliament had decreed that broad gauge tracks were not permitted to be laid further north than Birmingham. Clearly Brunel was convinced that with his reputation he could persuade The House that his gauge was superior and thus gain a foothold in the north west when the time came.

With little expectation of any cooperation with the London & Birmingham Railway (later L&NWR) at Rugby, the GWR abandoned progress on the Fenny Compton to Rugby line and promptly diverted its route to Birmingham via Leamington Spa. The advantage was obvious by providing a more direct route via the prosperous town of Leamington Spa on the way. Today this is the route of the Chiltern railway from London to Birmingham.

The GWR planned to gain access to Birmingham at Curzon Street Station, which was the GJR's original terminus from the north west. However, once the London & Birmingham Railway was connected to the capital, Curzon Street station became operationally awkward, requiring locomotives to be turned and run round their carriages before continuing their journey south. This led the L&NWR to build New Street Station, a short distance from Curzon Street, which allowed through trains to operate between London, Liverpool and Manchester.

Although an amalgamation of the L&BR and GJR was logical, talks had stalled, so something had to be done. So in order to bring matters to a conclusion, the following perplexing document was sent to the GJR shareholders on 11 June 1845, the crucial section of which was as follows:

'The question at issue has been represented as one entirely of Broad and Narrow Gauge; upon this point the Directors may observe that they do not anticipate any inconvenience whatever to arise from the introduction of Broad Gauge among Narrow Gauge Lines, or the mixture of gauges on the same Line. On the contrary, looking at Express Trains running at high speed, which are now being introduced on the leading roads, they deem it probable that many Companies possessing Trunk Lines on the Narrow Gauge principle may find it in their interest to adopt both; and the Directors have ascertained the perfect practicability of adding the Broad Gauge on the Grand Junction at a very reasonable cost.'

The document rambles on for several paragraphs in a similar vein and is signed by the GJR's company Secretary, Mark Huish, who was later to become its general manager.

At first it's difficult to find an explanation for this puzzling pamphlet, which is in effect, inviting a potential competitor to share its route between Birmingham and cities in the north west. By the mid-1840s, mixed gauge tracks were operationally troublesome and the GJR was proving popular with fast, reliable standard gauge trains, so why on earth would the company make life awkward for itself by worsening its position? The reason is not hard to find. The GJR was bogged with difficulties in amalgamating with the London & Birmingham Railway to its south, particularly in regard to the awkwardness of operating Curzon Street station as

Curzon Street Station, Birmingham, in early days. (Tony Hisgett)

described earlier. The GJR in a classic Machiavellian manoeuvre, surmised that this statement to shareholders would force talks to take place with the L&BR, which of course it did. The two companies amalgamated and were thereafter known as the L&NWR with trains planned to run seamlessly from London to the north west through New Street Station, which was then under construction. The GJR's Curzon Street Station was relegated to goods traffic in 1854.

This left the GWR in some difficulty because the L&NWR insisted that only standard gauge trains would be permitted on its lines, in effect preventing the GWR access to its dominant position in Birmingham. The GWR countered, challenging the L&NWR by citing the questionably legal agreement with the former GJR which had indicated support for broad gauge access to Curzon Street Station. In researching this complex affair even MacDermot, whose comprehensive book in three volumes of the *History of the Great Western Railway*, became overwhelmed by having to wade through some 700 Parliamentary documents on this subject alone. He reached the conclusion that broad gauge access to Curzon Street station was undoubtedly agreed as stated in the pamphlet, but later on the directors of the L&NWR claimed that this had been penned by managers and not by directors so therefore 'had no substance'. Meanwhile the GWR, by now in a sea of troubles, was desperate to complete its line from Oxford to Birmingham. Thus in 1851 headed by Brunel, the GWR sought Parliamentary powers to connect its line to that of the L&NWR by connecting rails close to the southern tunnel portal on the south side of New Street Station. This would be approximately 300 yards long. As expected the L&NWR aggressively challenged this proposal, citing that the junction with its own lines would seriously interfere with the smooth operation of trains at New Street and provide the GWR with a cheap way of bringing extra trains from its other routes being opened to the south west of the city. The L&NWR further emphasised that the GWR already had powers under its Act of 1846 to connect to Curzon Street. Although the GWR's plan to gain access to New Street Station was approved by Parliament it was subsequently thrown out by the House of Lords.

So, much against its will, the GWR was forced to build an expensive connecting viaduct from Adderley Street at the site of the present Bordesley station to Curzon Street, now of course owned by the L&NWR following the takeover of the GJR. But in spite of earlier hints to the GWR that the L&NWR would acquiesce, it took a hard stance and refused entry to Curzon Street, leaving it open to a legal challenge. Clearly exasperated by this endless quarrelling, the Court of Chancery intervened and settled the dispute once and for all. Its ruling was that the GWR was to gain access to the city centre by tunnelling under the L&NWR's lines to the east of New Street Station to a new station at Snow Hill and continue to construct the railway to Wolverhampton. In order to prevent Parliament having to intervene any further, the two company engineers, Brunel and Robert Stephenson, were ordered to work together to ensure that the Chancery's instructions were carried out. They were further instructed to seek independent arbitrators in the event of any disagreements.

Proposed Birmingham Curzon Street Station. (newcivilengineer.com)

In the meantime and prior to this final decision by the Chancery, the pointless viaduct continued to be constructed and was both

Detail of the map of the planned new development at Curzon Street HS2. ('Rcsprinter')

unloved and unwanted by all the players in this drama. This was well summed up by MacDermot in his history of the GWR referred to earlier, when he wrote, 'And so the derelict Bordesley Viaduct or most of it still stands, a melancholy monument to the ill-conditioned spite of a great Railway Company against a victorious rival in the old fighting days.'

In the fullness of time we must suppose that both sides in this battle can claim some victory. The GWR gained its foothold with its own stations at Snow Hill and Wolverhampton, but only through an expensively built tunnel. Ultimately it would lose its broad gauge status which prevented the company from continuing further to the north west. Before the end of Queen Victoria's reign, all its railways would have reverted to standard gauge. To this day the GWR is seen as a charismatic enterprise and its title has been retained by the present train operating company. As to the L&NWR it managed to get the better of the GWR by keeping it out of New Street Station and opening a new line to Oxford via Bicester. Philip Hardwick (1792–1870), the architect who designed Curzon Street Station, would be proud to see that this long abandoned listed building will soon be part of Great Britain's second High Speed Railway Station from London to the north of England.

Unused remains

Bordesley Viaduct. As referred to earlier, this viaduct ran from a point north west of Bordesley Station, crossing over Adderley Street and then close to a road junction with Upper Trinity Street. It then continued on a slight curve, crossing Lower Trinity, Bromley and Allcock Streets. It proceeded on the same curve to Liverpool and Great Bar Streets and over the Warwick & Birmingham Canal. From there it ran parallel to Montague Street, finishing a few yards from the Duddleston Network Rail viaduct and where Birmingham's cattle market was once sited.

As to the remains, these can be seen at the following places: Adderley to Liverpool Streets via Hack and Allcock Streets. A small section survives on the corner of Liverpool and Great Bar Streets. The rest of this iconic structure has been lost to industry, car parks and a waste disposal site.

Bordesley Viaduct. (Anne-Marie Hayes)

Bordesley viaduct old. (warwickshirerailways.com)

Earthworks at Fenny Compton. The ill-fated extension to Rugby was abandoned as referred to earlier, but the contractors to the GWR did partially complete earthworks to the north a little way west of Fenny Compton. These are visible to this day.

How to get there

The remains of this line are best visited by foot, bicycle or car, since Fenny Compton lost its railway station in November 1964. The area is rural and the proposed railway to Rugby would have branched right some two miles north west of Fenny Compton at a place called Knightcote, passing beneath a bridge which carries a farm track. It is recommended that the reader takes a large scale map indicating footpaths to ensure success.

CHAPTER 13

Isambard Kingdom Brunel's Hidden Dream

The author of this book would like to indulge readers with a subject that is not really related to railways, but does involve a man frequently mentioned in this book and who is nationally remembered, namely Isambard Kingdom Brunel.

Little is known about the private twelve-year period in Brunel's life beginning in 1847 when he visualised a grand home in Torquay planned to become his family's retirement home. He grew to love the area when he worked on the construction of new lines, particularly the atmospheric South Devon Railway, which were being developed along the coast. Later this resort would be stylishly known as part of the 'English Riviera'.

By all accounts, Brunel's comparatively short working life was frenetic, beginning with the construction of his first tunnel beneath the River Thames at Rotherhithe. This ambitious project for such a young man of twenty-one years nearly cost him his life when tunnelling reached half way beneath the Thames. Foul water catastrophically flooded the workings when his boring machine inadvertently breached the river bed. In spite of nearly drowning, a fate which befell some of his workers, this did not deter the young Brunel, who went on to design the Bristol Suspension Bridge, followed by what he is mostly famed for, the construction of the Great Western Railway between London and Bristol. He pioneered the broad gauge railway system and furthered his reputation by designing wonderful tunnels with castellated entrances and ornate stations, many of which endure to this day.

It should not be forgotten that later in life he became deeply involved with the design and building of iron ships at a time when wooden vessels ruled the waves. To Brunel, nothing was impossible and there is no doubt that his dedication to working excessive hours contributed to his early death at the age of fifty-three.

By 1847 Brunel was contemplating a retirement home near Torquay at a place he identified, which would take in dramatic views of Dartmoor to the north and a sweeping vista of Torbay on the seaward side. He would design a beautiful house and gardens from undeveloped land using all his talent to produce a wonderful home for his family in the years to come. The choice of the site was a place called Watcombe, which at the time would have made even the most ambitious think twice about taking on a venture such as this. The land's only saving grace apart from its views was its close proximity to the turnpike road on the east. Apart from that it was rocky, undulating with little topsoil and devoid of a ready water supply.

Nevertheless, his son Isambard records that 'my father would frequently step out of his coach and walk amongst the rocky outcrops, dreaming of his castle in the air'. It was clear that Brunel had already purchased some land here but in order to fulfil his dream, would need to buy further plots which by all accounts

Watcombe Estate map.

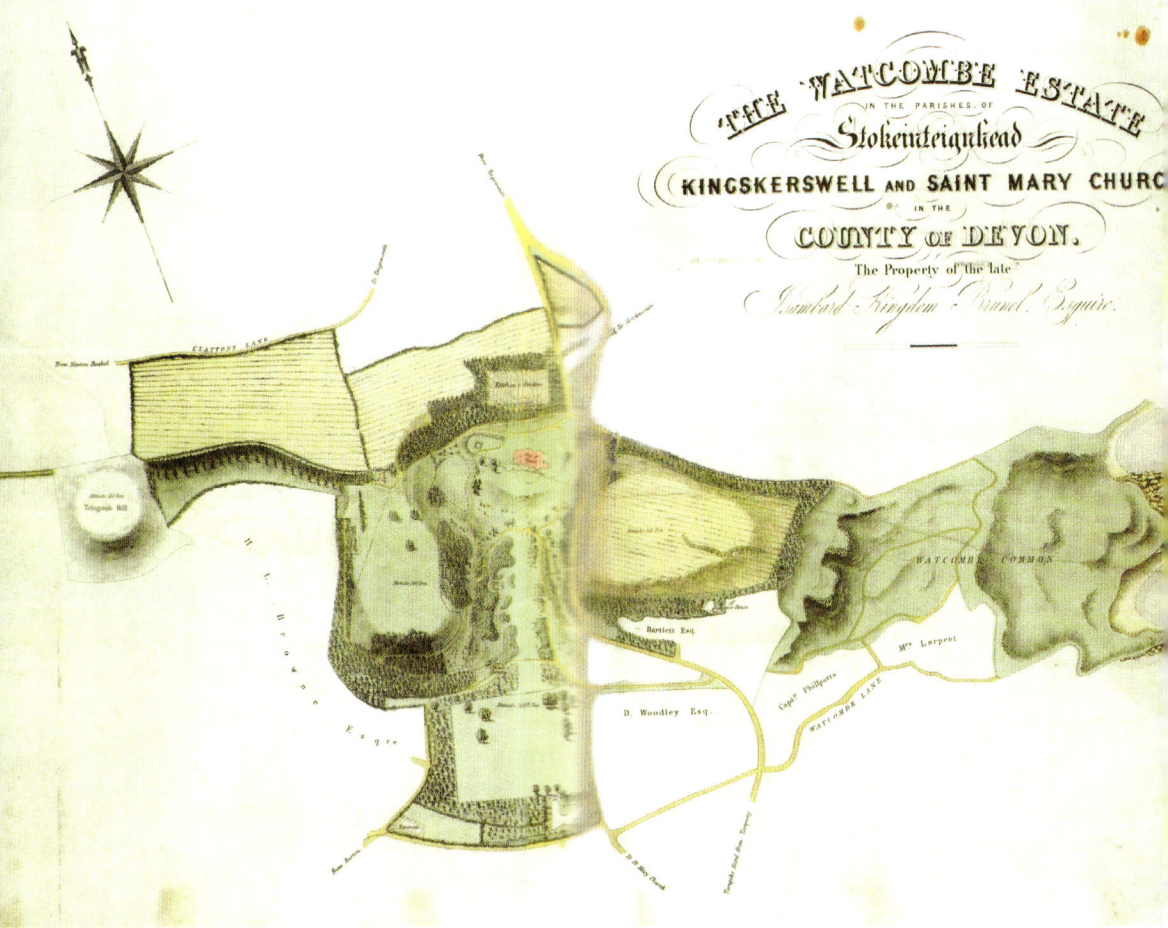

were difficult to acquire, in part because the owners could see their potential value in the burgeoning seaside resort of Torbay and would therefore, demand high prices.

There is no doubt that the late 1840s were troublesome for Brunel, particularly as railways had been expanding at too fast a pace, leading to within a few years, the bankruptcies of major banks and several railway companies. Brunel's schemes were just as vulnerable, although he was personally more financial secure. He was still facing significant problems though, with the most troublesome one being the atmospheric South Devon Railway (covered in Chapter 10).

Nevertheless, he started his plans for Watcombe and it is recorded that Brunel and his brother-in-law John Horsley set off in 1848 on an extended visit to France on one of his rare holidays to purchase furniture. Some may contemplate that this may have been putting the cart before the horse but Brunel was desperate for a rest and some distraction, particularly as the SDR's atmospheric railway on his doorstep was being abandoned.

Some six months earlier the indefatigable Brunel was at home on Christmas Eve in 1847 when most families were looking forward to the festivities, writing to Alexander Forsyth, a gardener of repute, to seek advice on the matter of plants to enhance his estate, by now called Watcombe Park. He realised that these would need to be established early so that his land would benefit from maturity when the house was eventually built. Shortly afterwards, Forsyth was persuaded by Brunel to take the job of Estate Manager and it is recorded that he moved house nearby.

Brunel was 41 when he started work at Watcombe, his initial task being to clear and reorganise the rocky landscape and secure the purchase of the remaining pieces of land, long before the building of his house. He was frequently away during this period, using solicitors and banks to handle legal and financial transactions with his eagle eye in overall control.

Unsurprisingly, Brunel regarded this project as little different to all the other great works that he had undertaken. Work involved the topography, dealing firmly with land transactions, provision of roads and paths as well as the sinking of wells. Whilst Brunel obviously had a love of trees and plants, he spent many hours studying their place in the landscape, no different to that of an engineering project, to ensure that scenically they would render the park a beautiful experience to be enjoyed.

Correspondence at the time indicates a close relationship with William Lawson, his surveyor and land agent. A surviving letter written to him by Brunel on 27 January 1848 indicates the level of trust placed in him, and reads:

'Drummonds (Bank) will tomorrow pay into Barclay and Co. to your account at the Exeter Bank £2,926.17.0 being the amount mentioned in your letter which is to be paid this week for certain lands purchased by Mr Brunel (signed in his absence).'

In the following spring he had described his plans for a pumping station to bring vital water supplies to the high ground and at the same time indicated the place where his grand house would be built.

As to the purchase of land, Brunel was fortunate to be able to buy a large proportion of his needs from Henry Landford Brown of Barton Hall, Kinkerswell. Brown needed the money to fund his expensive yachting pastime but it became clear during correspondence on this matter that Brunel, probably for the first time in his life, was financially challenged because Brown and others had to wait a while to be paid.

The reasons for Brunel's difficulties are not difficult to fathom. On the doorstep of Watcombe Park was the South Devon Railway's atmospheric system, which was forced to be abandoned as described elsewhere, which led to the loss of his investment. Additionally, his involvement with the Great Western Steamship Company involved his design and successful launch of the SS *Great Britain* ship in 1845, which undertook several successful sailings, the first of which was to New York in the same year. Unfortunately, the company was so severely in debt due to the high cost of the ship's construction that it was declared insolvent one year later, the final straw being an expensive rescue operation when the vessel grounded at Drummond Bay in today's Northern Ireland. The SS *Great Britain* continued work as a steamship and moved many emigrants to Australia before reverting to sail in 1881 and eventually retiring to the Falkland Islands, where it was used in several roles, including warehousing, quarantine and coal storage before being scuttled in 1937. In 2003 Sir Jack Arnold Hayward OBE generously funded the vessel's raising from the sea bed of the South Atlantic and subsequent tow back to the United Kingdom. It now resides, fully restored in a dry dock at Bristol and has become a major tourist attraction.

Brunel would have been proud to see his famous ship now so revered but at the time his need to fund his retirement home in Torbay and the collapse of the steamship company in which he was a major shareholder, had severely compromised his personal finances. He was forced to lay off several directly employed key engineers who were working on railways elsewhere that had gone bankrupt in 1849. Times were hard and shortly afterwards, several major banks collapsed, making life considerably more difficult.

He decided in the latter part of 1849 to reduce his role in the woes of the railway industry and spend a few months concentrating on Watcombe, one reason being to negotiate the alteration of a right of way, which was necessary to ensure his plans could proceed. This road near a local church crossed his proposed estate and permission to interfere with it was vehemently refused by local church commissioners and the Highways Authority, which deemed that 'this was not desirable'. Fortunately, Brunel had friends in high places and was able to negotiate this alteration.

In spite of his tenuous financial position, Brunel continued to buy parcels of land for the provision of gardeners' cottages, stables and a shelter of trees to offer protection from northerly gales. Once all the land had been acquired, history records that over fifty men were employed moving soil by carthorses, including gangs of railway navvies who were grateful for the work during the railway crisis.

Not surprisingly Brunel designed paths and tree banks in military fashion along a similar design to that of a new railway. The stone work is remarkable by use of retaining walls which to this day successfully prevent encroachment. The estate approach roads were made wide enough for carriages to pass, and in a truely Brunelian touch, viewing places were designed at strategic intervals. The edges of these roads were lined with pebbles, cartloads of which were laboriously hauled up slopes from the beach.

Fortunately for Brunel, his finances improved when he became heavily involved in 1851 with the Great Exhibition in London and new design of Paddington Station.

When he returned to Watcombe he needed to make a decision in regard to the water supply for his estate. For some time he contemplated one deep well at the top of the hill or alternatively several shallow wells at the foot of the valley, where he was confident that 'an abundance of water would be found'. Brunel wisely opted for the latter, providing seven wells and an adit which fed upwards to two reservoirs, one to provide water to the estate and the other for the benefit of the local population. The gas pump, a unique Brunel invention, was described as 'rather primitive' but it certainly worked well and by all accounts provided ample water to the estate. In this matter Brunel was fortunate because the ever burgeoning resort of Torbay was perennially short of water, with it rationed for a few hours each day and with the problem not resolved until the end of Queen Victoria's reign.

One problem that Brunel would have been well aware of was that of storms, particularly in the autumn and winter, which regularly dashed the coast and sometimes washed out the track bed of the coastal railway between Exeter and Newton Abbot. Early in the life of his Watcombe project he was making plans for shelter belts of trees because of the estate's exposure to these high winds. With the purchase of all but one piece of land complete, the trees were planted in strategic places before Brunel became embroiled in matters elsewhere.

These included completing the work on the Saltash bridge over the River Tamar and undertaking major works on the extension of the GWR into Cornwall. But undoubtedly his involvement with another great iron ship, the *Great Eastern*, would take him away from his beloved Watcombe and severely tax his energy for most of his remaining life. This was a huge undertaking requiring Brunel to fund, finance, construct and launch this vessel of the massive proportions which he noted in one of his early drawings to the East India Steamship company as 'say, 600 ft x 65 ft x 30 ft'.

Although this venture occupied Brunel's life during the early 1850s, he still managed to occasionally visit Watcombe and purchase the odd piece of land. In fact, as recently discovered records show in his Watcombe Garden Book, his visits and actions were not infrequent and would appear to be his only solace, particularly as the construction of the *Great Eastern* was testing him to the limit. By all accounts it would appear that Brunel had become a more kindly and generous man. He paid for his staff to visit the Great Exhibition in London with no loss of wages and his dealings with local tradesmen were courteous. Gone were the days when Brunel was regarded as aggressive and domineering; he now found peace with God.

In 1854 there was a first mention of Brunel's plan for an Italian garden in front of the proposed house, surrounded with yew trees which would be ideal for topiary ornamentation. He had on his travels to Italy, with this garden in mind, collected statues and urns to enhance its beauty.

In spite of his failing health, his mind turned to the design of his new house at Watcombe. His early idea was for a Gothic castle with a great turreted tower overlooking the sea but this was soon abandoned as being out of keeping in the area, more suited for a stormy rocky coastline such as those found in Scotland. Later he produced designs for an Italianate villa with a belvedere and colonnaded terrace but eventually opted, possibly because of his French origins, for a house along the lines of a Loire Valley Chateau.

In 1855 Brunel was actively specifying details of his house including stone facings and other architectural matters. It has often been stated that during this period, Brunel was wrestling with so many problems in regard to the progress of the *Great Eastern* that he neglected all else. However, there is ample evidence that his involvement with Watcombe was frequent and indeed continually offered sanctuary. In the spring of 1858, with the successful completion of his famous ship, he was still to be seen in the gardens and arranging finance with banks for the building of his new house. But by the autumn, with Brunel's health clearly failing, it is recorded that he was in Egypt for Christmas and dining with Robert Stephenson in Cairo. He returned to London in mid-May and readied himself for the final task of launching the *Great Eastern*. However, there was still much to be done, particularly in the raising of funds to prepare for trials at sea. By now realising the extent of his mortality, he began to prepare for his demise. His final dealings at Watcombe show his communication with Dawson in regard to the estate map in the late summer of 1859. This reveals the full extent of his purchases amounting to 136 acres, with thousands of trees planted, the foundations of the terraces and the cellars of his house. With all these matters in order, he died peacefully at the age of 53 on 1 December 1859 at his London home in Duke Street.

Remains of Watcombe

The original estate is today much reduced in size with land sold off for development over the years, and the gardens are the only tangible evidence of Brunel's painstaking hours of planning. They are well worth a visit as many of his trees still stand as testament to the well planned estate which was born out of a rocky landscape with little suitable topsoil. Unfortunately a severe storm in 1990 led to many trees being destroyed. The paths, which were much neglected in early times, have survived as has the rockery and access ways to the turnpike road. Today's terrace in front of the house was constructed and accurately follows Brunel's design that he would certainly recognise. The stunning views of the sea give the impression of a large lake attached to the estate and the trees were carefully chosen to offer a myriad of colour, particularly during the autumn. The steps to the pond are original.

Other places to visit include the water garden which Brunel notes in his garden book as 'Water Arrangements'. This was fed by the primitive gas pump described elsewhere. From here the ground continued down the hillside through the present day boundary fence into what today is appropriately named Brunel Woods. Alternatively, access to these woods designed by Brunel can be through the top of Seymour Drive or Brunel Avenue at the south end.

Near the water garden Brunel designed a 'Green Lane' which would have provided a beautiful vista between the trees to a meadow and lake below, but today this view has been compromised by a development of bungalows. Staying on the path which leads up a steep slope, some original Monterey Cypress trees may be seen to the left, one of which is reputed to be the biggest tree of its type in Western Europe. This path leads to a flight of steps to a tennis

Original plan of Watcombe house, which was never built.

court and it is here one can see some magnificent beech trees on the skyline behind the present house. This woodland forms part of the shelter belt designed by Brunel to 'protect the house, gardens and more tender trees from the savage winds that batter Devonshire in autumn and winter'.

The present trackways were strengthened by cobbles as can be seen, designed to add great strength to allow for heavily laden carts which brought in trees, soil and other essential materials.

The house that Brunel commissioned in the style of a French chateau was designed by the well-known country house architect, William Burn (1789–1870). It was deliberately intended to be a grand affair as the Brunels wanted to use this as a place of entertainment as well as a family home.

The present house was built in 1870, some eleven years after his death, to a more modest design, but in spite of that is a fine example of Victorian architecture. Watcombe has had many owners over

Brunel Manor.

Recent wooden carving of Brunel in the Estate gardens.

the years and latterly a Christian Holiday & Conference Centre occupied the property which oversaw the well-being of the gardens for the benefit of all visitors. At the time of writing the estate is on the market and it is to be hoped that the gardens will be protected in the years to come.

The Italian Garden.

How to get there

The future of the estate is not known as the property is on the market at the time of writing and it is likely that permission will be required to make a visit. It is worth making contact with the local tourist office in this regard.

Torquay is well served by rail which runs frequent services from Newton Abbot to Paignton and by steam trains to Kingswear, and there is a wide range of hotels and guest houses to accommodate visitors. Brunel Manor can be reached by bicycle, foot or car, on the Teignmouth Road, TQ1 4SF.

CHAPTER 14

Railways, Stations & Tunnels Beneath London

England's capital city is riddled with underground tunnels, which over many decades have been used for multiple purposes, and not just the London Underground Railway. These include air raid shelters, government and military headquarters, tunnels which were used for trams, horses, vaults, hydraulic pipes, postal delivery, mushroom cultivation and ancient streams, not forgetting of course one under the Thames flood barrier on the east side of London. Tunnelling through the clay sub strata is a continual process, the latest railway about to open being Crossrail at the time of writing. All this activity is best described as the equivalent of London sitting on a large truckle of Gruyère cheese.

The history of the London Underground is complex and the system was born from the need to make more space available at ground level. London's population dramatically increased from 1 million in 1800 to nearly 3.2 million in 1861 and the inadequate road system was heavily clogged with horse drawn traffic, so something had to be done.

Clearly there were only two realistic options. Firstly, to construct another level of traffic above the streets such as those that can be found in New York and Chicago and which the Americans call elevated railroads, or build railway tunnels beneath the streets for the movement of passengers. Promoters could choose either but the main advantage for overhead railways would have been that they were cheaper to build and that passengers could travel in comparatively clean air. By 1850 this idea had been rejected because it would create the despoliation of many of London's grand buildings and the inevitable cascading of hot ash from locomotives to pedestrians and horses on the streets beneath.

This left the second option, which was to lay a railway beneath ground level, the first of these being a section of the Metropolitan Railway, which opened in 1863 between Paddington, Euston, King's Cross and Farringdon. Early lines such as this were placed immediately beneath streets using the 'cut and cover' system. In essence this meant removing the road by excavating a large trench and placing iron tubes to carry trains, bolted together in sections before replacing the road surface over the top. Thus the early underground railways, later aptly known as 'tube lines', were largely constructed in this manner and to this day are close to the surface and follow streets, studiously avoiding tunnelling under buildings which could have been damaged in the process.

Over the following decades, this method of construction became increasingly difficult because of the large amount of underground activity, not only by railways but other penetrations such as sewage pipes, drains and cables which rendered sub-surface lines impossible to construct. Later schemes during the Victorian era and up to the present day meant that underground promoters have been forced to dig deep tunnels, which enable them to avoid the clutter of what had occurred earlier. The advantage of these deep excavations was that the unpopularity of digging up streets was avoided and the London clay at greater depth was of a more stable condition thus less likely to collapse.

However, there were problems such as the poor quality of air whilst work took place and of gaining access to work sites. These problems were largely overcome with the advent of ventilation shafts, frequently disguised as buildings, and the use of a new generation of tunnel boring machines. Earlier inventions worked well enough and the first of these was designed by I. K. Brunel, which made reasonable progress until it punctured and flooded the bed of the River Thames in 1828. Later boring machines, designed by Captain Thomas English (1843–1935), worked beneath the first Channel Tunnel from the shores of England and France, another contender being Edward Blackett Beaumont MP (1833–1899). However, it was Peter William Barlow (1809–1885) who was the first to patent a circular tunnelling shield in 1864. He later worked with a South African engineer, James Henry Greathead (1844–1896), who took a lead role in developing its efficacy and they were able to prove its worth by excavating the Tower Bridge Subway. So successful was Greathead's improved machine that it was used

James Henry Greathead.

on all the later tube lines in the early part of the twentieth century and which were lined with the familiar Cleveland cast iron segments which can easily be seen to this day.

Once underground railways had proved their success, the conversion from steam-hauled trains to electric power significantly increased their popularity with passengers. This led to a scramble of new lines to be built, mainly to the north of the Thames, where much of the construction meant that most of these new routes were cheaper to build because they could rise to the surface in areas that were then mainly agricultural. There was less incentive for companies to take their lines south of the river because the SER, LB&SCR and LSWR, amalgamated in 1923 as the Southern Railway, were innovators of third rail electric power, which they had already developed in the early part of the twentieth century.

North End Station

This station, also known as the 'Old Bull & Bush' and named after a local public house, was never completed and it can be found on London Underground's Northern Line between Hampstead and Golders Green.

In 1893 the Royal Assent was granted for the construction of the Charing Cross, Euston & Hampstead Railway. However, shortage of funds meant that no work was carried out for the next seven years. The ever eagle-eyed Charles Yerkes (featured in Chapter 9), headed a financial syndicate and purchased the ailing company. His plans included completing the railway to Hampstead as already approved and continue its construction under the Heath to Golders Green where a train depot would be provided. It had of course not escaped Yerkes's attention, that open farmland surrounded the route, which could be developed for property development. These plans were predictably vociferously opposed by local residents and others who made use of Hampstead Heath in their leisure time. It's interesting to note that rather like present construction schemes, the reason given for concern was the disturbance that a new tunnel would cause to ecology, rather than the real objection which was actually their loathing of new housing developments.

In spite of this the Metropolitan Borough of Hampstead, although initially objecting, later relented and the Royal Assent was granted for the extension of the line to Golders Green. In granting permission, a condition was that the company had to provide an intermediate station at North End on Hampstead Way. However, the residents' powerful opposition should not have been underestimated, particularly that of Henrietta Octavia Weston Barnett, later a Dame (1851–1936). This English social reformer, educationalist and author, who with her husband founded Toynbee Hall, a pioneering university for the poor in the East End of London, took great exception to the extension of the railway and particularly plans to develop the land for housing. She and Canon Barnett owned a house as a weekend retreat in what is now Hampstead Garden Suburb and they were vehemently opposed to their tranquillity being disturbed. They established several financial trusts which bought 243 acres along the railway route and for good measure, persuaded Sir Edward Lutyens (1869–1944) the renowned architect, to buy a further 800 acres, thus ensuring the peace of Hampstead Heath in perpetuity.

Tunnelling had begun at North End station in 1903 following Parliamentary permission and the larger section and low level passageways were excavated. At this stage it became obvious that Barnett and Lutyens had effectively scuppered Yerkes and any chance of housing development on the land that they had purchased. The works were abandoned apart from the main railway tunnel to Golders Green.

Had the station been completed it would have been London Underground's deepest at 221 feet. Three years later at the latter end of 1906, most of the ancillary tunnels for passenger movement to the base of the lift shafts had been excavated only to be completely abandoned. In 1907 the line to Golders Green was opened and trains have run through the remains of North End station ever since.

Dame Henrietta Barnett. (Toynbee Hall)

But this is not the end of the story. After the end of the Second World War when two atomic bombs had been dropped on Japan, the threat to Great Britain became a reality when it was feared that other nations could develop the technology for themselves. The magnitude of these weapons was of huge concern to the government and plans were put in place for shelters away from central

London, which would survive destruction from such attacks. Amongst several locations chosen was the abandoned North End station, complete with flood gates, which was regarded as the most favourable in view of its depth. On the edge of Hampstead Way the Manor House Hospital had been demolished and it was on this site that a surface blockhouse was constructed. It was built directly above a new ventilation shaft of 120 feet, complete with lift and spiral staircase sited on the northbound platform. It was within this complex that flood gate consoles, battery and relay rooms with a blast proof door had been added. No sooner had most of this work had been carried out than a new and more deadly threat emerged – the hydrogen bomb. As this weapon of complete destruction would destroy all that went before it, including London itself, North End station ceased to be of any strategic importance. However, the flood gates were maintained until being de-commissioned in 1984.

Remains of North End Station

Although out of bounds to the casual visitor, both the northbound and southbound tunnels can be witnessed from passing trains, albeit in the dark. The platforms have been demolished to track

Dame Barnett's house.

level and the only purpose of keeping access today is as an emergency exit for passengers, although from time to time, track materials are stored for the maintenance of the permanent way. The building now occupying the planned site of North End Station is heavily fenced but is clearly visible.

What may be of interest to visitors are sites associated with Dame Henrietta Octavia Barnett who fought so pugnaciously to preserve the finer features of Hampstead Heath. Their property, Heath End House NW3 7JE, that she and her husband bought in early years still stands overlooking the Heath near to the Spaniards Inn, which itself has a colourful history and dates back to 1585.

It had been in 1896 by sheer chance, while taking a holiday in Russia, that the Barnetts met Yerkes. He, somewhat unwisely as it transpired, told them of his plans to extend the London Underground northwards to Golders Green with North End Station being at 'a place near Wyldes Farm'. This led the Barnetts, with other philanthropists referred to earlier, to buy the land and frustrate Yerkes's plans. Barnett then set about building a garden suburb of mixed housing for the wealthy and artisan classes. The first two properties, today marked by a plaque, are at 140 and 142 Hampstead Way.

The first two houses which marked the development of the Hampstead Garden Suburb.

In the fullness of time Barnett might not be best pleased to see the garden suburb today. Property speculation and the controversial selling of what is today called social housing by the Hampstead Trust, would have greatly displeased Barnett, although it should be recorded from the outset, that there had been no provision for housing the unskilled labouring class. Her loathing of the underground railway and particularly the provision of the never to be completed tube station, is a pity as the invasion by cars has proved to be a nuisance in modern times.

How to get there
Apart from passing through the station's tunnels in darkness, access is not allowed under normal circumstances, but armed with an explorer map, this is a good way of visiting one of the few relatively unspoilt areas north west of London. Travel by London Underground on the Northern Line is recommended to either Hampstead or Golders Green stations.

Take a while to take in the rolling countryside and just imagine that were it not for the actions of this feisty lady, the scene today would be a sea of suburban housing, burying all the farmland of what once went before.

Moorgate Station
Moore-Gate, as its name was originally spelt, was the site of the final gate of the City of London and was built in 1650. It was so called after a marshy area known as Moorfields, a tract of land immediately to its north. The gate was demolished in 1762 and the surrounding area had become built up by 1834.

The first record of railway development was in 1863 when the Metropolitan Railway planned an extension from Farringdon to Moorgate as part of the City & South London Railway, the station opening in 1865. So successful was this short line that it soon attracted passenger and goods traffic from the Great Northern Railway, which constructed a four track railway, named the City Widened Lines, with a tunnel added at Clerkenwell.

A proposal by the Great Northern & City Railway (GN&CR) at the end of the nineteenth century was to construct a line from Finsbury Park to Moorgate. This bold scheme was to provide twin tunnels of larger loading gauge to accommodate main line locomotives and rolling stock. However, the GNR, the main backer of the scheme, withdrew its interest and there matters languished.

In spite of that, the GN&CR persisted in its plans by extending some of the line from Moorgate south to Lothbury, to become a new terminus. As so often, a lack of funds prevented further tunnelling and a short section of the southbound tunnel was dug before being abandoned in 1903. To this day the Greathead shield lies entombed a few yards in from the entrance, barely remembered by modern commuters who wait impatiently for their train to work or home.

How to get there
Take an underground train to Moorgate station and walk to the front of the train. The Greathead Shield, embedded in the face of the tunnel a few yards within, can just be seen. Its rotational cutting wheel rests quietly buried in the London clay, having completed its last revolution in 1903.

The ghosts beneath King's Cross Station
One of the more complicated histories of the London underground railway's developments was that in relation to the capital's northern

A myriad of tunnels ran beneath King's Cross Station, one of which, in spite of being laid with rails, was never used. (Alex Griffin (based on map from 'BackTrack' Oct 1997))

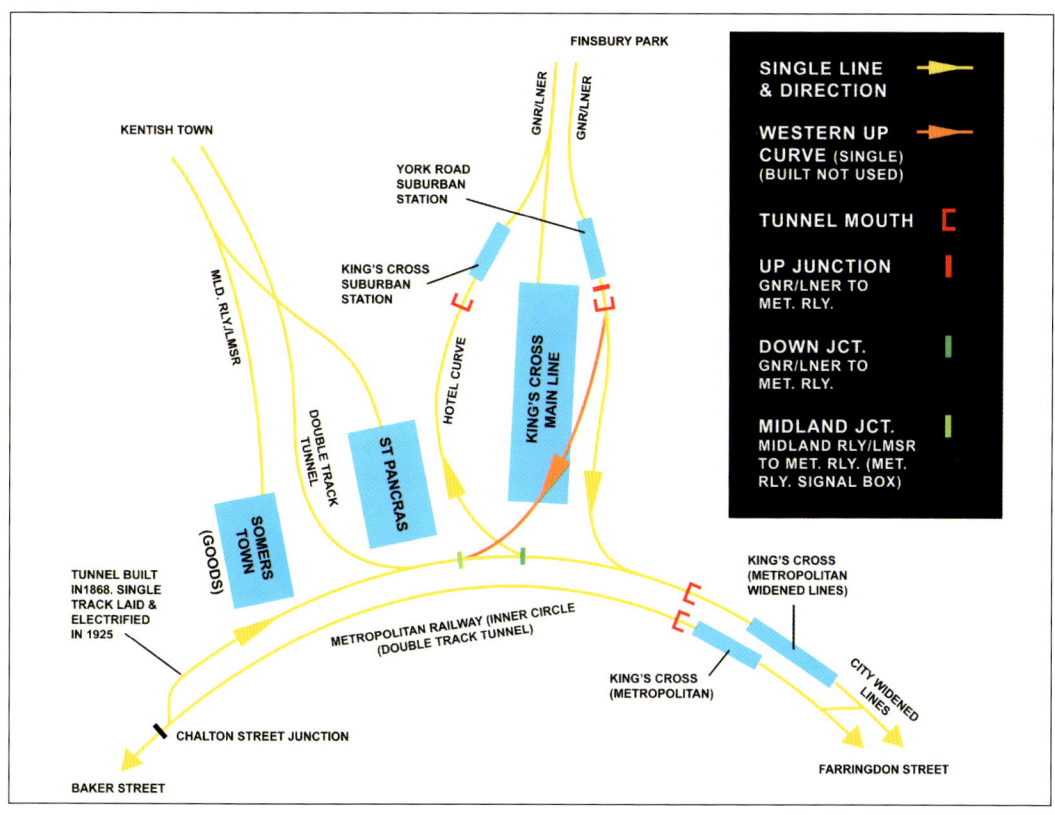

termini. In early days when human and horse traffic was becoming excessively congested, promotion of railways beneath street level was actively considered as a solution to this problem.

It was a comparatively unknown solicitor, Charles Pearson (1793–1862), who took up the case of providing improved railway connections in central London. Most of his life had been as a Liberal member of Parliament concerned with the abolition of the death penalty and other unfashionable causes. When the matter of street congestion raised its head, Pearson initially fought for a large underground station to be built in central London, which would be connected by tunnels to termini at that time sited on the periphery of the metropolis. Parliament had earlier decreed that the main line stations should not penetrate what was then outer London, which is why stations such as Euston, King's Cross, St Pancras, Marylebone and Paddington were built on the north side of Euston Road. Southern termini were placed on either side of the River Thames but close to the shore. Pearson's proposal was thrown out, thus exacerbating the continuing problem of handling passengers and in particular goods, such as farm produce and coal from the north of England.

Charles Pearson.

With these restrictions in mind, the Metropolitan Railway was formed to connect the north London termini from east to west, mostly tunnelling beneath the Euston Road near Farringdon and to the west at Paddington, eventually becoming part of the inner circle line that we know today.

King's Cross Station, built in 1863 on the Metropolitan Railway, was recently superseded on the same site by the present day Thameslink station and it has been so comprehensively rebuilt that very little of its original structure can be seen. The traffic generated into London from the Great Northern Railway soon swamped this cramped line and in spite of widening the tracks from two to four, it was clear that more drastic action was needed to create more capacity.

Thus was born the new King's Cross Station on today's site slightly to the north of Euston Road. The current building supersedes a temporary structure near York Road which survived for less than two years and it opened in 1852 on land that has an interesting history. As this part of London became built up during the early Victorian era, the presence of two obstacles preventing commercial growth were removed, the first being the River Fleet and the second an old cholera hospital. The river was rerouted to the west of what is now St Pancras Station in 1825 and then flowed into the Thames. Evidence of the course of this ancient waterway can still be seen in various locations where it has not been piped, although it latterly carries waste water so cannot be regarded with much romance by the casual visitor.

The place where the present King's Cross Station stands was originally a village called Battle Bridge, so named because this is where Roman invaders and the Celtic English Icene Tribe fought in early conflict. The English tribal leader Boudica, met a violent death and was allegedly buried beneath what are now platforms nine or ten. Unsubstantiated rumours persist to this day of her ghost being occasionally seen in several parts of the station.

The Great Northern Railway, faced with severe congestion, built several underground tunnels which were designed to carry goods traffic from north to south each side of King's Cross Station. These connected in several places on the Metropolitan line and allowed traffic to travel either from east to west and north to south. The large amount of soil excavated from these tunnels was used to provide embankments for GNR lines that were being constructed further north near Maida Vale.

This activity led to the provision of freight depots to be established in or near existing main line stations, which handled the bulk of goods needed for the population of the growing capital city.

In later years with continuing changes to London Underground's evolution and the improvement of roads, freight traffic began to decline from the 1930s and vanished completely by 1969. The last passenger trains were withdrawn ten years later. Gradually all these tunnels became disused, but the interesting one relevant to this book is the single line tunnel that ran from a place just south of York Road Station under the south east corner of the present King's Cross Station and connecting with the Metropolitan Railway near the south east corner of St Pancras Station. Destined to be only a southbound directional railway, it's difficult to justify the reason for its construction. Allegedly, the GNR belatedly realised that it would be operationally awkward and that its share of traffic would be severely compromised by competition from the presence of St Pancras, at that time under construction. Whatever the real reason the tunnel was laid with track but never formally opened to traffic.

It's worth taking a grandstand view from the southern side of Euston Road between King's Cross and St Pancras stations. The reader is looking at two tastefully restored main line termini and it is well worth taking the time to explore further.

St Pancras came to a whisker of being demolished in the 1960s but was rescued by a fine group of people headed by Sir John Betjeman. It received Grade 1 listed status in 1967 although it remained largely unloved and the haunt of petty criminals and drug addicts for many years. However, it has emerged today as one of the finest international stations in Europe. The presence of modern, international sleek electric trains, stylish shops and restaurants make a striking site beneath the Barlow's original arched roof and are rounded off by a large bronze statue of Sir John Betjeman.

The ground beneath St Pancras and King's Cross stations was heavily excavated with railway tunnels.

Similarly, King's Cross Station still contains much of its original fabric, but has been tastefully restored in the early part of the twentieth century, assisted by the removal of some later inappropriate buildings from the facade. Today apart from many

passengers, tourists flock to the station to take in the legend of J.K. Rowling's world of Harry Potter. She writes that Harry and his friends took the train from platform 9¾ to Scotland where Hogwart's school of Witchcraft and Wizardry was located. A luggage trolley is embedded in the brickwork between platforms 9 and 10, marking the place where pupils were able to gain access by passing through a solid wall.

Few people standing in Euston Road would realise that beneath the road surface are several tunnels *(see map)* including of course, the Western Up Curve which cuts under the south east corner of King's Cross station. Unloved and long forgotten it slumbers in peace and was never used by trains.

Elephant & Castle to Camberwell

Elephant and Castle underground station is the southern terminus of the Bakerloo line and in the early part of the twentieth century, plans were drawn up to extend the railway to Camberwell. As this part of London was poorly served by tube trains, the excessively worded 'London Electric Metropolitan District & Central London Railway Companies (Works) Act 1931', drew up its plans.

The railway between the two stations was to operate through two twin tunnels constructed with cast iron segments, the cost of the scheme estimated to be £5 million (over £320 million today). Some work on the tunnels commenced at Elephant & Castle station during 1937 and was soon abandoned because of rising costs and the looming prospect of the Second World War. A moratorium on further construction was in place until 1947 following a 'Special Enactments (Extension of Time) Act 1940'. In spite of this, no further work was carried out but the railway did for a while appear on London Underground Maps, alluding to this as a live scheme.

Plans were again revived in 2006 when Ken Livingstone, then Mayor of London, announced that the railway was being considered as a project that should be completed within twenty years. This remains at the proposal stage, currently uncommitted.

Were this line ever to be built it would represent an ever changing tapestry in the development of the history of Camberwell station. Opened in 1862 by the London, Chatham & Dover Railway, it was part of the city branch between Herne Hill and Blackfriars stations. Originally served by two lines, it was later increased to four in 1866 and the entrance was at street level, the station itself built on a viaduct. When first opened it was called 'Camberwell' and a year

The extension of the Bakerloo line to Camberwell was never constructed. Today a short tunnel section is used to stable trains.

Camberwell station, having changed its name more than once, presents a forlorn site from its former two storey building. This was and is planned to become the terminus of the underground railway from the Bakerloo line at Elephant & Castle station.

later renamed, 'Camberwell Green', a more apt location only to be changed back to its original name in 1908.

By this time the development of tram routes had severely undermined the viability of the station and it was closed in 1916 for passengers, and for goods traffic later in 1964.

Remains
Kensington South Station

This area of South Kensington west of London is largely a creation of the Victorian era. Its origins lay in medieval times and for centuries consisted of mixed farming and arable crops. Change was slow to come and even in 1800 the population was around 8,500, rising to about 25,000 in 1840. The nearby metropolis had created a ready market for food and by the Victorian era much of the land was used for market garden and glasshouse crops to meet this demand.

The area's first claim to fame was the coming of Kensington Palace, which was bought and commissioned by William the Third in 1689. This led directly to the establishment of the Square and the origins of what is now known as Kensington High Street. In spite of these developments it is recorded that at the dawn of the nineteenth century some 60 per cent of land was still being used for crops. Their need for fertiliser was provided by horse manure from the burgeoning traffic from the rapidly expanding urbanisation to the east.

Inevitably, by the mid-nineteenth century, the value of land for building outweighed that of farmland and the speculators moved in. The presence of the Great Exhibition of 1851 in nearby Hyde Park additionally acted as a catalyst for this event and the largely rural area around Kensington became part of the city of London from that date onwards.

These developments did not go unnoticed by railway companies and the first line into South Kensington was constructed by the Metropolitan District Railway (later known as the District Line) in 1868 and subsequently extended to Westminster. An additional line was provided by the Metropolitan Railway to Notting Hill, Kensington High Street and Brompton. By the early 1900s, the company was extending in to suburban areas, including Ealing, Richmond, Hounslow and Wimbledon. Inevitably, the success of these new railways led to severe congestion between South Kensington and Mansion House. This problem was forecast some years earlier but a lack of finance, the need to provide a new fast route to the city in a deep tunnel and steam-hauled trains all led to its abandonment.

By 1902 the Great Northern, Piccadilly & Brompton Railway (GNP&BR), later called the Piccadilly Line, put forward plans for a deep level underground railway from South Kensington to Piccadilly Circus. At much the same time the GNP&BR and Metropolitan railways came under the joint control of Charles Yerkes' London Electric Railways Company. This charismatic figure, featured in Chapter 8, never to be discouraged, forged ahead with plans which came to fruition with an additional line between Hammersmith and Finsbury Park, including a station at South Kensington which opened in January 1907. Yerkes determinedly forged ahead by electrifying the route, and complete with his recent acquisition of the GNP&BR, rendered the Metropolitan District express route superfluous. In spite of this, some tunnelling by the Metropolitan District Railway (MDR) had already taken place for its route adjacent to South Kensington station and added a series of interchange tunnels close to the lifts. Additionally, a large diameter tunnel was built to the west of the station where a junction between the express line and the GNP&BR was projected. If the MDR's plans had come to fruition, a complex method of operation would have been inaugurated, including the use of trains on two levels, so it was clear that the decision not to proceed was a sensible one.

Because the express route was never constructed, all the works associated with its plans were not needed, so several uses were found during the years that followed. Throughout the First World War, the tunnel was used for the storage of artefacts from the Victoria & Albert Museum and ceramics from the Royal Collection. A railway signalling school was later established in the disused tunnel between 1927 and 1939. And further use was made of the site when hydrophonic equipment was installed during the Second World War to act as a warning of bombs near the River Thames. This was designed to activate emergency flood gates should the underground railway tunnels be penetrated.

Escalators were installed at Kensington in the 1970s, their shafts penetrating the abandoned railway tunnel. Simultaneously the former lifts were removed, rendering the old surface buildings of the GNP&BR redundant. And from that time onwards, all passengers used the original MDR station for all trains.

CHAPTER 15

The Collywell Bay Railway

The origins of this railway, built and never opened, lay in its connection with that of former horse drawn lines and the early development of the thriving coal industry north of the River Tyne. History records the presence of steeply inclined waggonways from pit to coast, which were collectively incorporated under a Parliamentary Act of 1853. This led to a conventionally constructed railway which took coal traffic to Tynemouth Docks, mainly for export. The line, the Blyth & Tyne Railway, colloquially known as 'The Avenue Branch', was opened for goods in 1860 and passengers a year later. It operated between Hartley in the north and Whitley, Monkseaton and Tynemouth in the south. Later, in the early twentieth century when the line between Whitley Bay and Newcastle was electrified, interest was gathering to serve residential housing on coastal areas.

An early scheme to serve Seaton Sluice from a place called Dairy House on The Avenue branch was opened in 1853 but was unsuccessful and closed some ten years later. Clearly a lack of passenger traffic was to blame because the expected housing never developed, mainly because, it is claimed by local inhabitants, 'Who would want to live near a drain called Seaton Sluice?'

The second attempt at opening up a passenger link to the coast was more successful. The promoters had sensibly identified a location south of Seaton Sluice and named this more appropriately as Collywell Bay, which attracted housing development. Thus a Bill was deposited in Parliament in 1904, receiving the Royal Assent on 18 August 1910.

This short branch line was 1 mile 68 chains and branched north eastwards from a junction on The Avenue Railway at a place named Brierdene Junction, about one mile north of Monkseaton Station. The only other station, other than the terminus at Collywell Bay, was at Brierdene and the railway was planned to be electrified.

The contractor, C.M. Skinner, signed a formal agreement on 14 November 1912 to construct the line, with some further details drawn up since its inception some two years earlier.

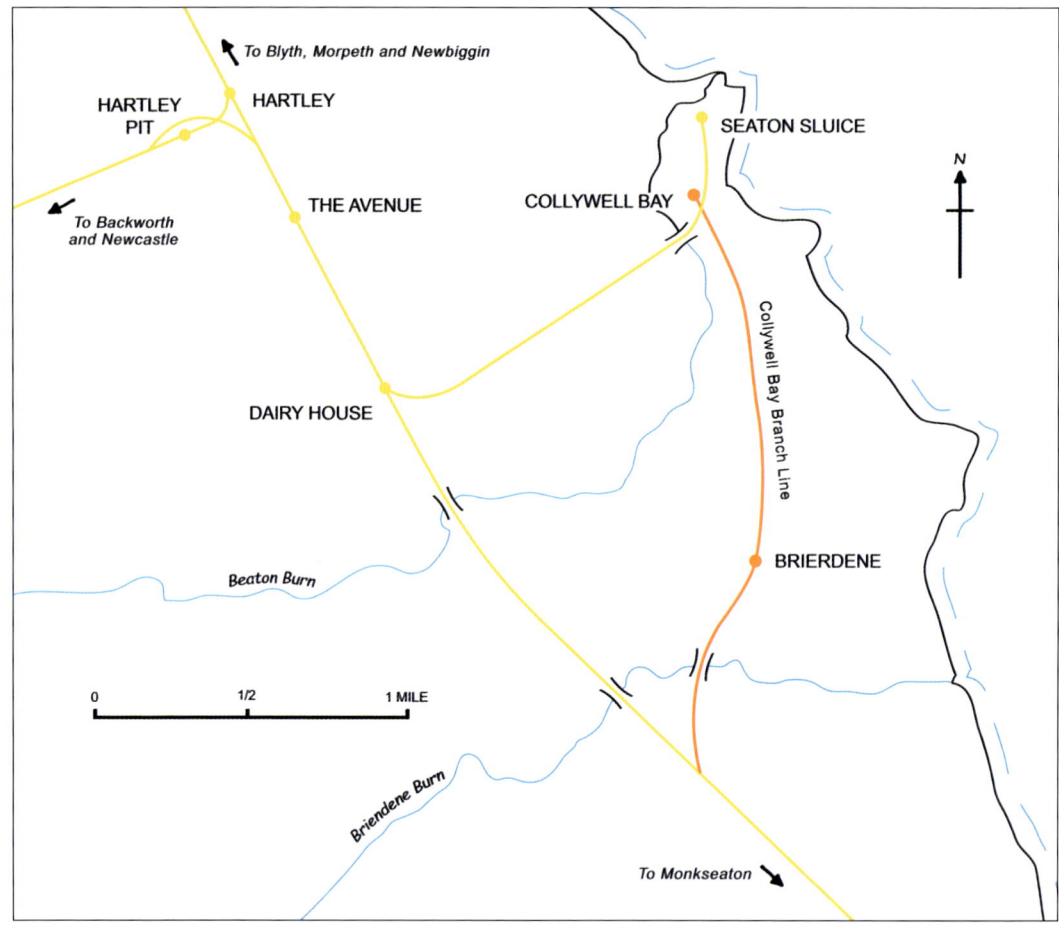

To Blyth, Morpeth and Newbiggin

HARTLEY
PIT

HARTLEY

SEATON SLUICE

THE AVENUE

COLLYWELL BAY

To Backworth
and Newcastle

N

DAIRY HOUSE

Collywell Bay Branch Line

BRIERDENE

Beaton Burn

0   1/2   1 MILE

Briendene Burn

To Monkseaton

The Collywell Bay Railway. (Alex Griffin (based on map by 'disused-stations. org.uk))

The length of the branch was planned to be increased by two miles to allow for an extension to Seaton Sluice to capitalise on the expected increase in housing. In order to facilitate the expected increase in train movements, the line was to be doubled between Monkseaton Station, which would be rebuilt, and Brierdene Junction. In 1913 Lord Hastings, who owned land at Collywell Bay, agreed to sell some 21.5 acres to the North Eastern Railway (NER) for £860, allowing 350 houses to be built near the terminus.

The NER planned to open the railway at the beginning of November 1914 and even went as far as altering the destination blinds at the front of the trains to read 'Colleywell Bay'. By all accounts construction was proceeding well, with track and passing loops, station platforms, bridges and signal boxes. Third rail electrification was underway at Brierdene Junction and its signal

The railway
under construction
at Collywell Bay
Station, 1914. (Jim
Rogerson/'Disused
Stations')

box made ready to operate trains to the terminus. Monkseaton Station's new build was almost finished and was completed the following year.

When the First World War broke out in August 1914 the scheme shuddered to a sudden halt, as did the expected development of housing on the coast. The situation was worsened by the Ministry of Munitions and the Railway Executive Committee, which decreed that essential materials, particularly steel, were required for the war effort. In the case of Collywell Bay all the track was lifted in 1917, a sad sight which was later partially reprieved by the railway's relaying of a mile-long single line with second hand rail. This was done to allow access by a rail mounted gun to provide coastal defence.

After the war the local authorities expected the railway to be completed. However, the London & North Eastern Railway (L&NER), which became part of the national railway amalgamation of 1923, reviewed its fate in 1924 and decided not to proceed because too few houses had been built to justify the continuation of the project. It did not make happy reading and in essence, the decision was to recommend abandonment, its seal of approval being drawn up by the L&NER and Lord Hastings. By 1932 the line and bridges were dismantled but the partially completed stations remained because of the cost of their removal.

What remains of the Collywell Bay railway

For many years much of the line could be explored from Brierdene Junction to Colywell Bay, but in the 1960s, housing development obliterated all trace of the railway at both ends.

Above: **Remains of** bridge at Hartley Road next to the site of Brierdene station. (Edward Parker)

Below: **Bridge remains** half a mile south of Collywell Bay station. (Edward Parker)

Today the main remaining feature is a substantial embankment and two partially demolished railway bridges. The southern bridge at Hartley Road, about three quarters of a mile north of Brierdene Junction, has one remaining wall with the other recently demolished on the present golf course. Brierdene station would have been built here, the only intermediate one on the branch.

The other bridge remains are to be found at about half a mile south of the site of Colleywell Bay station. The deck is missing and some demolition has taken place and it suffers from the inevitable presence of graffiti. Nevertheless restoration is possible and would provide a pleasant walking route to the south as far as Hartley Road.

How to get there

The best way to explore the remains of the Colleywell Bay railway is by use of the Nexus, the Tyne & Wear Metro system. The nearest station is Monkseaton, which has been served by trains since 1864. It was rebuilt on the present site by the North Eastern Railway in 1915, partially at that time with the potential opening of the Collywell Bay Railway in mind. Much of the station remains and is incorporated in to a modern building with two glass artworks which are featured in part of the original canopies. These were designed by Mike Davies and portray beaches and shipyards for which the area was well renowned. Armed with a Pathfinder map, the route and remains to Collywell Bay can be followed, and trains to and from Monkseaton are frequent.

CHAPTER 16

The Mistley, Thorpe &
Walton Railway

The north-eastern coast of Essex was first opened up by the Great Eastern Railway, which constructed a line between Colchester and the port of Harwich in 1854. After a long trading history with Holland, a regular ferry service to Rotterdam was provided by the Great Eastern Railway.

It was not long before the remaining Essex coastline to the south came to the attention of property speculators. With fine sandy beaches and bracing weather, the Victorian trend for healthy bathing was becoming fashionable and railway companies were showing interest.

Because Walton-on-the-Naze was inland from the coast, a new resort was being planned to take advantage of the sea, although it should be recorded that one of the earliest piers in England was constructed here in 1830. The Tendring Hundred Railway (THR) had already built a line from Colchester, reaching Wivenhoe in 1863, and completed the line eastwards to Thorpe-le-Soken and Walton in 1867.

In the meantime, before that line was completed, the monopoly of traffic to Walton was already being challenged by the Mistley, Thorpe & Walton Railway (MT&WR), which planned a new route from Mistley station in north west Essex. Although portrayed as a company which would provide services to and from the Ipswich direction, it was at a disadvantage from the beginning as construction of the Tendring line was well underway and would clearly reach the coast before its rival.

Fortunately, the promoter of the MT&WR was Robert Free, a comparatively young man at the time but very ambitious. He had already established a malting business on the quay at Mistley with long term plans to establish a similar business in later years at Thorpe-le-Soken. It was therefore in his interest for the railway to profitably serve his businesses at two places on the forthcoming railway.

The Mistley, Thorpe & Walton Railway's Bill was deposited in Parliament at the end of 1862. This somewhat wordy document described the objective as:

'A railway to commence by a junction, in the Parish of Mistley, in the county of Essex with the Harwich Branch of the Great Eastern Railway, at a point sixty yards to the east of a bridge constructed for carrying the said Harwich Branch over a certain tramway leading from such Branch to certain coke ovens, now or formerly the property of John Mann and John Stuck Barns, or one of them; and to pass through or into the several places following, or some of them:- Bradfield, Wix, Little Bentley, Tendring, Weeley, Beaumont-cum-Mose, Thorpe, otherwise Thorpe-le-Soken, Great Holland, Frinton and Walton, otherwise Walton-le-Soken, otherwise Walton-on-the-Naze: and to terminate in Walton aforesaid in a field called 'Davis's Field', lying west of the churchyard of Walton aforesaid, and belonging to the Trustees of the Widow Dennis, and in the occupation of John Barton.'

The MT&WR was duly incorporated by an Act dated 21 July 1863. The amount of authorised capital was £60,000 in ten shilling shares and £20,000 on loan. The compulsory purchase of necessary land was to take place within two years and power was granted to acquire additional land of up to six acres. Five years were allowed for the completion of works and under arrangements with the GER that company was authorised to provide £20,000 under its corporate funds to appoint two directors at 48 per cent of receipts. There were two registered offices, one at Manningtree and the other at Bishopsgate in London. Captain H.J.W. Jervis (1825–1881), Deputy Chairman of the GER, was appointed Chairman of the MT&WR, which was not without controversy. By all accounts Jervis cut a combative figure by apparently ruffling more than a few feathers in his own company by raising concerns about the poor management of the GER. This led to his being removed as Deputy Chairman during his absence in 1865, and whilst a subsequent enquiry proved that some of his accusations were accurate, he faced censure for his actions. In spite of this episode he remained on the MT&WR board and also served as a Conservative MP from 1859–1880.

One of the first problems that the directors needed to address was which course the final six miles from Thorpe-le-Soken to Walton would take, particularly as the Tendring and Mistley companies were indicating separate routes as shown on the map. The minutes of an early meeting stated that:

'Upon the two companies coming to an agreement to continue their respective lines as far as Thorpe and from thence to Walton by one

Mistley, Thorpe & Walton Railway including alternative proposed routes. (Google. Imagery ©2021 TerraMetrics, Map data ©2021. By Alex Griffin)

line, as laid down by the Mistley company, this company (GER) will be prepared to arrange terms for contributing a portion of the capital required for both lines and for the working of them when completed, but upon the express understanding that plans for the two lines of railway are to be subject to the approval of this Company's engineer, and that the contract for works is also to be approved by him.'

On this basis the MT&WR Act was passed.

Eventually, as the original plans indicated that the two companies' lines were planned to be a mere half mile apart, when it came to construction the THR route became the preferred option.

At the second general half-yearly meeting of the shareholders, which took place at the Hart Inn at Manningtree, it was resolved that construction should commence immediately and so it was that the opening event of the 'cutting of the first sod' took place on 6 April 1864. It was reported that this jamboree of a ceremony was largely due to the ebullient personality of the contractor, William Munro. He was already known as a competent contractor, having worked on the recently constructed Colne Valley and Brightlingsea railways, as well as in Crimea some nine years earlier. Under Robert Free's stewardship as the original promoter of the MT&WR, no pains had been spared to make the day a memorable success. A special train from London conveyed the contractor and his friends, together with the company directors. Amid festoons of bunting the Colchester Volunteer band attended the arrival of the train at Mistley and large crowds of children were gathered at the station. The site chosen for the ceremony was where the projected railway was to cross under the Harwich Road. To this place a number of vehicles made their way from the station, 'preceded by a mounted platform draped with a crimson cloth on which a handsome barrow of polished oak and an elegant silver spade'. The *Essex County Standard* newspaper report continued:

'At the ground itself crowded by spectators, speeches were made and appropriately finished with the following prophetic words by the Reverend George Burmester MA, Rector of Little Oakley who offered up a prophetic prayer which ended, "Should difficulties arise in the construction of the work, make us willing to suffer anything rather than seek relief by dishonourable means".'

The proceedings then continued with Mrs Jervis, the Company Chairman's wife, cutting the first sod followed by a toast proposed by George Josselyn, a director of the GER. Speeches were made with much applause and the guests made their way homewards in anticipation of the railway to come.

It did not take long before the words of the Rector came to haunt them. Within a year a dispute arose which culminated in recourse to violence. Apparently the Company and its engineer, James Cooke, expressed their dissatisfaction with the slow pace of construction. This led to Munro being forced to assign the remaining works to Frederick Furness, a new contractor. However, in his defence Munro complained that the expiry period allowed for the completion of the line was nearly due before he was able to take possession of about half the land. In addition to strengthen Munro's case, between the autumn of 1864 and the spring of 1865, Mr Mustard of Tendring Green had summarily driven the workmen from a portion of his land required for the railway because the purchase remained uncompleted. Understandingly, Munro felt extremely angry at the whole affair and was not inclined to assist the new contractor. Part of the arrangement of reassigning the works was that Furness should take over rails and other materials, a condition that he objected to. To make matters worse, Munro submitted a final invoice for £2,000 for works completed. This was rejected by Cooke with his suggestion that as his bill included one nought too many, he should receive a mere £200. Not surprisingly, Munro refused to give up possession of the sites and Furness was called upon by the Company to ensure that work could continue. Finally, the decision was taken to dislodge Munro by force and so 11 April 1865 was the day set for this event.

The battle lines were drawn and on one side were some fifty navvies under the command of Fryer, Munro's agent. On the other were about sixty longshoremen, also known as lumpers, from Harwich under the leadership of James Cooke acting on behalf of the Company. Fryer, not wanting to be caught in the rear, chose the head of a cutting for his defence and skirmishes were engaged with initially no decisive result. Cooke then made a direct appeal to the lumpers who rushed Fryer with the intention of ejecting him but they were met with equal determination by the army of navvies. Cooke then tried the same tactic again and after several skirmishes managed to capture 'General Fryer' whilst his supporters fled in disarray. Fryer was then ignominiously lifted over the company's boundary but was not arrested. This left Fryer free to have one last try and by all accounts he partially regrouped his navvies but it was clear that they were not up to fighting these superior forces and submitted to the inevitable.

In defence of the unfortunate Mr Munro, it was clear that not all the land on the northern extension where the battle took place had been purchased. Certainly, Mr Mustard, referred to earlier, was almost certainly in dispute over the question of land ownership, which was hardly the fault of Munro. However, it is equally clear that Munro was overstretched because he was still being employed to complete the Tendring Hundred Railway at Brightlingsea and thus unable to please two masters.

Furness, the contractor, breathed new life into the embryonic railway and at the half yearly meeting in London on 30 August 1865 it was reported that over £26,000 had been spent, a large proportion of which was for the purchase of land on the northern section. It was further reported that this section would be ready by the end of November the same year. A resolution was carried which authorised work to be carried out immediately on the Tendring to Thorpe route and that the shareholding be reduced from £60,000 to £36,000, leaving a further £12,000 to be raised by a mortgage to complete the railway.

November came and went but it was clear that the line was far from complete. In spite of this the company was undaunted and astonishingly sought to launch plans for an extension. This application included the construction of a railway along the south side of the Stour Valley from a junction with the GER at Manningtree to the GER's Branch line at Bures. Unsurprisingly, nothing came of this project.

In spite of this distraction, their rival Tendring Hundred Railway had been progressing rapidly. By the summer of 1866, the line had been extended to Thorpe-le-Soken and the station there was opened on 28 July. The speedy progress by the THR led to a lack of confidence in the MT&WR which, in spite of changing contractors, was still proceeding at a tardy pace. At the end of 1868 debts to Furness amounted to £12,000, which led to work ceasing completely. By that time four bridges on the northern section of line between Mistley and Tendring Green had been constructed and were open to road traffic, with two partially completed ones further south. The proposed stations at Bradfield and Tendring & Weeley had not been built. Following cessation of the works, Furness obtained a judgement against the company which resulted in his being granted a quantity of sleepers that had been laid along the route of the line in readiness for rails that were never supplied.

It was clear by this stage that the company was hopelessly insolvent and the period allowed for completion had expired a year earlier. At a shareholders' meeting held at Bishopsgate in the summer of 1869, it was resolved to make an application to the Board of Trade for abandonment of the railway. This was granted under the provisions of the Abandonment of Railways Act 1850.

During this time, Furness had arranged for the disposal of the Company's goods upon which execution had been levied. The sale was held at the Thorn Inn, Mistley, on 11 August 1869 with the following items to be auctioned: 150 tons of rail at 21 feet long, a quantity of fishplates, some iron girders and 3,600 sleepers. These chattels realised £2,000, and with a sum of money from the company, brought it up to £5,816. Any hopes of receiving money from the sale of property were dashed when a summary of land values was outlined by the parish overseers of Tendring, Wix and Bradfield as follows, ' For just under 36 acres, £22 5s, of which 6 acres in the parish of Mistley, mostly in a deep cutting, is deemed to be of no value at all.'

Furness, faced with these gloomy figures, almost certainly would have ruled out any prospect of further litigation in a court of law. But in a strange way the railway survived a while longer and was resuscitated by a new company, which like the fabulous bird Phoenix, was borne from the ashes of the former MT&WR. The new company, now renamed the East Essex Railway Company, was incorporated in 1873, and the former plan to connect the line to Thorpe-le-Soken was abandoned. The new route would utilise the track bed from Mistley to a point just north of the planned Tendring & Weeley station site and then turn south to join the GER line east of Weeley station as shown on the map. In spite of a Bill being deposited in November of 1873, nothing further was heard and the plans, rather like the earthworks and bridges, faded into oblivion through the decades, sleeping peacefully on to the twentieth century.

However, when Great Britain was facing a serious threat of invasion in the early part of the Second World War, the railway came to the attention of the Army General Staff whilst they studied maps of the east of England. They came across a map that indicated the course of an 'abandoned railway'. Perhaps they mused, this line of the proposed railway would be ideal as an anti-tank ditch. Of the four miles built, about a quarter was in cuttings, so the army set about excavating the new cuttings to provide an ideal method of stalling the progress of tank movements. It was reported that the western side of these ditches was excavated and heaped up to provide an escarpment where it was thought German tanks would find their progress frustrated.

As for the original promoter, Robert Free would have at least taken comfort in knowing that in one sense at least, his railway did provide an active defence of the realm even though it was never tested in anger. Surviving records indicate that he became disillusioned with the ramifications of the railway and withdrew from its affairs when he realised that further investment in the scheme was pointless. History reveals that after the railway was abandoned, he formed a partnership and then traded as Free Rodwell, expanding his malting empire throughout the remaining part of the Victorian era. He designed several innovative processes which were patented, and by the time of his death in 1902, had branched out into the wider food industry. His memory lives on in Mistley in the form of the large EDME works, still on the quayside, which continues to manufacture foodstuffs to this day.

But before we confine the story of the MT&WR to the history books, there are some observations the author would like to share with the reader. The first is, why did the scheme fail? Well certainly it was underfunded, which caused major problems but which were in spite of this perhaps not insurmountable. Secondly, maps indicate that the rural area was flat with most roads of a minor nature, so why didn't the original promoters make plans for level crossings? After all, East Anglia has to this day, more level crossings than other areas in the United Kingdom. The bridges that were constructed in their place necessitated the construction of expensive major earthworks each side to raise road levels over the railway, not of course forgetting the cost of bricks and skilled labourers. And thirdly, what was the company thinking when in the midst of all its difficulties in November of 1865, it proposed the construction of a new railway extension from Manningtree to Bures on the Stour Valley line to the west?

But now we need to turn our attention to the unfortunate William Munro, whose navvies and agent Fryer were unceremoniously ejected from the site after major disagreements. The author, having investigated this affair in some detail, is sure that, although fault lies with both sides, Munro was treated unfairly. It is important to recall that on at least one occasion, Munro was prevented from entering land and working on it because the purchase of the property had not been completed by the company. If Mr Mustard, the farmer named in this dispute was affected, one must assume that other landowners had been similarly treated and to expect the contractor to have worked under those conditions was unfair. Thus when Munro complained that access to land was restricted, which led to the date of the railway's completion being compromised, the author tends to agree with him. And clearly none of this was helped by a major personality clash between Munro and James Cooke, the company's engineer.

History records that Munro had been actively involved with the construction of the Colne Valley Railway in Suffolk and the Brightling Railway in Essex, as well as works in Crimea, where no stain on his character has been recorded. He clearly was overstretched at the time with the Tendring Railway and after the debacle on the MT&WR it is recorded that Munro bid for a contract on the Athenry to Ennis Junction Railway in County Galway where he excavated a thirty-six mile line. Although closed during the Irish railway rationalisation in the latter part of the twentieth century, this railway is once again being discussed as a possible re-opening project. Munro would at least be pleased about that.

Remains of the Mistley Railway Bridge under the B1352.

Remains of the Mistley, Thorpe & Walton Railway

How to get to the remains of the MT&WR

Most of the construction work on the railway was carried out at the northern end of the line, so it is suggested that visitors travel to Mistley station and walk or cycle from there. The last time remnants of the works were recorded was in 1946, when Thomas B. Peacock wrote a history of the railway with photographs. Since then, all of the bridges with the exception of the one beneath the B1352 road have been demolished. Similarly the earthworks, including the wartime tank trap, have been subjected to the plough, so there is little to be seen on the landscape. It's worth taking a look at the remaining bridge and standing in the place near the would-be junction, where all those people celebrated the cutting of the first sod of the railway that was never built.

The cutting of the first sod took place here near the junction with the Mistley to Harwich railway.

CHAPTER 17

The East Kent Light Railway

In the late period of the Victorian era most of the United Kingdom was covered by a comprehensive railway system. Like the spokes of a wheel, lines radiated from London to all corners of the country and these were supplemented by branch lines to serve many of the remaining communities. Yet in spite of this, there were areas of the country where railways had not been provided because of a lack of financial investment and a low level of population. Parliament was keen to rectify matters and introduced a new Act called 'The Light Railways Act 1896'. This legislation allowed for lines to be built cheaply in rural areas by allowing an easing of gradients, a reduction in the need for earthworks, ungated level crossings and simplified signalling. In return, operators had to adhere to a maximum speed limit of 25 mph with fewer rules and regulations than was normally the case.

It was at the start of this Act that Colonel H.F. Stephens first made his name in the era of light railways. This entrepreneur, the son of an eminent pre-Raphaelite art critic, had been apprenticed to the Metropolitan Railway and cut his teeth with the South Eastern Railway during the construction of the Hawkhurst line. He then set up as an engineer and promoter of railways, developing lines throughout England and Wales. The first to be constructed after the passing of the Act was the Kent & East Sussex Railway which, when completed ran from Robertsbridge to Headcorn, opening in stages between 1900 and 1904.

Most of Colonel Stephens' Railways have closed but evidence of their existence remains in many places and are well worth a visit.

Stephens became involved with the construction of the East Kent Light Railway when an opportunity arose during the early years leading up to the outbreak of the First World War.

It's not widely known that the county of Kent was once the subject of major interest for its possible deposits of coal. Awareness of this was not realised until the Victorian era when the South Eastern Railway discovered coal seams during its construction of the second shaft of the proposed channel tunnel. It had long been expected that coal reserves probably existed in Kent but few speculators were prepared to risk finance on sinking speculative shafts that might not bear fruit. The former workings were subsequently purchased after attempts to complete a tunnel under the English Channel were abandoned, with high hopes of establishing a mine. But the continual problems with flooding and the presence of only narrow bands of coal rendered the site of little use. By all accounts only one trainload of coal was ever excavated at the foot of Shakespeare Cliff.

However, this setback was not severe enough to deter promoters and interest continued throughout the period leading up to the First World War, by which time a considerable quantity of coal had been discovered at Tilmanstone. Following a meeting in October 1910 in Canterbury between the promoters and Light Railway Commissioners, approval was given to build a line. The Act was to construct the railway, complete with extensions to various collieries on the route. The railway would operate from Shepherdswell on the South Eastern and Chatham Railway (SE&CR)'s Dover line to Wingham (Canterbury Road). Collieries were planned at Guilford, Tilmanstone, Hammill, Staple and Wingham.

The line under construction near Wells Farm, Eastry. (Col. Stephens Museum)

East Kent Railway (ask.) 1913.

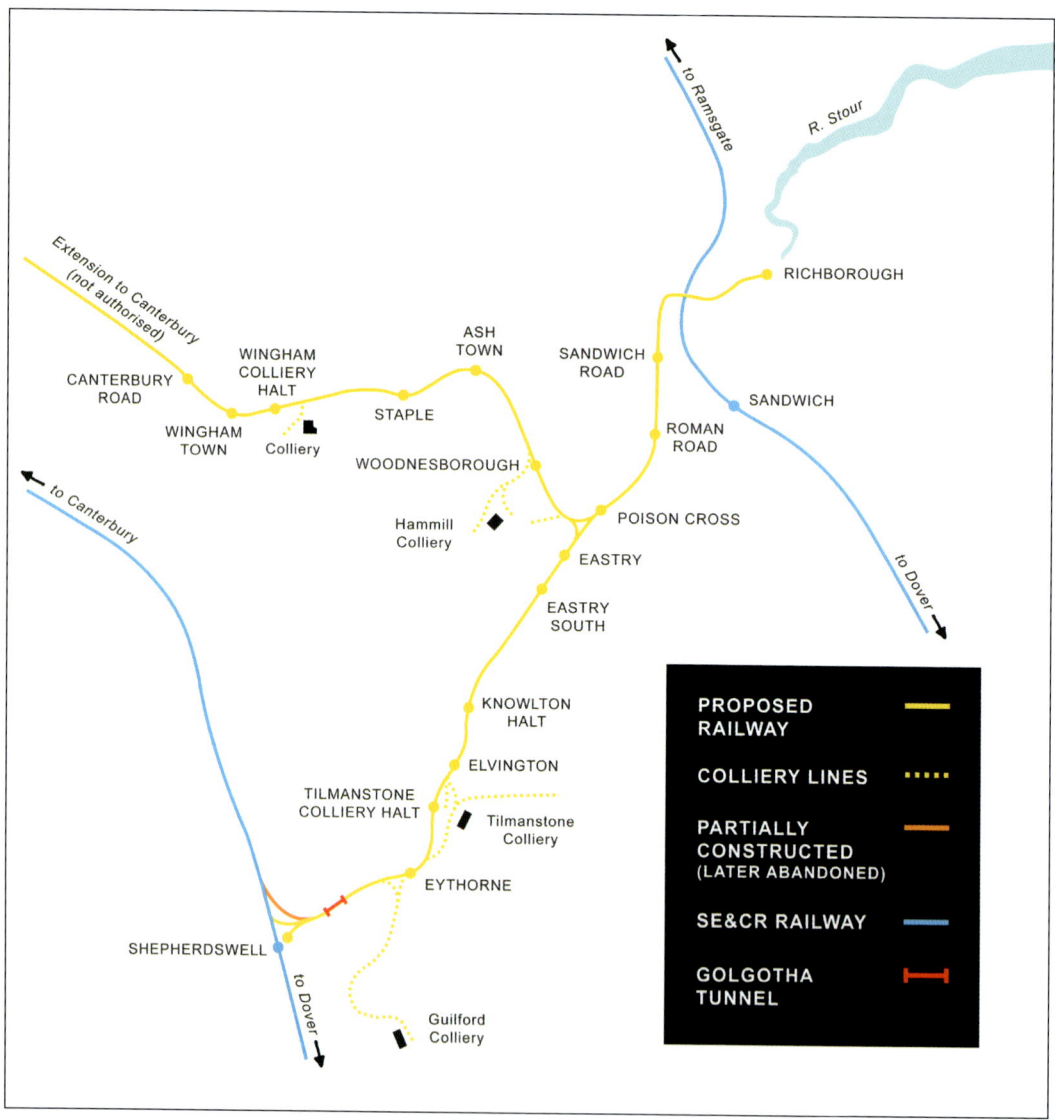

Extent of East Kent Light Railway. (Alex Griffin (based on that from *Colonel Stephens' Railways* – John Scott Morgan))

By 1916 the railway was largely constructed as planned but an extension from Wingham (Canterbury Road) to Hackington level crossing near Canterbury West station was never authorised. Most of the collieries proved to be unviable and gradually faded into oblivion. The only one on the East Kent Light Railway (EKLR) that survived into the era of British Railways was Tilmanstone, which closed in 1986.

Wingham Canterbury Road Station. The extension of the railway from here to Canterbury was never authorised. (Col. Stephens Museum)

The railway was not profitable and like several other of Colonel Stephens' railways continued to be run on a shoestring. As the mines were gradually abandoned, farm produce replaced coal but the passenger service could be best described as 'minimal'. However, a new opportunity appeared on the horizon during the First World War when the port of Richborough to the north of Sandwich was developed. The purpose was to provide staging facilities for the movement of stores and heavy equipment to the armed forces in France. By the end of the war in 1918, the harbour was almost out of use but this did not go unnoticed by Colonel Stephens. He envisaged a substantial new port which would include cross-channel services and a dramatic increase in trade. With this in mind he promoted a new railway which would run from Eastry to Richborough with stations at Poison Cross, Roman Road and Sandwich Road, passing over the SE&CR to a platform at the port. The Parliamentary Act was passed, with the line opening

Richborough Port station, although constructed, was never used for passenger traffic. (Col. Stephens Museum)

in 1925 but even by the Colonel's standards the stations were very primitive, little more than garden sheds without running water or lavatories. The train service was so minimal that few passengers were ever tempted to use it. In fact the port was never used by passenger trains and unsurprisingly, passenger services between Eastry and Sandwich Road were withdrawn in 1928.

In spite of setbacks such as these, the EKLR continued to serve the community with an increase in coal traffic during the Second World War. The railway was nationalised in 1948 but the writing was on the wall as far as passenger services were concerned, being completely withdrawn less than a year later. The section of line between Eastry and Richborough was closed in 1949 but in reality had remained largely out of use since the end of the war. All traffic ceased between Eastry and Canterbury Road in 1950 and a year later the same fate was wrought on the railway between Eythorne and Eastry.

However, the remaining section of the branch between Eythorne and Shepherdswell survived, prospering with coal traffic until 1986 when the mine was closed. The national miners' strike a year earlier sealed the fate of this once proud colliery.

Remains of the East Kent Light Railway and what to see

Today, much of the EKLR, particularly in the north, has disappeared without trace and largely returned to the plough. Even a substantial community such as Ash has so completely lost its railway that the site of the station can only be found by detailed map references. Even so, the line is fondly remembered by some elderly folk who can recall many anecdotes from its heyday. The author, with a fondness for his adopted county of Kent, has mixed feelings about the East Kent enterprise. Yes, in earlier times, there is no doubt that, had a large coalfield been discovered to match those in Wales or the north of England, the wealth of the region would have been assured. However, the few collieries that did survive meant that the scars on the landscape were kept to a minimum. Today the area is still primarily that of mixed farming with only distant memories of the pits that once were there. The author begs the reader's forgiveness in pondering that history will demonstrate that this Colonel Stephens railway would have spoilt a significant area of county had large deposits of coal been discovered.

Golgotha Tunnel

When the line was first constructed, Tilmanstone colliery was already established and immediate steps were taken to connect it to the main London, Chatham & Dover Railway at Shepherdswell. In 1911 a line was built to the mine with minimal earthworks around Golgotha hill, but because of the severe gradients, presented a severe risk to heavily loaded coal trains, thus leading to the abandonment of the route. The company then embarked on a new course by the construction of Golgotha Tunnel, 550 yards through a chalk hill on an easier gradient. The name Golgotha is interesting and local history does not reveal its origins except to suggest that it may contain ancient burial sites. In biblical terms Golgotha is described as 'a hill in the shape of a skull and the place where Jesus Christ was crucified'. Whether the EKLR hill is in the shape of a skull is a matter of conjecture, but through this chalk the railway constructed its tunnel, which did not reveal any graves.

Clearly the early promoters of the railway had high hopes for the coalfield's success, because Golgotha Tunnel was planned to accommodate a double line. The brick-built portals clearly indicate

Above left: **Golgotha Tunnel** was built to serve a double track railway. (Nick Catford)

Above right: **Inside the** tunnel indicating the southern side which was never excavated. (Nick Catford)

this and the approaches through the chalk were of generous proportions. The tunnel contract was let to Rigby, a contractor well-known to Stephens, who was tasked to build the southern part of the EKLR. Work commenced by the boring of a shaft in the centre, which allowed excavation to take place in four places, both directions within the centre of the tunnel and at the east and west portals. Because the EKLR was under pressure to complete the works, the four work sites considerably speeded up progress. In addition a decision was taken on cost grounds to only cut a sufficient passage for single line running within the tunnel with a further saving made by adding only a brick lining to the roof. This allowed the presence of chalk on each side to take the tunnel's structural load, with the opportunity of excavating further should an increase in traffic justify the need. As the single line was adequate throughout its operational days, the tunnel remained in its unfinished state, so today, the chalk remains can be studied with interest.

Guilford Colliery branch

This colliery was constructed in 1911, complete with a full set of substantial buildings and three shafts partially sunk. But surprisingly the connecting railway was not built until 1913. By that time the French owners had decided to abandon the colliery before any coal was mined and the railway was never used.

Guilford Colliery just after construction, 1910. (Subterranea Britannica)

A triangular junction had been provided near Eythorne and the tracks remained in place for a number of years, although the only traffic seen was that of stored rolling stock in various states of decay in later years.

North Bank Junction

When the railway first opened, the connection from the EKLR to the main line at Shepherdswell was established through the sidings owned by the SE&CR. Clearly this arrangement was regarded as unsatisfactory by the EKLR, which found itself in conflict with the goods traffic generated by its more powerful neighbour. Rigby was instructed to construct earthworks for a new junction further north, which would allow coal trains to gain direct access to the main line by a north facing junction. Some heavy earthworks were undertaken, which was surprising because no agreement had been made with the SE&CR, thereby making these developments somewhat speculative. Clearly the SE&CR took a dim view of this development and made its objections clear by placing a new signal box on the place where the branch railway would have formed the junction with the main line.

The planned extension to the main line north of Shepherdswell station was never used because of objections from the SE&CR. (Col. Stephens Museum)

This issue was never resolved and trains continued to operate somewhat awkwardly through Shepherdswell Station's goods yard until closure in 1986.

The partially completed remains of the earthworks remain to this day and are occupied by a siding.

The East Kent Railway Heritage Trust (www.eastkentrailway.co.uk)

Formed in 1987, the East Kent Heritage Railway was established at Shepherdswell, adjacent to the main line station. Its aim is to preserve the remains of the EKLR as a working museum. On high days and leisure days, the restored line runs from its own rebuilt terminus for 2.4 miles to Eythorne station, with future plans to reach the site of Tilmanstone colliery.

Services are mainly run by diesel hauled trains or multiple units and as the journey includes a ride through Golgotha Tunnel, the details of its construction can be seen from the train. The remains of the triangular junction of the railway to Guilford colliery can be seen to the south before arriving at Eythorne.

A museum, refreshments and miniature railway add to the interest of visitors.

How to get there

As all of the partially surviving remains are at or around Shepherdswell, taking a train is the best way of viewing the sites. The station is well served by trains from Dover in the south and London via Canterbury to the north. The country lanes are quiet and exploration by foot or bicycle is recommended.

CHAPTER 18

The Cleveland Extension Mineral Railway – Paddy Waddell's Railway

To outsiders with little detailed knowledge of the North York Moors, it may come as a surprise to learn that this remote region, consisting mainly of base rock from the Jurassic period, has been heavily influenced by the presence and activities of man over many centuries.

As long ago as 8000 BC during the Mesolithic period, man's migration from Europe led to the settlement of tribes on the moor, which in those days was heavily wooded. By all accounts, the first significant change to the landscape occurred in 5000 BC when what would be Great Britain became an island following the incursion of seawater in the south, which formed what became the English Channel. Agricultural activity took place, which led to the beginning of deforestation of the landscape, and by the Bronze Age of 2000 BC the indigenous inhabitants continued to farm and had removed much of the remaining forest for this purpose. The effect of this action led to the top soil being washed away and the loss of naturally occurring minerals, thereby preventing the re-establishment of woodlands that had earlier been widespread. By 600 BC, ironworks were established on a small scale and remnants of this activity in the form of slag heaps are visible to this day. The British invasion by the Romans from AD 71 led to a legacy of superior stone roads, many of which survive today. Even so, these entrepreneurial immigrants found Great Britain a tough place to rule and finally called it a day after they built what is now Hadrian's Wall, a comparatively short distance north of the moors between Newcastle-upon-Tyne and Carlisle.

The final invaders, apart from the Normans who fought the English at the Battle of Hastings in 1066, were the Vikings and Danes who sailed across from northern Europe. Eventually, they amicably settled and farmed the moor and established the Christian church at York in AD 627. Today it is widely believed that the present Yorkshire dialect stems from the settlers of these countries.

The long period of peace that followed led to the development of the Catholic faith and construction of monasteries. Much of the land was farmed by monks from the Christian community, but this era of tranquillity was brought to a brutal end when Thomas Cromwell decreed that all monasteries and other places of Catholic worship be destroyed, this occurring between 1536 and 1541.

Once a parliamentary democracy was later established, the area was subject to the industrial revolution, with iron ore production then the development of railways in the twentieth century.

Today, it is hard to believe that the activities of man could have been quite so widespread. The early loss of this heavily wooded region has resulted in wonderful rolling scenery, sheep farming and the survival of historic towns. The evolution of the North York Moors has led to its latest industry which shows no sign of abating, and that of course is tourism, which is vital to the economy.

Our story begins during the railway period of Queen Victoria's reign. Surprisingly, when one considers the low population of the moors, they were subject to several significant railway developments, the first of which was engineered by George Stephenson (1781–1848) in 1835. This line ran from Whitby to Grosmont and Pickering, was operated by horses and clearly built with the burgeoning iron ore industry in mind. It was later converted to steam and became part of the North Eastern Railway in 1854. Other lines followed which served Picton, Battersby, and a long east to west railway from Middlesbrough to Grosmont. The final route was a coastal railway that ran from Whitby, to Guisborough, Nunthorpe and the industrially developed north coast at Redcar.

The birth of the Cleveland Extension Mineral Railway (CEMR) can be traced back to 1860 when F.K. Robinson, whilst writing *Whitby, its Abbey and Principal Parts of the Neighbourhood*, referred obliquely to a proposed railway which uncannily described the route which was broadly similar to that which was eventually partially constructed. The purpose of the railway was to provide inward transport to exploit iron ore deposits, which were to be hauled from a place east of the present Leaholm station on the Whitby to Middlesbrough line, to processing works at Staithes and Port Mulgrave on the North Sea coast. The finished iron was then to be taken by ship to industrial areas further north. Although this project was not developed, the mineral wealth was subject to further ambitious schemes in the area, taking advantage of this naturally occurring mineral. Eventually, as each project fell by the

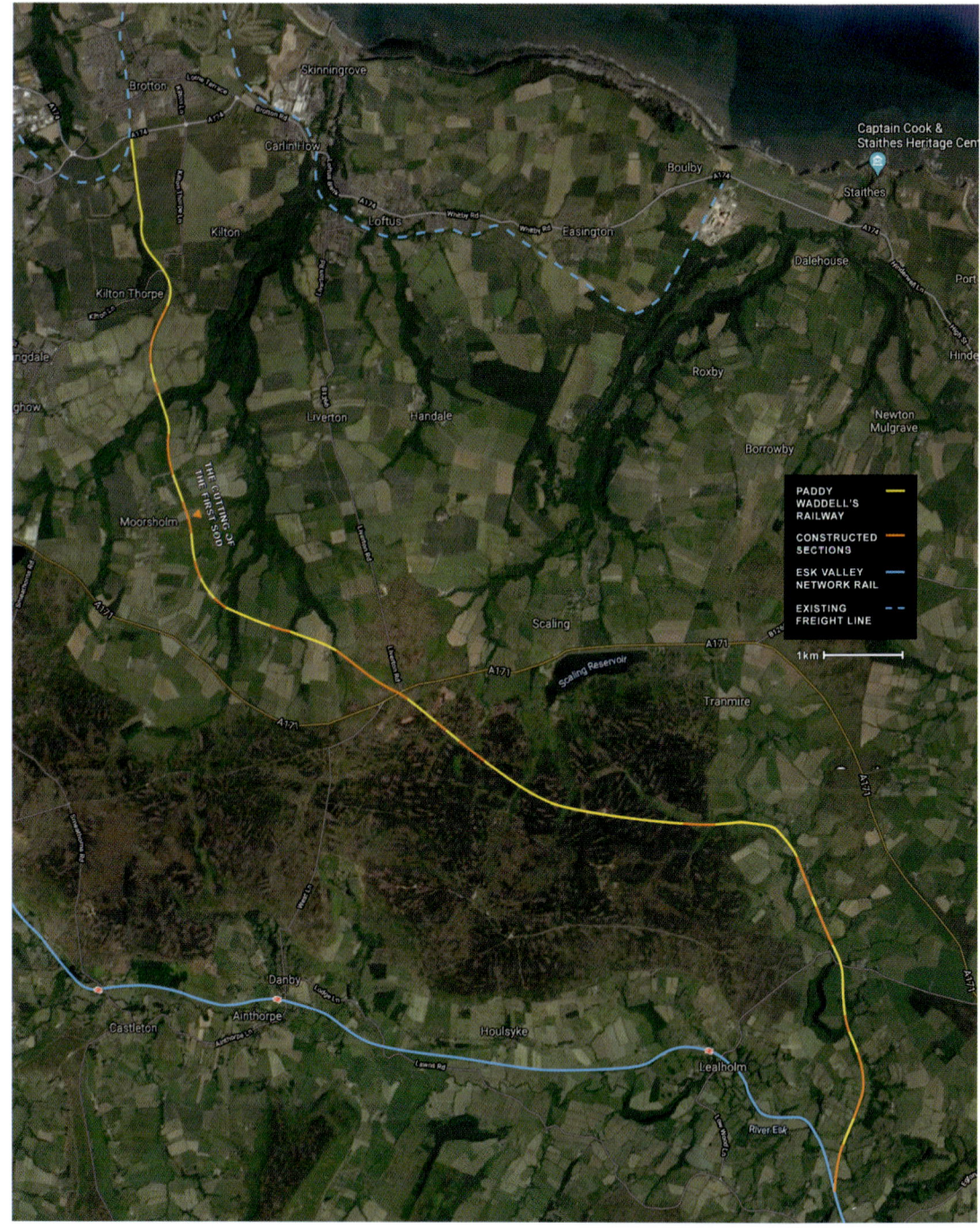

The Cleveland Extension Mineral Railway, otherwise known as 'Paddy Waddell's Railway'. (Google. Imagery ©2021 CNES / Airbus, Infoterra Ltd & Bluesky, Landsat / Copernicus, Maxar Technologies, The GeoInformation Group, Map data ©2021. By Alex Griffin)

wayside through lack of finance, the pioneering spirit of those early entrepreneurs faded.

The first mention of Paddy Waddell appears in print towards the end of the 1860s. History records that he walked the proposed railway from one end to the other and became well known to inhabitants and farmers while he surveyed the route.

So who was Paddy Waddell? Well, unusually in this case the truth is stranger than that recorded, and not a great deal was known about him in early days. Understandably, an immediate reaction was to assume that he was Irish because of his Christian name. But it's now generally agreed that an Irishman of that name was not the contractor in charge of the works but a Scotsman, John Waddell from Edinburgh. At the time of the proposed CEMR, Waddell was about to complete earthworks on the Loftus to Whitby coastal railway in July 1881. However, this line required a large amount of additional work necessitating a lot more of Waddell's time and as a result was not formally opened until 3 December 1883, some two years later.

Historians now believe that Waddell's chief engineer of works, a man called Gallaher, whilst working on the Loftus to Whitby Railway, was seconded to survey the CEMR on behalf of Paddy Waddell. Confusion over his Irish name became legend and local landowners who witnessed Irish navvies at work, gradually adopted Paddy Waddell's name to describe the forthcoming railway being constructed over their land. History records that Gallaher was well received by the farming community, and to this day is fondly remembered by relatives of long deceased landowners who have repeated memorable anecdotes that have been passed down through the ages. By introducing himself to the local community as a representative of the railway he cemented this misconception, so from then on the project was always better known as Paddy Waddell's Railway.

When it came to Bills petitioned in Parliament, three railway schemes were outlined with a wordy presentation clause which read:

'To authorise the Company to make and maintain the railways following, or some or one of them, and some part or parts thereof, together with all necessary and convenient or incidental works, stations, bridges, approaches, roads or communications (that is to say)-

'**No 1.** A railway commencing in the township and parish of Skelton, in the North Riding of the county of York, by a junction with the Saltburn Extension Branch of the North Eastern Railway Company at or near a point thereon about 330 yards measured in a northerly direction from a farmhouse belonging to John Thomas Wharton Esq. and occupied by Thomas Hall, called East Pastures marked on the Ordnance map of the county of York with the number 18 then passing from, in, through and into the several townships, parishes and extra-parochial or other places following, or some of them (that is to say): Skelton, Brotton, Kilton, Stanghow, Little Moorsholme, Great Moorsholme, Girrick, Easington, Liverton, Liverton Moor, Lofthouse, Wapley and Wapley Moor and terminating on Liverton Moor, belonging or reputedly belonging to Viscount Downe, at or near a point adjoining and on the northern side of the public highway leading to Guisborough to Whitby, about 704 yards measured in a westerly direction from Wapley New Inn, which point is situated in the township of Liverton, in the parish of Easington, in the North Riding of the county of York.

'**No. 2.** A railway commencing in the township of Liverton and parish of Easington aforesaid, at or near a point adjoining and on the northern side of the said public highway leading from Guisborough to Whitby, about 704 yards measured in a westerly direction from Wapley New Inn aforesaid, thence passing from, through into and in the several parishes, townships and extra-parochial and other places following, or some of them, that is to say Easington, Liverton, Liverton Moor, Lofthouse, Wapley, Wapley Moor, Scalingdam, Easington High Moor, Hinderwell, Rousby, Rousby High Moor, Rousby Low Moor, Black Dike Moor, Lealholme Moor, Newton Mulgrave, Ugthorpe, Green Houses, Stonegate, Lealholm Rigg, Lealholm Side, Egton, Lythe, Short Wait, Danby and Glaisdale, and terminating by a junction with the North Eastern Railway in the township of Glaisdale, in the parish of Danby, in the North Riding of the county of York, at or near point on such railway about 70 yards measured in a westerly direction, from a house called Rake House, marked on the Ordnance map of the county of York with the number 31.

'**No. 3.** A railway wholly in the said township and parish of Skelton, commencing in the township and parish of Skelton, aforesaid by a junction with Railway No. 1, in a field belonging to the said Thomas Wharton, Esquire, and occupied by the said

Thomas Hall, and terminating by a junction with the Cleveland Branch of the North Eastern Railway at or near a point about 250 yards measured in a south easterly direction from the said farm house called East Pastures'.

Those readers with an eagle eye will notice one or two minor errors in the above descriptions but in the end, these were of no lasting consequence, as will be seen later. Railway No. 3 was abandoned prior to construction.

Joseph Dodds (1819–1891) was the promoter of the Cleveland Extension Mineral Railway when the Bill came before Parliament in 1872. Born the son of a farmer at Winston near Barnards Castle, he was educated at Gainford Academy and became articled to a firm of solicitors in Stockton. Once qualified, he practised as a solicitor and attorney, later becoming a councillor and mayor to Stockton Town Council.

His other interests lay in the development of industry, which grew at a rapid pace in the decade following 1864. Dodds could see the potential for substantial profits in iron ore and became both a director and promoter of the CEMR. At this stage he already owned

Joseph Dodds.

the Stockton Forge Ironworks, mines at Boosbeck, and had involvement with Durham coalfields and the improvement of drainage channels of the River Tees. He was colloquially known at the time as 'The Industrial Tycoon' and as if that were not enough, was elected Liberal Member of Parliament for Stockton in 1868 and again five years later. As it was necessary to attend Parliament on a regular basis, he persuaded the North Eastern Railway to run a through train from Stockton and Middlesbrough to London, colloquially known as 'Dodds' Express'.

At first all seemed to be proceeding smoothly. The Bill was first presented by three local luminaries, Messrs Pease, Millbank and Beaumont, to Parliament during February of 1873. However, a month later Sir Francis Goldsmid, a member of Railway Bills, reported in the Commons

Journal 'that in the case of the CEMR Bill they had examined the allegations contained in the preamble of the Bill, but the same had not been proved to their satisfaction'.

This unexpected turn of events was quickly laid at the door of a competitor in the form of the Whitby, Redcar and Middlesbrough Union Railway. One of its supporters was the shadowy figure of John Thomas Wharton who, it may be recalled, owned property near the proposed CEMR No. 1 Railway. Wharton appeared to have changed sides by formally objecting to the CEMR Bill.

Dodds moved quickly and reviewed the Bill's progress, which had within a few weeks, moved to the House of Lords. After consideration by the Examiners and two readings, the Bill finally received the Royal Assent on the 26 June 1873. It soon became clear that the earlier difficulties could now be explained. During 1873 Wharton had acted underhandedly during the Parliamentary process by constructing his own private railway from a junction with the Cleveland Railway. This embraced the northern section of the proposed Railway No. 1 between Kilton North and Lindale junctions where the private railway branched south east to Kilton Thorpe and later south west to Lingdale mines. Although this duplicitous action placed Wharton at odds with his former colleagues, ultimately a pragmatic view was taken and this railway passed into the hands of the North Eastern Railway. Simultaneously, Railway No. 3 was formally abandoned.

The capital of the CEMR was to be £170,000 in ten pound shares, the subscribers being The Right Hon. Lord Downe, Thomas Richardson, Joseph Dodds, C.F. Bolckow, A.L. Maynard, John Robinson, David and William Petch. The first directors were Thomas Richardson, Joseph Dodds, John Robinson and Peter Graham. Under the Act, a sum of £8,306 15s 6d was held by HM Paymaster General on behalf of the Court of Chancery in the event of bankruptcy of the undertaking. The Act further clarifies the nature of sidings and related works on Wharton's land at Grange Farm, Girrick and Girrick Moor areas which were rich in iron ore.

True to railway tradition, the 'turning of the first sod' took place at Moorsholme at the end of October in 1874. It is recorded that a large party of gentlemen connected with the iron trade in Cleveland was present when it was announced:

'The line will be between 10 and 11 miles in length and proceeds through the richest part of the hitherto undeveloped ironstone district, passing over a mile of the estate of Mr J.T. Wharton of Skelton Castle. Next it goes through Capt. Linskill's Moorsholm Estate, where a ravine 120 feet deep is crossed by a viaduct, on to Great Moorsholm and Girrick where the ironstone is proved to average 20,000 tons per acre, over Liverton and Danby Low Moor Estates of Lorde Downe to Easington Low Moor, owned by T.M. Palmer MP., skirting the estates of Mr E. Turton the Marquis of Normamby, through the valley of Greenhouses Beck to the Esk, where a junction will be made with the North Yorkshire & Cleveland Railway, about a half mile from Glaisdale and 10 miles from Whitby.

'Danby Moor is one of the highest points in Cleveland, and the line will have an inclination in each direction, so that loads of ironstone will be carried with minimum engine power. The ceremony of turning the sod was performed on the estate of Mr D.T. Petch, at Moorsholm, a remote, bleak and at this season, almost inaccessible portion of the district.

'Mr Dodds stated that within a mile of each side of the line, and over a distance of three miles, from Hagg Beck to Girrick, there was a deposit of not less than 80,000 tons of stone available for working.'

This promising report was clearly aimed at prospective investors because money had not been forthcoming at levels the promoters were expecting. Hopes of an early start were dampened with a reference to a viaduct at Moorsholm which suggested that it had been built, but which was patently untrue. However, Dodds remained enthusiastic by purchasing 'a large and valuable tract of ironstone at Girrick and Moorsholm on the route of the proposed Cleveland Extension line.'

The Act of 1873 allowed for completion of the works within five years from 7 July of that year. In spite of all the early enthusiasm, three years were to pass with little to show and on 1 July 1876 a press announcement was made to 'remind those interested that the CEMR company had been formed for the purpose of constructing a line from the Kilmanthorpe Branch of the NER to terminate at Glaisdale by a junction with the North Yorkshire & Cleveland Branch of the NER'. In spite of a report some three months earlier that work would commence quickly with contractor Miles Tallett, appointed, it would appear that nothing was done and he was never heard of again.

If, however, the promoters of the CEMR thought that the machinations of the Whitby, Redcar and Middlesbrough Railway referred to earlier had gone away, they were to be sorely tried by new events. It would appear that just before 1887, Mr Leeman, Chairman of the NER, engaged Mr A.S. Hammond of Birmingham to plan for a rival railway to compete with the CEMR for ironstone traffic between Brotton and Ellerby. Plans were duly presented along with a bill of £1,500 for the work carried out, but in due course the scheme was dropped. However, Hammond had not been paid. He took the matter to court, which found in his favour, but Leeman passed the matter to the Exchequer Division of the High Court of Justice, which also found against him. This action against the Chairman of the NER was obviously an embarrassment and plans to compete with the CEMR were quietly abandoned.

Meanwhile, the CEMR's Act of 1873 had by now expired and at the end of December 1877, there was a notice of intention to bring in a Bill for an extension of time and revival of powers. These allowed for the compulsory purchase of land, the final date being 7 July 1881 to allow completion of the railway. Problems were exacerbated by the absence of the CEMR's contractor John Waddell, who was unable to start work because of his commitments on the Whitby to Loftus railway which itself had run into great difficulties. Eventually, on 17 December, the CEMR contemplated an abandonment order due to a lack of capital but by a narrow majority vote this was rejected. The third bill was read in the House of Lords in February 1881 and two months later the power to complete the works was extended to 7 July 1884.

Meanwhile Waddell was inundated with work elsewhere, which apart from the Loftus, Whitby and Scarborough line now included a new bridge across the River Thames at Putney.

In spite of this there then followed a drum roll of publicity. Engineers from the CEMR enthusiastically began to set out a new line at Kilton Thorpe by excavating a deep cutting at the junction with the NER, followed by a substantial viaduct some 127 feet over a ravine. After passing Moorsholm there were to be two further viaducts over ravines before the railway set across the moor. At a place where the nearby hamlets of Scaling Ugthorpe were reached, a range of works were to be carried out in the form of cuttings, embankments, viaducts and bridges in the direction of Glaisdale. Here a substantial 400 yard tunnel was to be excavated in freestone, followed by a heavy embankment and a large number of heavy culverts and bridges before reaching the junction with the NER. An early decision was made to excavate the tunnel before tackling the remaining works and great play was made of the fact that the district through which the railway passed was notable for significant mineral wealth.

This upsurge of activity in April of 1882 did not go unnoticed and to add a further injection of enthusiasm, the CEMR produced a new prospectus graphically extolling this investment opportunity. Unfortunately, in its attempt to attract support the company was less than truthful in its claims that 'Cleveland ironstone yields 45 per cent metallic ore'. The best ore in the area was at Rosedale further west and that only produced an output of 35 per cent. In spite of the company's best efforts, investors were conspicuous by their absence and the lack of finance was still proving to be a major obstacle.

In the meantime, where was the elusive contractor, John Waddell? Clearly, he was under a lot of pressure on projects elsewhere but in spite of this, felt he should honour his commitment to the CEMR, which was to bear his name. For the first time, history records that he was seen on site with his navvies during the autumn of 1882, tackling the onerous task of constructing the Stonegate Tunnel. Unfortunately, work spluttered to a halt when it became obvious that 'the money had run out' and any prospect of completing the tunnel or remaining viaducts evaporated into thin air. Waddell immediately took other paying contracts, which included the completion of works between the Scarborough to Whitby railway and the Mersey Tunnel between Liverpool and Birkenhead.

Whilst time marched on, routine matters such as level crossings and the provision of stations were discussed and aired at local level. However, what could not be resolved were the lack of finance and the date of the line's completion.

By 1884 there were widespread doubts that the CEMR would ever be completed, so a final desperate attempt was made to salvage something from the ashes. The proposal was a considerably scaled down version of the railway's earlier ambitions and a new completion date was extended to July 1887 with no real prospect of its being achieved. But the board took the decision to use its dwindling resources to complete the railway between Lingdale Junction and Moorsholm, a distance of 1.75 miles. This line was actually part of Railway No. 1 already authorised under Acts of 1873, 1878 and 1881. The railway was to be constructed by 28 July, which would coincide, it was stated, with the whole line being complete to Glaisdale on the same date.

As no public money was involved, the CEMR had to resort to use its own dwindling resources. But at least, they reasoned, some income could be gained by exploiting the ironstone at the end of this short branch. However, even this desperate measure could not cover the cost of an expensive viaduct over Hagg Beck, so this final throw of the dice brought the whole sorry venture to an end. As if to seal its fate completely, the value of iron ore fell from between 50 and 120 shillings per ton to 33 shillings, which ruled out any further exploitation of this once valuable mineral. Little was heard of the CEMR as the company's works gently hibernated on the moor, apart from strangely enough, the granting of a further extension of completion time until 1890.

John Waddell died at his home in Edinburgh, some six months after the passing of the CEMR Act of 1887. He was described in the *Whitby Gazette* as a well-known Scotch contractor with a resume of his working life outlined. He was sixty years old.

Meanwhile the tenacity of the CEMR could only be admired, as the company applied for one more extension of time to complete the line, taking it up to 7 July 1896. In spite of the attempt to re-invigorate the railway, no spark of life was detected and the partially completed earthworks remained slumbering on the Moor. And yet, in spite of appearing on a list of expired Acts in 1896, the CEMR, in its final death throes, put out an ebullient statement seeking finance to complete the works with all the appeal that could be mustered. But not surprisingly, this rousing report failed to attract any interest and the CEMR faded in to history.

We should not close this chapter without referring to the promoter, Joseph Dodds MP, referred to earlier in this chapter as 'the industrial tycoon'. He continued to amass wealth as witnessed by his buying land on the route of Paddy Waddell's Railway in 1873 and his continuing to invest in the iron ore industry. His popularity continued unabated and he was again re-elected as Member of Parliament for Stockton in 1886 by a majority of 4,991, one of the largest in the country.

But even he could not avoid the looming recession and depressed prices of iron ore. His personal circumstances waned and he was facing bankruptcy when one of his trusting clients, Jane Meynell, an old lady, entrusted Dodds with her life savings. This consisted of her property in Stockton High Street and a large sum of money. One of her cheques, on the advice of Dodds, was made out to Tees Conservation Committee for the sum of £2,000. He promptly countersigned this with the word 'Bearer', and took the cash. Nevertheless, this crime was a matter even Dodds would have to confront. At his trial in 1888, Judge Baron Hadlestone summed up the affair by recording:

> 'Here an old lady 76 years of age, places herself entirely in the hands of her solicitor, a gentleman whose public position most fully justified the confidence which she placed in him, and he has basely abused that confidence and embezzled £13,800.' *[about £1.35 million today]*

According to newspaper reports after the hearing, 'he hurriedly left town and it is not known where he has since been living'. Three years later in 1891 he died a broken man and his betrayal was so complete that his passing was barely reported in the *Stockton Echo*, his local newspaper.

After this sorry episode it is left to others to sum up the reason for the failure of the railway. Firstly, it lay in the public's reluctance to invest, not helped of course by quoting inflated estimates of the quantity of ore in the district. Secondly, the closing of Glaisdale Ironworks in 1876 removed a large potential for rail born traffic, and thirdly, reports of declining rail traffic on other nearby lines alarmed potential investors. Even so, the generosity of local landowners should be recorded because unusually, some of them allowed railway construction to take place on their property without the purchase being completed.

What remains to be seen

From south to north the route of the line begins at Rakes Farm at a place between Glaisdale and Leaholm stations on the Esk Valley Railway. Remaining works can be seen north of Thorn Hill and between Stonegate and Redmire Farm. Small sections can then be seen at Hardale Head, Easington High Moor and the A171 at the road junction with the B1366. Other abandoned sections can be found at Avens Wood, South Lane Farm, Moorsholm, Throstle Nest, Little Moorsholm Farm and Buck Rush Farm on the approach to Kilton Thorpe.

Above: **Remains of** the railway at Lodge Farm. (Graeme Aldous)

Below: **Early drainage** channel, under the trackbed at Moorsholm. (Graeme Aldous)

Above: **Bridge over** railway at Rake House. (Graeme Aldous)

Below: **Flooded cutting** near Stonegate tunnel. (Graeme Aldous)

How to get there and what else to see

Travel by train is recommended, particularly for those in good health. There is a regular service between Whitby and Middlesbrough and the southern site of Paddy Waddell's Railway is close to Leaholm station. The line can be walked or cycled with the help of an OS Explorer map and as the area is remote, exploration by car is a quite understandable alternative. Certainly, the challenge of the early railway builders can be appreciated during one's exploration of Paddy Waddell's Railway.

The North York Moors Railway

A visit to this heritage railway should be top of anyone's list who is visiting North Yorkshire. This line, once a horse drawn tramway, runs between Grosmont and Pickering and main line locomotives regularly haul trains with refreshments in high season. Its terminus at Grosmont station is additionally served by trains from the Esk Valley Railway referred to earlier, so a visit by rail is recommended.

Whitby

This attractive seaside town is well served by trains on the national railway network and in high season steam-hauled services from the North York Moors Railway. With a wealth of shops and restaurants and references to the elusive Count Dracula, an interesting day out can be assured. Car parking is challenging at peak times, so use the train if you can!

CHAPTER 19

The Battles of Saxby

When the railway network was being developed in its prosperous period during the 1840s, lines were planned in many places in order to take advantage of substantial profits that could be generated as the country became connected. Perversely, although railways brought wealth to Great Britain, which was widely regarded as beneficial, the aristocracy occasionally took an opposing view, especially when their own land was directly affected. There are many examples where railway companies were forced to build unnecessary tunnels or deviations, simply to screen stately homes from intrusive steam trains, which were perceived by the aristocracy to carry a cross-section of undesirable members of the public.

During the 1840s, the Midland Railway was planning new routes, one in particular being the Syston to Peterborough Railway through Melton Mowbray. This railway would prove to be a profitable cross-country connection between the Midlands and East Anglia with no major construction difficulty anticipated. However, the MR had clearly underestimated the problems it would encounter at Stapleford Hall at Saxby, owned by Robert Sherard, the 6th Earl of Harborough. This stately home, built originally during the Norman period, had over the centuries been enlarged and improved. It is recorded that banquets were held on a lavish scale and the surrounding land was regarded as some of the finest hunting ground in the East Midlands.

Aiming towards this aristocratic seat near Saxby was the Midland Railway (MR) on the chosen route to the east of Melton Mowbray. The first problem encountered by the MR was its lack of an Act to build the line, so before taking the proposal to Parliament, the company had to survey the route. It was made very clear from the outset that the Earl would have nothing to do with any person connected with the railway.

In general the Earls of Harborough had proved over the centuries to be gentlemen not renowned for making trouble and had lived in reasonable harmony with their neighbours. However, this did not apply to the 6th Earl who has been colourfully described as

Stapleford Park.
(Pride of Britain Hotels)

'The Naughty Earl', less generously as a 'hellion of the aristocratic type' and at worst 'a barbarian'. However, Harborough did have a weakness for a pretty face and quite by chance during the early 1830s, met Emma Sarah Love, a well-known actress and opera singer from the Drury Lane theatre in London. She had been unhappily married to a certain Granby Calcroft for a mere eight months when she was introduced to Harborough after an evening's performance at the theatre in Nottingham. Without delay he took her to his estate and built her a cottage near the lake in the ornamental woodland to the east of Stapleford Hall. The wronged husband sued Harborough for enticement and received the paltry sum of £100, the presiding magistrate intimating to Calcroft that he 'should have known better than by marrying such a woman from a theatrical background'.

Her presence on the estate attracted unwanted attention from the local population who were apt to gawp at Emma whilst walking near her cottage. The outraged Earl closed all the footpaths and re-routed them around the outside of his estate. And for good measure, he purchased some bears from a travelling circus and released them into the woods to deter would be trespassers. He placed gamekeepers as guards on the gates, in effect imprisoning his mistress. In spite of this treatment she remained loyal, later bearing him three sons and remaining in her cottage until the Earl's death in 1859.

In the early 1840s the Midland Railway revealed its plans to construct the Syston & Peterborough Railway and in October 1844, Harborough was approached by surveyors from the MR, at which time he made it abundantly clear that he wanted nothing to do with them or the proposed line.

The MR had in a rather cowardly manner avoided this looming problem, but now realised that time was short in gaining approval by Parliament, so the company decided to carry out surveys on Stapleford Park without the permission of its owner. This drove the Earl to 'fight the battle against the levelling spirit of the age' through his park which became known forever as 'the Battles of Saxby'.

Emma Sarah Love.

Early studies had indicated that the best route of the railway lay in the valley of the River Eye, which ran through the eastern boundary of Stapleford Park. Upon getting wind of this plan, his Lordship forbad all cooperation and emphasised that no MR employee would be allowed to gain entry to the park. In spite of this, on 12 November 1844 the route was surveyed in some detail by gaining access on the towpath of the Oakham Canal up to the point where it met the boundary of the park as shown on the map. It was here that the Earl's men flatly refused entry, at which point one of the MR's surveyors allegedly threatened them with a pistol.

This was met by Harborough's gamekeeper who invited the armed man to 'shoot away!' The challenge led to a wrestling match in which nine surveyors were captured, tied up, loaded into a cart and taken to Cold Overton Hall near Oakham where a Justice of the Peace was known to live. As the JP was unavailable, and advice given that holding them would be regarded as unlawful, the surveyors were ignominiously tipped out of the cart and dumped

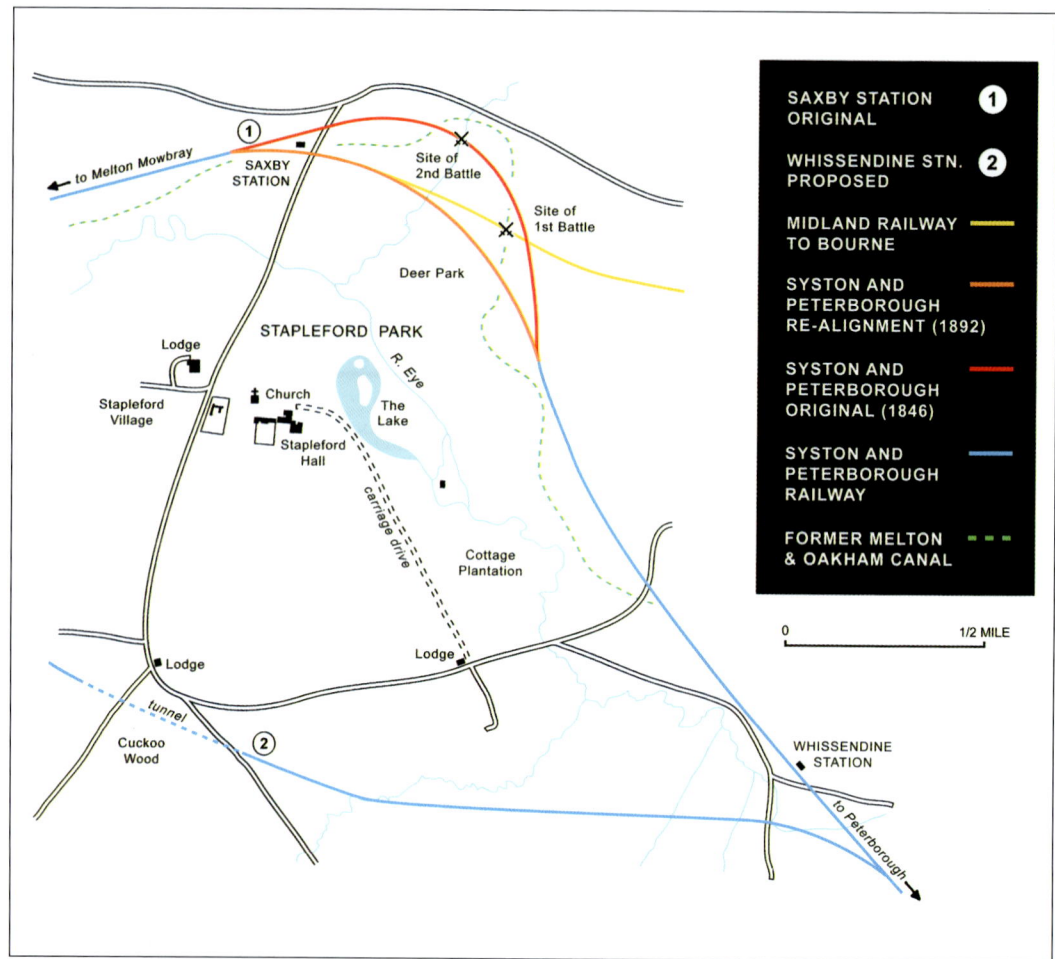

Routes Considered by the Midland Railway and points of interest. (Alex Griffin)

outside the estate in a dishevelled heap. This was the first round of the Battle of Saxby.

This action did not dissuade the MR from making a further attempt. Within two days the company returned with solicitors and a group of burly railway navvies, including three prize fighters from Nottingham. This time they met at Saxby Pile Bridge, which crossed the River Eye just outside the park, where they were confronted by the Earl's men and his legal team. At first a heated verbal confrontation took place but when it was clear that the exchange was going nowhere, a group of surveyors tried to force their way past the Earl's men. They were unable to continue because the other end of the bridge was heavily barricaded. It now looked as though a pitched battle was about to take place but this was avoided by the arrival of the County Police who threatened to arrest anyone who committed a physical assault. However, they were prepared to allow the act of *'pushing'* which meant that both sides would have to lay down their clubs and iron pointed staves and rely on pressure alone. This debacle was witnessed by C.E. Stretton, an early Midland Railway historian who recorded what happened next:

> 'A grand stand was then made by Lord Harborough's party below the bridge and nearest Melton, who stood wedged together, forming a living and very formidable barrier. The surveyors next placed rows of their men with their backs to the faces of the Earl's party, and set others in an opposite position to force the way. An almost incredible scene now took place. The railwayists exerted their utmost strength, but so firmly did his Lordship's party retain their ground, that more than one was actually forced high in the air, rolling over the heads of the contending party. Others were forced through the hedge, tumbling over each other, and nearly filling the ditch beneath, amidst the shouts of the leaders and the laughter of the numerous spectators. Great confusion now ensued, the two parties mixing together and in the tumult and dirt becoming almost indistinguishable by each other.'

The intensity of the conflict allowed some of the surveyors to break from the turmoil and begin to take measurements within the park. However, it was not long before they were spotted and chased away leaving their surveying equipment which was subsequently smashed to pieces and hurled in to the canal.

It was generally agreed that the Earl of Harborough had won this, the second battle of Saxby, and both sides for the time being, laid down their arms whilst court proceedings took place. In spite of this and before any hearings could take place, rumours were leaked to Harborough that his adversaries were preparing for a third battle. The Earl's solicitor wrote to the MR warning that 'we have barricaded the towing path and have in readiness a few cannons from His Lordship's yacht. If you force us to use them, as a last resort, the blood be upon your heads'.

This threat did not deter the MR and in the early hours of 16 November a small group of railwaymen attacked the Earl's barricade, clearly aiming to create a diversion. This allowed about a 100 strong surveying party to scale the perimeter fences of the 800 acre parkland, where they then began surveying in earnest. The Earl's men found it impossible to round up most of the surveyors and were thus unable to prevent the work taking place. By now the shenanigans at Saxby were attracting the attention of the national press and a correspondent from *The Times* newspaper took up the story two days later:

> 'By the time the surveyors had reached opposite his Lordship's beautiful cottage, where he resides, Mr Fabling, Lord Harborough's steward, on a pony, came up, bringing with him a few of his troops. Mr Cope, the chief surveyor, told him that if he wished not to be hurt, he had better retire; and on refusing to do so the railwaymen were ordered to remove him. Mr Fabling ordered the measuring chains to be taken up. His situation at that moment was perilous; but being much respected by his Lordship's tenants and servants, they rallied round him for protection, began to feel confidence in their leader and their own strength, and the fight became general.'

At this stage of proceedings, C.E. Stratton, the MR's historian, reported:

> 'The noise was so great it was heard in the village two miles off. The spikes of the railway party were thrust into the sides of the defenders of the park, and after a battle of five minutes, and many broken heads, wounded sides and faces, the lower grade of intruders got away.'

It is recorded that the park's fire engine was employed to dowse the surveyors and the Earl's cannons added a further threat to the proceedings. However, it was later revealed that these were fakes but at least they looked threatening enough. For the first time during these forays, Lord and the recently betrothed Lady Harborough, (*nee* Eliza Temple), put in an appearance but he was suffering from a severe illness which prevented his taking part in the conflict. The estate's men were paid 2s. 6d a day, a significant sum in those days, which explains why they took part in the battle with such enthusiasm. In retrospect it is astonishing that some of those involved in the fighting were not killed in the process.

An unofficial truce then followed which allowed time for matters to come to trial. Minor infringements were dealt with in the local magistrate's court in Melton Mowbray but the more serious charges were heard in Leicester Assizes in the spring of 1845. A correspondent from *The Times* was present as by now this case had attracted national attention. At stake lay the fundamental right of an individual against a large company and naturally, the greater interest of the state itself. The court's initial charges were:

> 'Warrants for the apprehension of several of the rioters have been granted, and shortly some will be brought before the magistrates, when it will be ascertained whether the agents of a powerful Railway Company can thus act with impunity.'

The Chief Justice summed up the hearing with the following verdict:

> 'Lord Harborough's people had been justified in using force to eject the trespassers from the park, although the actions brought against his men for damage to surveying equipment and a number of specific personal assaults were upheld.'

Unfortunately, the matter of whether the railway could be surveyed in the park remained unresolved, which led to the continuation of further conflict. In spite of the court case, further disruption was caused a year later in 1845 when the surveyors were still investigating alternative routes around the park. Lord Harborough, clearly having recovered from his illness, was seen to drive a horse and carriage up and down the high road whilst his men in a cart, obstructed the view from the surveyor's theodolite by holding up sheets of calico between them. The Earl had not lost his appetite for a fight when he drove a brake against the surveyors' cart in an attempt to saw off the wheels in a fashion not dissimilar to that portrayed during the chariot race in the film, *Ben Hur*.

Although it would appear that a running battle was continuing to take place, there were in reality, periods of comparative peace when each side were considering their positions. The MR had invested too heavily in the Syston & Peterborough line, as well as purchasing the largely defunct Melton & Oakham canal, to withdraw. The MR was led by its Chairman George Hudson, whose colourful personality has been described in chapter eleven of this book. The Earl instinctively loathed this belligerent individual with his coarse manners, so the stage was set for as much as anything else, a battle based upon a clash of personalities as well as the material matters of the dispute.

It was clear that the case for building the railway through any part of the park would be continually resisted and time was not on the side of the Midland Railway. A further uneasy truce was brokered in 1845 when the company planned to take the railway across the south west corner of the estate as shown on the map. The route would have branched west from a place south of Whissendine station, which opened in 1848 and closed in 1955, heading towards the south west corner of Stapleford Park. This alternative siting of Whissendine station as indicated on the map, was to have been built on the east side of Stapleford Road, placing it at a considerable distance from the village it purported to serve. The railway would then enter a shallow tunnel under the Earl's Cuckoo tree plantation before emerging between Cuckoo Hill and Sawgate Roads. This route had the advantage of avoiding a sharp curve on the original route planned and more importantly, completely screening the view of trains from Stapleford Hall.

Although the Earl was not placated, there is no record of his actively interfering with the tunnel then under construction, although there is no doubt that he had his spies watching like hawks from the sidelines. Then disaster struck when part of the tunnel under Cuckoo wood collapsed, destroying some seventy beech, elm and oak trees. The outraged Earl physically attacked one of the surveyors, which led to the abandonment of this latest attempt to complete the railway.

Finally, the MR had little choice but to take the railway close to the route originally planned to the east and north of Stapleford Park, but carefully avoiding any penetration of the estate's boundary. The Parliamentary Act was duly passed with the Earl receiving £22,000 in compensation, presumably in part for the loss of his trees in Cuckoo Wood, and the line opened some two years later in 1848.

Thus, the Midland Railway had eventually acquired its line and the final section was completed, but for decades it was forced to operate main line express trains that had to greatly reduce speeds before negotiating the severely tight radius on the approach to Saxby station. It was to be nearly fifty years before a re-alignment was negotiated and constructed, long after the death of his Lordship in 1859. As for Harborough, this was a Pyrrhic victory, because for the remainder of his days, trains were visible and audible from the northern and eastern boundaries of his estate. His beloved

Oakham canal in which he had a controlling interest had been sold to the Midland Railway, and filled in to allow construction of the new Saxby station in 1892. At least Harborough did not live to see this ultimate indignity, having passed away years earlier. Perhaps though, he did allow himself the flicker of a smile at Hudson's plight when he was declared bankrupt and imprisoned shortly after the Midland Railway's financial crash of 1850.

What remains to be seen

Stapleford Park opened as a luxury country house hotel in 1982 although its appearance is largely unchanged since the 1700s, with the exception of a Jacobean style alteration that was added to its southern side during the late Victorian era. The parkland was considerably improved between 1818 and 1834 by Lancelot Brown, better known as Capability Brown. To the east of the Hall an oval lake with serpentine tail was excavated and woodlands planted, with the addition of a lodge, which is today a listed building. The Earl ensconced his mistress in a new cottage on this part of the

Harborough Cottage after rebuilding at Whissendine. (Alan Murray-Rust)

estate in the mid-1830s , releasing bears into the barricaded woods to deter unwanted visitors. Upon Harborough's death in 1859, his widow had Emma Love evicted from her cottage but allowed the building's materials to be sent to nearby Whissenden so that it could be rebuilt. The remains of footings still remain in the woods and the rebuilt home was named 'Harborough Cottage', which is where Emma lived out her days.

The site of Saxby Pile Bridge which was obliterated when Lord Harborough's Curve was built. (John Sutton)

The places where the battles took place are marked on the map. The first location can be seen next to the course of the former canal just above the abandoned railway to Bourne and indicates the place where the towpath met the Stapleford boundary. The site of the second battle was known as Saxby Pile Bridge but this was completely obliterated when 'Lord Harborough's Curve' was

eventually constructed. The wooden bridge and its right of way over the River Eye were buried under this substantial embankment, remains of which can be seen today.

The route of the original railway ran outside the park's boundary until abandoned in 1892 and can easily be traced today with the aid of an OS Explorer map. The final attempt by the Midland Railway to tunnel under Cuckoo Wood left a depression after the collapse which has never been filled in.

The village of Saxby was served by two stations, the first at the end of 'Lord Harborough's Curve' being shortly after the line opened in 1848. This closed in 1892 to be replaced by a station at the junction of the realigned route, with the railway to Bourne opening at the same time. Today Saxby station is no more, having been closed by British Railways in 1962 and completely demolished in 2014. Ironically, the first station at the commencement of 'Lord Harborough's Curve' became part of the goods yard and is today converted to a residential house.

How to get there

A visit to Stapleford Park is recommended, particularly as it could include a holiday break in the former 6th Earl of Harborough's residence. This hotel, which has been restored to a fine standard, welcomes visitors who may like to recall anecdotes about the Earl and his forays as they enjoy their break.

At certain times of the year, usually in June and August, a 10.25 inch miniature railway runs at the Eastern side of the park. With beautifully engineered locomotives running through tunnels and over streams, this fine attraction raises money for charity. It is recommended that a visit coincides with an operating day to heighten one's enjoyment. What would the estate's predecessors have thought of that?

A visit by rail is recommended as a first choice as Melton Mowbray station is only three miles away and provides a taxi service. Trains are frequent from Peterborough in the east and Leicester to the west. The journey is worth the effort as it will take the passenger through many miles of unspoilt rolling scenery and Victorian stations, many of which retain some of their original features.

Sources

Chapter 1. The Cranbrook & Paddock Wood Railway
Brian Hart, *The Hawkhurst Branch*.
David Hodgkins, *The Second Railway King*.
Kent County Library Archives.
The Diaries of William Courtenay Morland, Heather Dyke, Gt.
  Granddaughter of W.C. Morley.

Chapter 2. The Ouse Valley Railway
J.T. Howard Turner, *The London, Brighton & South Coast Railway*.
The Keep Museum Brighton.
Image, Samuel Laing (NRM/Science & Society Picture Library).

Chapter 3. The Mysterious Second Tunnel Portal near Cowden Station
David Gould, *The Croydon, Oxted & East Grinstead Railway*, Oakwood
  Press.
Timothy Boyles, *Mark Beech – The Unknown Village*.

Chapter 4. The Chessington to Leatherhead Railway
C.E. Klapper, 'Sir Herbert Walker's Southern Railway', *Railway
  Magazine* (July 1938).

Chapter 5. Kent's International Airport Railway
C.E. Klapper, 'Sir Herbert Walker's Southern Railway'.
David Staines, 'The Ghost at Lullingston', *Rail Magazine* 2019.

Chapter 6. The First Channel Tunnel
Donald Hunt, *The Tunnel, Story of the Channel Tunnel 1802–1994*.
David Hodgkins, 'The Life and Times of Sir Edward Watkin
  1819-1901', *Subterranea Britannica*.

Chapter 7. The Didcot, Newbury & Southampton Junction Railway
T.B. Sands, *The Didcot, Newbury & Southampton Railway*.
P. Karau, M. Parsons & K. Robertson, *The Didcot, Newbury &
  Southampton Railway*. Hampshire Records Office, Winchester.

Chapter 8. Edgware to Watford – Trains, Films and Military Planes
Tony Beard, *By Tube Beyond Edgware*.
John Franch, *Robber Baron, the Life of Charles Tyson Yerkes*.

Chapter 9. The Mid-Suffolk Light Railway
N.A. Comfort, *The Mid-Suffolk Light Railway*.
P. Paye, *The Mid-Suffolk Light Railway*.
P. Paye, *The Southwold Railway*.
Bealings & Playford Parish Records.

Chapter 10. The South Devon Atmospheric Railway
Charles Hadfield, *Atmospheric Railways*.
E.T. MacDermot, *History of the Great Western Railway, Volume 1*.
Historic England, *Engine Houses*.
Didcot Railway Centre.

Chapter 11. George Hudson's Virgin Viaduct at Tadcaster
Brian J. Bailey, *George Hudson. The Rise and Fall of the Railway King*.
Historic England, *The Viaduct at Tadcaster*.

Chapter 12. The Birmingham & Oxford Junction Railway
E.T. MacDermot, *History of the Great Western Railway, Volume 1*.
Oxford County Council History Centre.
New Civil Engineer.
Warwickshire Railways.com

Chapter 13. Isambard Kingdom Brunel's Hidden Dream
Geoffrey Tudor, *Brunel's Hidden Kingdom*.
Devon County Council Record Office.
The Royal Institution of British Architects.

Chapter 14. Stations and Tunnels Beneath London
Alan A. Jackson, *London's Local Railways*.
Nick Catford, *Secret Underground London*.
Backtrack, October 1997.

Chapter 15. The Collywell Bay Railway
Alan Young, disused-stations.org.uk.

Chapter 16. The Mistley, Thorpe & Walton Railway
Thomas B. Peacock, *The Mistley, Thorpe & Walton Railway*.
The Great Eastern Railway Society.

Chapter 17. The East Kent Light Railway
M. Lawson Finch & S.R. Garrett, *The East Kent Railway, Volumes 1 & 2*.
The Colonel Stephens Museum, Tenterden.

Chapter 18. The Cleveland Extension Mineral Railway – Paddy Waddell's Railway
R.F. Moore, *Paddy Waddell's Railway*, including additional evidence at Moorsholm provided by Graeme Aldous.

Chapter 19. The Battles of Saxby
Peter Smith, *The Syston & Peterborough Railway*.
Tim Warner, *Backtrack Vol. 2, No. 4, winter 1988*.
genealogy.com

A special thank you to all uncredited photos taken by my family: Elizabeth, Frances, James, David, Paul, Alex and Alison.